Billy Graham

THE HOLY SPIRIT

Activating GOD'S Power in Your Life

(with Built-In Study Guide)

WORD PUBLISHING
Dallas · London · Sydney · Singapore

The Holy Spirit

Unless otherwise indicated, Scripture quotations are from *The New American Standard Bible* (copyright 1960, 1962, 1968, 1971 by the Lockman Foundation and used by permission). Scripture quotations marked LB are from *The Living Bible Paraphrased* (Wheaton: Tyndale House Publishers, 1971). Quotations marked NIV are from the New International Version of the Bible—New Testament (copyright © 1973 by the New York Bible Society International). Those marked RSV are from The Revised Standard Version of the Bible, copyright 1946, 1952, © 1971, 1973 by the Division of Christian Education of the National Council of the Churches of Christ in the United States of America, and are used by permission. Those marked *Phillips* are from *The New Testament in Modern English* (rev. ed.), copyright © 1958, 1960, 1972 by J. B. Phillips. Quotations marked NEB are from *The New English Bible,* © 1961, 1970 The Delegates of the Oxford University Press and The Syndics of the Cambridge University Press. Those marked KJV are from the King James Version of the Bible.

ISBN 0-8499-3072-3

Library of Congress Catalog Card Number: 77-075458

Printed in the United States of America

6 7 8 9 LBM 23 22 21

Contents

Preface   7

Introduction: Man's Cry—God's Gift   11

  1. Who Is the Holy Spirit?   16

  2. When the Holy Spirit Has Come   24

  3. The Holy Spirit and the Bible   39

  4. The Holy Spirit and Salvation   50

  5. Baptism with the Spirit   62

  6. The Seal, the Pledge, and the Witness
     of the Holy Spirit   74

  7. The Christian's Inner Struggle   81

  8. The Fullness of the Spirit   96

  9. How to Be Filled with the Holy Spirit   109

 10. Sins against the Holy Spirit   123

 11. Gifts of the Spirit   131

 12. Further Gifts of the Spirit   148

 13. The Sign Gifts   157

 14. The Fruit of the Spirit   180

 15. The Fruit of the Spirit: Love, Joy, Peace   187

 16. The Fruit of the Spirit: Patience, Kindness,
     Goodness   195

 17. The Fruit of the Spirit: Faithfulness,
     Gentleness, Self-Control   202

 18. The Need of the Hour   212

Notes   221

Study Guide   225

Preface

An old American Indian legend tells of an Indian who came down from the mountains and saw the ocean for the first time. Awed by the scene, he requested a quart jar. As he waded into the ocean and filled the jar he was asked what he intended to do with it. "Back in the mountains," he replied, "my people have never seen the Great Water. I will carry this jar to them so they can see what it is like."

Before he died, Pope John was asked what church doctrine most needed reemphasis today. He replied, "The doctrine of the Holy Spirit."

A number of years ago, my wife and I had the privilege of spending a brief vacation in Switzerland as the guests of Dr. Karl Barth, the noted Swiss theologian. During the course of our conversations I asked him what he thought the next emphasis on theology would be. He replied without hesitation, "The Holy Spirit."

Attempting to write a book on so vast a subject as the Holy Spirit is like trying to capture the ocean in a quart jar. The subject is so infinite—and our minds are so finite.

This book really began as part of my personal spiritual pilgrimage. Throughout my ministry as an evangelist I have had a growing understanding of the ministry of the Holy Spirit. In recent years my attention has been drawn in a fresh way to the ministry of the Holy Spirit because of the renewed interest in His work in many parts of the world. Sensing my own need for further understanding, I began a systematic study of what the Bible teaches about the person and work of the Holy Spirit. It was not my original intention to write a book, but as I began to examine the subject in more depth I became concerned over the misunderstanding and even ignorance in some Christian circles concerning the Third Person of the Trinity.

In some ways I have been hesitant to write this book. But writing it has given me new insight into the ministry of the Holy Spirit; it has also helped me understand some of the movements of the Holy Spirit in our world today. My hope and prayer is that this book will be informative and clarifying for many Christians. I also pray it will be a unifying book. The Holy Spirit did not come to divide Christians but, among other reasons, He came to unite us.

My sole concern has been to see what the Bible has to say about the Holy Spirit. The Bible—which I believe the Holy Spirit inspired—is our only trustworthy source, and any reliable analysis of the person and work of the Holy Spirit must be biblically-based. As never before I have realized that there are some things we cannot know completely, and some issues are open to differences of interpretation by sincere Christians. About areas where there are honest differences among Christians I have tried not to be dogmatic.

I am thankful the Holy Spirit is at work in our generation, both in awakening the Church and in evangelism. May God use this book to bring renewal and challenge to many.

I owe a great debt to many people who have helped me during the writing of this book. I am grateful for my colleague Roy Gustafson who first suggested writing on this subject. Several people have been especially helpful in reading early drafts of the manuscript, either in part or the whole, and making constructive suggestions—including Dr. Harold Lindsell (former editor of *Christianity Today*), Mr. Paul Fromer (Wheaton College), Canon Houghton (former chairman of British Keswick), Dr. Thomas Zimmerman (General Superintendent of the Assemblies of God), Dr. Merrill C. Tenney (Dean Emeritus, Wheaton Graduate School), and Dr. Donald Hoke (Secretary, Lausanne

Committee for World Evangelization). I am also thankful for the graciousness of Mr. and Mrs. Bill Mead, whose generosity enabled my wife, Ruth, and me to join them for several periods of work on the book. I will never forget those days of sitting around in a circle with the Meads and my longtime colleagues, the Cliff Barrows, the Fred Dienerts, and the Grady Wilsons, discussing various chapters of the book. I am also thankful for the suggestions of my colleague, Dr. John Akers, the help of the Reverend Ralph Williams of our Minneapolis office, and of Sally Wilson in Montreat who suggested illustrations and Scriptures to add to my original notes. My secretary, Stephanie Wills, has patiently typed and retyped the manuscript through its various drafts.

Introduction: Man's Cry — God's Gift

Man has two great spiritual needs. One is for forgiveness. The other is for goodness. Consciously or unconsciously, his inner being longs for both. There are times when man actually cries for them, even though in his restlessness, confusion, loneliness, fear, and pressures he may not know what he is crying for.

God heard that first cry for help, that cry for forgiveness, and answered it at Calvary. God sent His only Son into the world to die for our sins, so that we might be forgiven. This is a gift for us—God's gift of salvation. This gift is a permanent legacy for everyone who truly admits he has "fallen short" and sinned. It is for everyone who reaches out and accepts God's gift by receiving Jesus Christ as his Lord and Savior. Paul calls it God's "indescribable" gift (2 Cor. 9:15).

But God also heard our second cry, that cry for goodness, and answered it at Pentecost. God does not want us to come to Christ by faith, and then lead a life of defeat, discouragement, and dissension. Rather, He wants to "fulfill every desire for *goodness* and the work of faith with power; in order that the name of our Lord Jesus Christ may be glorified in you" (2 Thess. 1:11, 12). *To the great gift of forgiveness God adds also the great gift of the Holy Spirit.* He is the source of power who meets our need to escape from the miserable weakness that grips us. He gives us the power to be truly good.

If we are to live a life of sanity in our modern world, if we wish to be men and women who can live victoriously, we need this two-sided gift God has offered us: first, the work of the Son of God *for* us; second, the work of the Spirit of God *in* us. In

11

this way God has answered mankind's two great cries: the cry for forgiveness and the cry for goodness.

As a friend of mine has said, "I need Jesus Christ for my eternal life, and the Holy Spirit of God for my internal life."

If you believe in Jesus Christ, a power is available to you that can change your life, even in such intimate areas as your marriage, your family relationships, and every other relationship. Also, God offers power that can change a tired church into a vital, growing body, power that can revitalize Christendom.

Unfortunately, this power has been ignored, misunderstood, and misused. By our ignorance we have short-circuited the power of the Holy Spirit.

Many books are written about this power, many prayers are said pleading for this power. Scores of Christians would like to have it, but they aren't sure what it is.

When the world looks at a Christian, certain mental clichés come to mind: it sees the believer as a stiff-necked, sober-faced person without a sense of humor; a person who can't make it himself so he uses "God as a crutch"; one who has left his brains in kindergarten.

Now, if this cold stereotype applies in any way to us or the Church, then we need to know about the exciting, revolutionary power available exclusively to Christian believers. No one can buy it, claim it, or use it without first knowing its source.

The Holy Spirit Was Promised

When Jesus was teaching His disciples, preparing them for what He knew was the end, His heart ached for them because He knew they were confused and sad. I can imagine that He moved from one to another, putting His arms around them. To each He explained in simple fashion, as we do to our children, the important truths He wanted them to understand. At one point He said, "But now I am going to Him who sent Me; and none of you asks Me, 'Where are You going?' But because I have said these things to you, sorrow has filled your heart. But I tell you the truth, it is to your advantage that I go away; for if I do not go away, the Helper shall not come to you; but if I go, I will send Him to you" (John 16:5–7).

There was a promise! The coming of the Spirit was based

upon the word of the Lord Jesus Christ. No conditions were attached. Jesus didn't say that He would send the Helper (or "Comforter") to some believers and not to others. Nor did He say that we had to belong to some special organization or be higher on the scale of spiritual performance than someone else. He simply said, "If I go, I will send Him to you."

When Jesus Christ makes a promise, He does not break or forget it. We may doubt the promises of friends or family; we may even doubt our own promises to others. But we have never been given a promise by Jesus that has not been a certainty.

Some people dismiss Jesus Christ as a "great teacher" or one of the outstanding religious leaders of the world. However, when it comes to promises, it's interesting to contrast His words with other great religious and philosophical leaders. For example, as the founder of Buddhism was bidding his followers farewell he said, "You must be your own light." Or when Socrates was about to take that fatal cup, one of his disciples mourned that he was leaving them orphans. The leaders of the world's religions and philosophies were unable to promise that they would never leave their followers.

The disciples of Jesus Christ, however, were not left alone. He said, "I will not leave you as orphans; I will come to you" (John 14:18). It is interesting that the Greek word for "orphans" is the same as the word used by the disciple of Socrates when he realized that his master was going to leave him alone.

The Promise Fulfilled

Jesus said He would leave His disciples for a while, and He did. During the dreadful hours of the crucifixion, death, and burial, agonizing doubt gripped the minds of those who loved Him. He had not yet been "glorified," so the promise of His Spirit was not yet a fact.

But we know what happened. God raised Him from the dead and gave Him glory. Addressing Christians, the Scriptures say that Christ came "for the sake of you who through Him are believers in God, who raised Him from the dead and gave Him glory, so that your faith and hope are in God" (1 Peter 1:20, 21).

God had said to "wait" for the Spirit to come. Jesus rose from the dead and was seen by His disciples. Unable to grasp what was happening, they failed to recognize Him at first, and were frightened because they thought they were seeing a ghost. To confirm His physical reality, Jesus told them to touch Him, and even asked for something to eat. A spirit didn't have flesh, did it? A ghost couldn't eat, could it?

So this was truly Jesus, not the Spirit He had promised. However, He told them still to wait! The time was not yet.

Fifty days later the promise was fulfilled at Pentecost. What a day it was! It is difficult for us to imagine, with our practical, earth-bound, scientific mentality, the amazing happening of that day.

"And when the day of Pentecost had come, they were all together in one place. And suddenly there came from heaven a noise like a violent, rushing wind, and it filled the whole house where they were sitting. And there appeared to them tongues as of fire distributing themselves, and they rested on each one of them. And they were all filled with the Holy Spirit and began to speak with other tongues, as the Spirit was giving them utterance" (Acts 2:1–4).

The one for whom they were asked to "wait" had come!

What a difference the emphasis of one word makes in the description of a happening of such world-shaking importance! Before the day of Pentecost the emphasis was on the word "ask." "If you then, being evil, know how to give good gifts to your children, how much more shall your Heavenly Father give the Holy Spirit to those who *ask* Him?" (Luke 11:13, italics mine).

After Pentecost the emphasis was on the word "receive." In his powerful sermon that day, Peter said, "Repent, and let each of you be baptized in the name of Jesus Christ for the forgiveness of your sins; and you shall *receive* the gift of the Holy Spirit" (Acts 2:38, italics mine).

This is the good news: we are no longer waiting for the Holy Spirit—He is waiting for us. We are no longer living in a time of promise, but in the days of fulfillment.

The members of the early Church, those men, women, and children who knew the reality of the Holy Spirit as a force, were totally transformed. The rush of power they experienced on the day of Pentecost is characteristic of the age that gave us the New Testament. The Holy Spirit was promised, the promise was fulfilled, the disciples were changed, and the glory of it for us is that He is present in every true believer today. And so His power is available today.

Who is this Person whom Christ promised to send to earth in His place? Who is this Person whom He uses to transform human nature? Who is this Person who can give you supernatural power to face any crisis? And how can you and I know His power in our lives day by day?

We will find out.

1. Who Is the Holy Spirit?

Some years ago a teacher in a fifth-grade class asked his students if anyone could explain electricity. One boy raised his hand. The teacher asked, "How would you explain it, Jimmy?" Jimmy scratched his head a moment and then replied, "Last night I knew it, but this morning I've forgotten." The teacher shook his head sadly and said to the class, "What a tragedy. The only person in the world ever to understand electricity, and he's forgotten!"

That teacher's position may describe you and me when we study the doctrine of the Trinity. We accept the fact that the Holy Spirit is God, just as much God as God the Father and God the Son. But when it comes to explaining it, we are at a loss.

In recent years people have talked more about the Holy Spirit and written more books about Him than possibly any religious theme other than the occult. This has come about largely because of the influence of the charismatic movement, which has been called Christendom's "third force" alongside Catholicism and Protestantism. The more recent charismatic movement, which has some of its roots in historic Pentecostalism and stresses the Holy Spirit, is now deeply entrenched in most of the mainline denominations and in Catholicism. We may feel that it is such a vast subject and we know so little about it. Nevertheless, God in His Word has revealed all we should know.

Many questions will arise in this book for which answers are being sought by puzzled and at times untaught believers. In fact, millions of Christians on every continent are now asking these questions. They are seeking and deserve biblical answers.

For example: What is the baptism of the Holy Spirit? When does it take place? Is speaking in tongues *possible* or necessary today? Is there an experience called a "second blessing"?

To start our study, we need to ask a critical question at the very beginning: Who is the Holy Spirit?

The Holy Spirit Is a Person

The Bible teaches that the Holy Spirit is a *person.* Jesus never referred to "it" when He was talking about the Holy Spirit. In John 14, 15 and 16, for example, He spoke of the Holy Spirit as "He" because He is not a force or thing but a person. Whoever speaks of the Holy Spirit as "it" is uninstructed, or perhaps even undiscerning. In Romans 8:16 the King James Version refers to the Holy Spirit as "itself." This is a mistranslation. Nearly all of the newer translations have changed "itself" to "himself."

We see from the Bible that the Holy Spirit has intellect, emotions, and will. In addition to this, the Bible also ascribes to Him the acts we would expect of someone who was not just a force, but a real person.

He speaks: "He who has an ear, let him hear what the Spirit says to the churches. To him who overcomes, I will grant to eat of the tree of life, which is in the Paradise of God" (Rev. 2:7).

"And while they were ministering to the Lord and fasting, the Holy Spirit said, 'Set apart for Me Barnabas and Saul for the work to which I have called them'" (Acts 13:2).

He intercedes: "And in the same way the Spirit also helps our weakness; for we do not know how to pray as we should, but the Spirit Himself intercedes for us with groanings too deep for words" (Rom. 8:26).

He testifies: "When the Helper comes, whom I will send to you from the Father, that is the Spirit of truth, who proceeds from the Father, He will bear witness of Me" (John 15:26).

He leads: "And the Spirit said to Philip, 'Go up and join this chariot'" (Acts 8:29).

"For all who are being led by the Spirit of God, these are sons of God" (Rom. 8:14).

He commands: "And they passed through the Phrygian and Galatian region, having been forbidden by the Holy Spirit to speak the word in Asia; and when they had come to Mysia, they were trying to go into Bithynia, and the Spirit of Jesus did not permit them" (Acts 16:6, 7).

He guides: "When the Spirit of truth comes, he will guide you into all the truth; for he will not speak on his own authority, but whatever he hears he will speak, and he will declare to you the things that are to come" (John 16:13 RSV).

He appoints: "Be on guard for yourselves and for all the flock, among which the Holy Spirit has made you overseers, to shepherd the church of God which He purchased with His own blood" (Acts 20:28).

He can be lied to: "But Peter said, 'Ananias, why has Satan filled your heart to lie to the Holy Spirit, and to keep back some of the price of the land? While it remained unsold, did it not remain your own? And after it was sold, was it not under your control? Why is it that you have conceived this deed in your heart? You have not lied to men, but to God' " (Acts 5:3, 4).

He can be insulted: "How much severer punishment do you think he will deserve who has trampled under foot the Son of God, and has regarded as unclean the blood of the covenant by which he was sanctified, and has insulted the Spirit of grace?" (Heb. 10:29).

He can be blasphemed: "Therefore I say to you, any sin and blasphemy shall be forgiven men, but blasphemy against the Spirit shall not be forgiven. And whoever shall speak a word against the Son of Man, it shall be forgiven him; but whoever shall speak against the Holy Spirit, it shall not be forgiven him, either in this age, or in the age to come" (Matt. 12:31, 32).

He can be grieved: "And do not grieve the Holy Spirit of God, by whom you were sealed for the day of redemption" (Eph. 4:30).

Each of the emotions and acts we have listed are characteristics of a person. The Holy Spirit is not an impersonal force, like gravity or magnetism. He is a Person, with all the attributes of personality. But not only is He a Person; He is divine as well.

The Holy Spirit Is a Divine Person: He Is God

Throughout the Bible it is clear that the Holy Spirit is God Himself. This is seen in the attributes which are given to the

Holy Spirit in Scripture, for example. Without exception these attributes are those of God Himself.

He is eternal: This means that there never was a time when He was not. "How much more will the blood of Christ, who through the eternal Spirit offered Himself without blemish to God, cleanse your conscience from dead works to serve the living God?" (Heb. 9:14).

He is all-powerful: "And the angel answered and said to her, 'The Holy Spirit will come upon you, and the power of the Most High will overshadow you; and for that reason the holy offspring shall be called the Son of God'" (Luke 1:35).

He is everywhere present (that is, omnipresent) at the same time: "Where can I go from Thy Spirit? Or where can I flee from Thy presence?" (Ps. 139:7).

He is all-knowing (that is, omniscient): "For to us God revealed them through the Spirit; for the Spirit searches all things, even the depths of God. For who among men knows the thoughts of a man except the spirit of the man, which is in him? Even so the thoughts of God no one knows except the Spirit of God" (1 Cor. 2:10, 11).

The Holy Spirit is called God: "But Peter said, 'Ananias, why has Satan filled your heart to lie to the Holy Spirit, and to keep back some of the price of the land? While it remained unsold, did it not remain your own? And after it was sold, was it not under your control? Why is it that you have conceived this deed in your heart? *You have not lied to men, but to God*'" (Acts 5:3, 4, italics mine).

"And we all, with unveiled face, beholding the glory of the Lord, are being changed into his likeness from one degree of glory to another; for this comes from the Lord who is the Spirit" (2 Cor. 3:18 RSV).

He is the Creator: The first biblical reference to the Holy Spirit is Genesis 1:2 (Moffatt) where we are told "the spirit of God was hovering over the waters." Yet Genesis 1:1 says, "In the beginning God created the heavens and the earth." And in Colossians 1 where Paul is writing to the Church at Colossae about the Lord Jesus Christ, among other tremendous truths he tells us, "For in Him all things were created, both in the heavens and on earth, visible and invisible, whether thrones or dominions or rulers or authorities—all things have been created through Him and for Him. And He is before all things, and in Him all things hold together" [cohere] (Col. 1:16, 17).

Thus, God the Father, God the Son, and God the Holy Spirit were together creating the world. To understand and accept these facts is of the greatest importance to every Christian, both theologically and practically.

One day I made a few of these assertions about the Holy Spirit to some seminary students. One asked, "But He is usually mentioned last. Doesn't that imply inferiority?" Yet in Romans 15:30 He is not mentioned last: "Now I urge you, brethren, by our Lord Jesus Christ and by the love of the Spirit, to strive together with me in your prayers to God for me." And in Ephesians 4:4 Paul says, "There is one body and one Spirit, just as also you were called in one hope of your calling."

But more than this, the usual placement of the three persons of the Trinity in the New Testament has to do with their order and function. Thus we say that we pray to the Father through the Son and in the power of the Holy Spirit. Moreover, I have already shown that *functionally* the Father came first, then the Son became incarnate, died and rose again. Now the Spirit does His work in this age of the Spirit. The order has nothing to do with equality, but only with function and chronology.

The Trinity

When I first began to study the Bible years ago, the doctrine of the Trinity was one of the most complex problems I had to encounter. I have never fully resolved it, for it contains an aspect of mystery. Though I do not totally understand it to this day, I accept it as a revelation of God.

The Bible teaches us that the Holy Spirit is a living being. He is one of the three persons of the Holy Trinity. To explain and illustrate the Trinity is one of the most difficult assignments to a Christian. Dr. David McKenna once told me that he was asked by his small son, Doug, "Is God the Father God?" He answered, "Yes." "Is Jesus Christ God?" "Yes." "Is the Holy Spirit God?" "Yes." "Then how can Jesus be His own Father?" David thought quickly. They were sitting in their old 1958 Chevrolet at the time. "Listen, son," he replied, "under the hood is one battery. Yet I can use it to turn on the lights, blow the horn, and start the car." He said, "How this happens is a mystery—but it happens!"

The Bible *does* teach us the reality of the Trinity, both in the Old and New Testaments. Let us look at some of the major passages.

God unfolds His revelation of Himself in the Bible progressively. But there are indications from the very beginning of the Book of Genesis that God subsists in three persons—the Father, the Son, and the Holy Spirit—and that these three persons constitute the one God. Christianity is trinitarian, not unitarian. There is only one God, not three, so it is clear that the Christian faith is not polytheistic.

The Bible begins with the majestic statement: "In the beginning God created the heavens and the earth" (Gen. 1:1).

Hebrew scholars have told me there are three numbers in the Hebrew language: Singular, one; dual, two; plural, more than two. The word translated "God" in Genesis 1:1 is plural, indicating more than two. The Hebrew word used here is *Elohim.* Matthew Henry says it signifies "the plurality of persons in the Godhead, Father, Son, and Holy Ghost. This plural name of God . . . [confirms] our faith in the doctrine of the Trinity, which, though but darkly intimated in the Old Testament, is clearly revealed in the New."[1]

As we have seen concerning creation, even from the beginning God gives us glimpses of the truth that the Godhead consists of more than one person. I have italicized some of the key words. In Genesis 1:26, God said, "Let *us* make man in *our* image, according to *our* likeness; and let them rule over the fish of the sea and over the birds of the sky and over the cattle and over all the earth, and over every creeping thing that creeps on the earth." Further, in Genesis 3:22 the Lord God said, "Behold, the man has become like one of *Us,* knowing good and evil." And in Genesis 11:6, 7, the Lord said, "Behold, they are one people, and they all have the same language. And this is what they began to do, and now nothing which they purpose to do will be impossible for them. Come, let *Us* go down and there confuse their language, that they may not understand one another's speech." When Isaiah heard the voice of the Lord saying, "*Whom shall I send, and who will go for us?*" he answered, "Here am I. Send me!" (Isa. 6:8).

The New Testament's doctrine of the Trinity is much more

fully developed than that of the Old Testament. Since revelation is progressive, more light is thrown on this subject as God more fully disclosed Himself at the time of Christ and the apostles.

The last command of Jesus before His ascension is recorded in Matthew 28:18–20. In it He ordered His followers to "make disciples of all the nations," baptizing converts "in the name of the Father and the Son and the Holy Spirit, teaching them to observe all that I commanded you; and lo, I am with you always, even to the end of the age." Here Jesus taught that after He left this earth, His followers were to carry His gospel message to all nations. The Holy Spirit was to use them to call out a people for His name. This trinitarian commission to baptize associates the Holy Spirit with God the Father and God the Son as their equal. He is God the Holy Spirit.

It is thrilling to note that Jesus says believers will not be left alone. Through the Holy Spirit whom He and the Father sent, He will never leave us nor forsake us (Heb. 13:5). He will remain with every believer right to the end. This thought has encouraged me a thousand times in these dark days when satanic forces are at work in so many parts of the world.

Along this line the apostle Paul also said, "The grace of the Lord Jesus Christ, and the love of God, and the fellowship of the Holy Spirit, be with you all" (2 Cor. 13:14). This benediction clearly indicates that the Holy Spirit is one with the Father and one with the Son in the Godhead. *It is not one plus one plus one equals three. It is one times one times one equals one.* The Holy Spirit is one with the Father and the Son. If the Father is God, and Jesus is God, then the Holy Spirit is also God.

The chief problem connected with the doctrine of the Trinity concerns Christianity's claim to be also monotheistic. It rejects polytheism, the belief in more than one God. The answer is that trinitarianism preserves the unity of the Godhead, and at the same time it acknowledges that there are three persons in that Godhead which is still of one essence. God is one, but that oneness is not simple—it is complex.

This is a terribly difficult subject—far beyond the ability of our limited minds to grasp fully. Nevertheless, it is extremely important to declare what the Bible holds, and be silent where the Bible is silent. God the Father is fully God. God the Son is fully God. God the Holy Spirit is fully God. The Bible presents this as fact. It does not explain it. Nevertheless, many explanations have been suggested, some of which sound logical, but they do not preserve the truth of Scriptural teaching.

One Christian heresy in the early church was called "modalism." It taught that God appeared at different times in three different modes or forms—as Father, then as Son, and finally as Holy Spirit. Those who held this view thought it preserved the unity of monotheism. But it also meant that when Jesus prayed, He had to be talking to Himself. Further, to say, as Acts 2 does, that the Father and the Son sent the Holy Spirit, makes little sense if we accept modalism. Moreover, it violated the clearest presentation of the Trinity-in-unity as expressed in Matthew's statement by Jesus in the Great Commission. It was Jesus who said that His disciples were to baptize their converts "in the name of the Father and the Son and the Holy Spirit." The Greek construction makes it clear that Jesus is referring to three separate persons. He clearly taught the doctrine of the Trinity.

We have seen that the Holy Spirit is a person, and is God, and is a member of the Trinity. Anyone who fails to recognize this is robbed of his joy and power. Of course a defective view of any member of the Trinity will bring about this result because God is all important. But this is especially true for the Holy Spirit, for although the Father is the source of all blessing, and the Son is the channel of all blessing, it is through the Holy Spirit at work in us that all truth becomes living and operative in our lives.

The most important point I can make in summary is this: there is nothing that God is that the Holy Spirit is not. All of the essential aspects of deity belong to the Holy Spirit. We can say of Him exactly what was said of Jesus Christ in the ancient Nicene Creed: He is very God of very God! So we bow before Him, we worship Him, we accord Him every response Scripture requires of our relationship to Almighty God.

Who is the Holy Spirit? He is God!

2. When the Holy Spirit Has Come

As I was writing this chapter, my wife and I sat on the porch in the hot spring sun, and we talked about the refreshment of the wind as evening came. We especially discussed the power and the mystery of the wind.

It is interesting that in Scripture, in both the original Hebrew and Greek languages, the word used in speaking of the Spirit is the word that can also mean "wind." In like manner, the Holy Spirit works in different ways in our lives, and in different times in history.

I have seen tornadoes in Texas and Oklahoma, and even in my home state of North Carolina when I was a boy. Yes, I have seen the power of the wind. I have seen the air-brakes that use the wind, or the air, to stop the giant truck going down the highway. That same force can lift a giant airplane.

"The manager of a granite quarry in North Carolina said: 'We supplied the granite for the municipal building in New York City. We can lift an acre of solid granite ten feet thick to almost any height we desire for the purpose of moving it. We do it with air. We can do it as easily as I can lift a piece of paper.'

"Air! Air—this invisible envelopment in which we live and move, this substance so immaterial that we can move our hands through it as though it had no reality at all. But the power it possesses! How great, how terrible!"[1]

We have seen something of the nature and personality of the Holy Spirit. Now we must catch a vision of His distinctive work in each of the great ages of time. But first, to place it in perspective, we must see how the Triune God is at work in every age.

The elements of mystery in this make it difficult for the human mind to comprehend fully. Simultaneously the Father, the Son, and the Holy Spirit have different functions to perform that are distinctive to each. For instance, it was not the Father or the Holy Spirit who died on the cross of Calvary. It was God the Son. We need to understand such facts, especially when we think of this present age and the work of God in it.

As we study the Bible, the work of God the Father is especially emphasized in the Old Testament. The work of God the Son is emphasized in the Gospels. From the day of Pentecost until the present, however, the emphasis is on the work of God the Holy Spirit. And yet the Bible also tells us God the Holy Spirit has been at work throughout history, from the beginning of the world. Therefore, we begin our study of the work of the Holy Spirit by examining briefly His activities in the eras before Pentecost, before concentrating on His unique ministry since then.

The Spirit's Work from Creation to Bethlehem

As we have seen in the previous chapter, the Holy Spirit was at work in creation. According to Genesis 1:2, "The earth was formless and void, and darkness was over the surface of the deep." Immediately, we are told that "the Spirit of God was moving over the surface of the waters." The Hebrew word for "moving" means "brooding" or "hovering." Just as a hen broods over her eggs for the purpose of hatching them and bringing forth new life, so the Holy Spirit brooded over the original creation of God for the purpose of filling its void with life in various forms. The creation recorded in the rest of Genesis 1, together with Genesis 2, resulted. Thus, from the beginning the Holy Spirit was active in creation along with the Father and the Son.

When God "formed man of dust from the ground" (Gen. 2:7), the Holy Spirit was involved. We learn this indirectly in Job 33:4, "The Spirit of God has made me, And the breath of the Almighty gives me life." A play on words here shows how intimately God's Spirit and our breath are related: both "Spirit" and "breath" are from the same Hebrew word.

Genesis 2:7 also says that the Lord God "breathed into his nostrils the breath of life; and man became a living being." While the Hebrew word translated "breath" here is not the one also meaning spirit, clearly man owes his very life to God according to this passage. And the breath of God that started man on his earthly journey was, in fact, the Holy Spirit, as Job 33:4 tells us.

Psalm 104:30 carries our understanding of the Spirit in creation a step further. Not only was the Spirit at work in the formation of the earth and the first man, but the Spirit is always the creator of life. "Thou [God] dost send forth Thy Spirit, they are created; And Thou dost renew the face of the ground." Who are the "they" whom the Spirit creates? The entire psalm clarifies this, but just in verses 18–26 we learn that included are wild goats and rock badgers (18), beasts of the forest such as young lions (20, 21), man (23), and whatever lives on the earth or in the sea (24, 25).

Understanding that the Spirit gives life, a married woman in the Old Testament who was unable to bear a child would go to the tabernacle or temple. There either she prayed or the priest petitioned God to open her womb. Now, such a woman knew the basic facts of life just as we do, although she did not possess as much scientific knowledge about the birth process as we do today. Yet even to us it is still one of the mysteries of nature and one of nature's miracles that sperm can penetrate an ovum and initiate a new life. This is simply a medical or biological way of describing the touch of God's hand in the creation of life.

Hannah is a classic illustration of this. She went to the tabernacle to pray for a son. Eli, the high priest, thought at first that she was drunk, but she informed him she was a woman in sorrow who had poured out her soul to the Lord. Eli responded, "Go in peace; and may the God of Israel grant your petition that you have asked of Him" (1 Sam. 1:17). She later conceived and Samuel the prophet was born. While in the story itself God's spirit is not mentioned, our understanding of His place according to Psalm 104:30 (and Job 33:4) shows us that the life-giving function distinctively belonged to God's Spirit.

Yet Psalm 104:30 says more than just that we owe our creation to the Spirit. The face of the ground is also renewed by Him. God feeds what He creates.

So believers in the Old Testament were rightly convinced that God had something to do with the growing of crops. They attributed a good harvest to Him: "He causes the grass to grow for the cattle, And vegetation for the labor of man, So that he may bring forth food from the earth" (Ps. 104:14). In Deuteronomy 28 the conditions for blessing or cursing in the promised land were enunciated. If Israel obeyed God there was the promise: "Blessed shall be the offspring of your body and the produce of your ground," and "The Lord will make you abound . . . in the produce of your ground" (Deut. 28:4, 11). Israel's Feast of Firstfruits formally recognized that God was responsible for abundance. Today as we bow our heads before meals to thank God for the food we continue to acknowledge God as the One who sustains us.

However, God both blesses and curses, delivers and punishes. The Old Testament often attributes the salvation of Israel to the Spirit of God. He strove with people before the flood (Gen. 6:3). I believe that He is striving with people today exactly as He did before the flood. Jesus said, "And just as it happened in the days of Noah, so it shall be also in the days of the Son of Man" (Luke 17:26). The same sick perversions, moral decay, and erosions are prevalent today. The Holy Spirit is mightily striving but the vast majority of the human race will not listen.

Then from time to time the Holy Spirit took possession of certain men in order to deliver God's people. For instance, in the Book of Judges alone, He came upon Othniel (3:10), Gideon (6:34), Jephthah (11:29), and Samson (13:25).

The three main expressions used in the Old Testament for the work of the Holy Spirit on human beings are:

(1) He *came* upon men: "Then the Spirit of God came on Zechariah" (2 Chron. 24:20). (2) He *rested* on men: "the Spirit rested upon them" (Num. 11:25). (3) He *filled* men: "I have filled him with the Spirit of God" (Exod. 31:3).

The Spirit used not only judges and prophets to deliver Israel, but also kings. They were anointed with oil, a symbol that they were empowered with the Holy Spirit. So when Samuel anointed David in 1 Samuel 16:13, "the Spirit of the Lord came mightily upon David from that day forward."

Yet the next verse sounds a note of solemnity. While in Judges the Spirit often departed when the select person's task was done, He also might withdraw when the chosen one disobeyed. This occurred to Saul according to 1 Samuel 16:14, and also to

Samson, as we see by comparing Judges 14:19 with 16:20. David's concern that the Spirit might withdraw from him occasioned his prayer, "Do not take Thy Holy Spirit from me" (Ps. 51:11).

God's great deliverance, of course, came not with a human anointed king, but with the Messiah, a title that means "Anointed." Isaiah had recorded prophetically that the Messiah would say, "The Spirit of the Lord God is upon me, Because the Lord has anointed me" (Isa. 61:1). And Jesus, reading this in the synagogue 800 years later, said, "Today this Scripture has been fulfilled in your hearing" (Luke 4:21).

It is not always easy to separate the roles of the Father, the Son, and the Holy Spirit in the Old Testament. But we do know that Jesus appeared from time to time in "theophanies" which are simply appearances of our Lord before the Incarnation. We also know that the use of the name of God in the Old Testament can refer to different members of the Trinity.

In summary, we have seen that the Holy Spirit was at work before the world began. Then He renewed and fed His creation. He was active throughout the Old Testament, both in the world of nature and among His people, guiding and delivering them through the judges, prophets, kings, and others. And He told of a coming day when the Anointed One would come.

The Spirit's Work from Bethlehem to Pentecost

During the period of time covered by the four Gospels, the work of the Holy Spirit centered around the person of Jesus Christ. The God-man was begotten of the Spirit (Luke 1:35), baptized by the Spirit (John 1:32, 33), led by the Spirit (Luke 4:1), anointed by the Spirit (Luke 4:18; Acts 10:38), and empowered by the Spirit (Matt. 12:27, 28). He offered Himself as an atonement for sin by the Spirit (Heb. 9:14), was raised by the Spirit (Rom. 8:11), and gave commandments by the Spirit (Acts 1:2).

Without a doubt one of the most awe-inspiring passages in Scripture relates what the angel said to Mary: "The Holy Spirit will come upon you, and the power of the Most High will overshadow you; and for that reason the holy offspring shall be called the Son of God" (Luke 1:35). Overly skeptical people, and others with too limited a view of science, may scoff in utter disbelief, but the angel dispelled all doubt when he said, "For nothing will be impossible with God" (Luke 1:37).

For Christians, any suggestion that God the Holy Spirit was not capable of bringing the virgin birth to pass is nonsense. If we believe that God is God—and that He rules His universe—nothing is too great for His limitless power. At all times God does whatever He chooses. When He planned the Messiah's birth, He performed a miracle. He bypassed one link in the normal physiological chain of birth: no human male participated. The life that was formed in the womb of the virgin was none other than the incarnate life of God the Son in human flesh. The virgin birth was a sign so extraordinary that it was obviously God and not man at work in the Incarnation. There are some so-called theologians today who deny the Incarnation—they reject the deity of Jesus Christ. In so doing they come very close to blaspheming the Holy Spirit!

The Holy Spirit was also at work among the disciples of Jesus before Pentecost. We know this because Jesus said of them, "He [the Holy Spirit] abides with you" (John 14:17). Jesus also said to Nicodemus, "Unless one is born of water and the Spirit, he cannot enter into the kingdom of God" (John 3:5). Again, He said, "You must be born again" (John 3:7).

Yet the operation of the Spirit among men in Jesus' day differed from His work today. For in John 7:39 we are told by the apostle John concerning the word of Jesus: "But this He [Jesus] spoke of the Spirit, whom those who believed in Him were to receive; for the Spirit was not yet given, because Jesus was not yet glorified."

Exactly what the difference was the Bible does not reveal completely. However, we know that the coming of the Spirit at Pentecost was in a far greater measure than anything they had ever experienced before. At any rate, we have seen that the Holy Spirit was at work in various ways in the birth and life of our Lord Jesus Christ and in the lives and ministries of His disciples.

The Spirit's Work from Pentecost till Now

In Acts, Luke records the ascension of Jesus into heaven (Acts 1:9–11). In chapter 2 he depicts the descent of the Holy Spirit to earth (Acts 2:1–4). Jesus had said, "If I do not go away, the Helper [Holy Spirit] shall not come to you; but if I go, I will send Him to you" (John 16:7). It was in fulfillment of this promise that Peter, speaking of the glorified Christ, said, "Therefore having been exalted to the right hand of God, and having received from the Father the promise of the Holy Spirit, He has poured forth this which you both see and hear" (Acts 2:33).

Many years ago a great Arctic explorer started on an expedition to the North Pole. After two long years in the lonely northland he wrote a short message, tied it under the wing of a carrier pigeon, and prepared to turn it loose to make the two thousand mile journey to Norway. The explorer gazed around him at the desolation. Not a creature to be seen. There was nothing but ice, snow, and never-ending bitter cold. He held the trembling little bird in his hand for a moment and then released her into the icy atmosphere. The bird circled three times, and then started her southward flight for multiplied hundreds of miles over ice and frozen ocean wastes until at last she dropped into the lap of the explorer's wife. By the arrival of the bird, his wife knew that all was well with her husband in the dark night of the arctic North.

Likewise the coming of the Holy Spirit, the Heavenly Dove, proved to the disciples that Christ had entered the heavenly sanctuary. He was seated at the right hand of God the Father, for His atoning work was finished. The advent of the Holy Spirit fulfilled Christ's promise; and it also testified that God's righteousness had been vindicated. The age of the Holy Spirit, which could not commence until Jesus was glorified, had now begun.

Unquestionably the coming of the Holy Spirit on the day of Pentecost marked a crucial turning point in the history of God's dealings with the human race. It is one of five past events, all of which are essential components of the Christian gospel: the Incarnation, the Atonement, the Resurrection, the Ascension, and Pentecost. A sixth component is still future: the Second Coming of Jesus.

The Incarnation as the first event marked the redemptive entrance of God into human life as true man. The second event in the series was the means by which God could remain just and yet justify guilty men—the Atonement. The third, the

Resurrection, demonstrated that man's three great enemies—death, Satan, and hell—had been dealt their death blow. The fourth—the Ascension—showed that the Father had accepted the atoning work of the Son and that His righteous demands had been met. Pentecost, the fifth, assures us that the Spirit of God has come to achieve His certain purposes in the world, in the church, and in the individual believer!

The Jewish religious calendar centered in a number of annual feasts. However, the three most important were those in which all males were required to appear before the Lord (Deut. 16:16). These were the feasts of Passover, Tabernacles, and Pentecost.

"The Feast of Passover" commemorated the time when the Israelites were miraculously freed from a long period of slavery in Egypt. After killing an "unblemished" lamb (Exod. 12:5), the Israelites placed the blood over the door of each Israelite house and the lamb was roasted and eaten. The blood of the lamb brought about deliverance from God's judgment. The Old Testament passover found its final fulfillment in the death of Christ on Calvary, "For Christ our Passover also has been sacrificed" (1 Cor. 5:7). The Book of Hebrews teaches us that there is therefore no more need for the offering of the blood of bulls and goats. Jesus Christ, once and forever, offered Himself for the salvation of men by shedding His blood.

"The Feast of Tabernacles" (the present-day word for tabernacle is "booths" or "tents") reminded Israel of the days during the exodus from Egypt when the people lived not in houses, but in booths made of cut branches. The celebration came when the harvests were in, so it is called the "Feast of Ingathering" in Exodus 23:16. Perhaps celebration of deliverance from Egypt was fulfilled in the greater deliverance and blessing that came with redemption in Christ. John 7:38 may suggest that the coming of the Holy Spirit quenches thirst as neither the water of the desert nor the rain needed for harvest could do.

Pentecost was known as the "Feast of Weeks" because it was celebrated on the day following the passage of seven sabbaths —a Week of Weeks—from Passover. Because it fell on the fiftieth day, it gained the name "Pentecost," from the Greek word for "fiftieth." The Feast of Pentecost celebrated the beginning of the harvest; in Numbers 28:26 it was called "the day of the first fruits." In a real sense, the Day of Pentecost in the New Testament on which the Holy Spirit came was "a day of first fruits"—the beginning of God's harvest in this world, to be completed when Christ comes again. Pentecost in the New Testament marked the commencement of the present age of the Holy Spirit. Believers are under His guidance even as the disciples of Jesus were under Him. From heaven Jesus still exercises lordship over us, but, not being physically with us now, He transmits His directions by means of the Holy Spirit who makes Christ real to us. Since Pentecost the Holy Spirit is the link between the first and second advents of Jesus. He applies the work of Jesus Christ to men in this age, as we will see in the pages that follow.

When I began studying about the Holy Spirit shortly after I became a Christian, one of the first questions I asked myself was: Why did the Holy Spirit have to come? I soon found the answer in my Bible study. He came because He had a work to do in the *world*, in the *Church*, and in the individual *Christian*, as we will now discover.

The Holy Spirit's Present Work in the World

In regard to the world, the Spirit's work is twofold. First, He has come to reprove it of sin, righteousness, and judgment (John 16:7-11). The Bible teaches us, and we know from experience, that all have sinned and are coming short of the glory of God (Rom. 3:23). Sinful man cannot inherit eternal life. Everyone who has ever been born recapitulates Adam's fall. Everyone is born with the seed of sin within him which, with the coming of the age of accountability, culminates in a multitude of sins. There is a difference between sin and sins. Sin is the root, sins are the fruit.

However, a person may not be consciously aware that his deepest problem is sin, or that his sin has separated him from fellowship with God. Therefore, it is the work of the Holy Spirit to disturb and convict him in his sin. Until this takes place he cannot experience salvation. In our crusade meetings I have seen people walk out shaking their fists at me as I was preaching. They are not actually hostile toward me, I know, but they have been brought under conviction by the Holy Spirit. Often people like this later return to find Christ.

But the Holy Spirit not only convicts of sin, He convinces

men that Jesus is the righteousness of God. He shows sinners that Jesus is the way, the truth, and the life, and that no one comes to the Father but by Him.

The Holy Spirit also convicts the world of judgment, because the prince of this world is judged, and all will be judged if they refuse God's offer of everlasting life. When the apostle Paul testified before Agrippa, he said that on the Damascus road at the time of his conversion God had told him the nature of his ministry. It would concern Gentiles and be "to open their eyes so that they may turn from darkness to light and from the dominion of Satan to God, in order that they may receive forgiveness of sins . . ." (Acts 26:18).

At the moment Jesus Christ died on the cross, Satan suffered an overwhelming defeat. That defeat may not be apparent as we read our newspapers and watch the television screens, but Satan is a defeated enemy in principle. He still wages his wicked warfare, and his total destruction and removal from the earth are near at hand. But until then, he will intensify his activities. It is quite apparent to Christians all over the world that new demons are abroad. Perversions, permissiveness, violence, and a hundred other sinister trends are now rampant on a world-wide scale perhaps unknown since the days of Noah. The Holy Spirit has come to show us these things, for He is deeply involved in biblical prophecy, as we will see later.

The Holy Spirit's work in the world is not confined to the ministry of conviction concerning sin, righteousness, and judgment, however. His *second work* in the world is to hinder the growth of lawlessness, that is, to engage in the ministry of preservation. The apostle Paul said, "For the mystery of lawlessness is already at work; only he who now restrains will do so until he is taken out of the way" (2 Thess. 2:7).

The Scripture makes it clear that this planet would already be a literal hell on earth were it not for the presence of the Holy Spirit in the world. The unbelieving world little knows what it owes to the restraining power of the Holy Spirit.

Several theologians to whom I have talked recently, both in Europe and America, hold the view that the Holy Spirit is gradually being withdrawn from the world as we enter what may be the climactic moments of the end of the present age. When He is totally withdrawn "all hell will break loose." The world will experience wars, violence, eruptions, perversions, hatred, fear—of which we are only seeing glimpses today. The human race will be in a hell of its own making. Free from the restraints of the Holy Spirit the Antichrist will reign supreme for a short period until he is crushed by the coming of the Lord Jesus Christ and the armies of heaven!

The Holy Spirit also *acts through* the people of God, who are called the salt of the earth and the light of the world by Jesus in His Sermon on the Mount (Matt. 5:13, 14). These are apt metaphors because salt and light are forces that operate silently and unobtrusively, yet with great effect. Salt and light speak of the influence Christians can exercise for good in society. We who are believers sometimes find it difficult to understand what influence we can have when we are such a minority, are so often divided, and are disobedient from time to time. By the power of the Spirit, however, we can restrain evil and do good!

To spell out the metaphors further, salt and light are essential in our homes: light dissipates the darkness, and salt prevents decay. The Bible tells us that the state of the world will grow darker as we near the end of the age. The world has no light of its own—and it is marked by a process of accelerating decay. However, Jesus taught us that we who are His followers, though weak and small in number, act as salt so that we can hinder the process of decline. Christians at work in the world are the only real spiritual light in the midst of great spiritual darkness. In studying the Old Testament prophets we discover that a part of the judgment on the wicked is the destruction of the righteous.

This places a tremendous responsibility on all of us. Only as the world sees our good works do they know that a light is shining. Only as the world senses our moral presence are they conscious of the salt. This is why Christ warned against the salt losing its saltness, and the light dimming. He said, "Let your light shine" (Matt. 5:16). If you and I filled this role faithfully, there would be a dramatic but peaceful revolution in the world almost overnight. We Christians are *not* powerless. We have the mighty power of God available through God the Holy Spirit, even in this world.

The Holy Spirit's Work in the Church

The Spirit is active not only in the world, but also in the Church. When speaking of the Church, I am not talking about the Presbyterian, Baptist, Methodist, Anglican, Lutheran, Pente-costal, or Catholic churches, but the whole body of believers. The word "Church" comes from the Greek word that means "called together ones."

Although the Church was veiled in mystery in the Old Testament, yet Isaiah proclaimed, "Therefore thus says the Lord God, 'Behold, I am laying in Zion for a foundation a stone, a tested stone, a precious cornerstone, of a sure foundation' " (Isa. 28:16 RSV). The New Testament speaks of Christ as that "sure foundation" of His Church, and all believers are little building stones built into a holy temple in the Lord (1 Peter 2:5). Christ is also the head of His body, the universal Church. And He is the head of every local congregation of believers. Every person who has repented of his sin and received Jesus Christ as Savior and Lord is a member of this body called the Church. So the Church is more than a religious organization. It is an organism with Christ as its living head. It is alive, with the life of Christ made living in each member.

What part does the Holy Spirit play in this? *First,* the Bible beautifully tells us that the Church was brought into being by Him: "For by one Spirit we were all baptized into one body, whether Jews or Greeks, whether slaves or free, and we were all made to drink of one Spirit. For the body is not one member, but many" (1 Cor. 12:13, 14).

Second, by the Spirit God lives in the Church: "And in him [Christ] you too are being built together to become a dwelling in which God lives by his Spirit" (Eph. 2:22 NIV). God does not dwell today in temples made with hands. But if we recognize that in our church gatherings God is really in our midst personally, it will deepen our worship.

One point about the relation of the Holy Spirit and Jesus Christ needs clarification. The Scriptures speak of "Christ in you," and some Christians do not fully understand what this means. As the God-man, Jesus is in a glorified body. And wherever Jesus is, His body must be also. In that sense, in His work as the second person of the Trinity, Jesus is now at the right hand of the Father in heaven.

For example, consider Romans 8:10 (KJV), which says, "If Christ is in you, the body is dead because of sin." Or consider Galatians 2:20, "Christ lives in me." It is clear in these verses that if the Spirit is in us, then Christ is in us. Christ dwells in our hearts by faith. But the Holy Spirit is the person of the Trinity who actually dwells in us, having been sent by the Son who has gone away but who will come again in person when we shall literally see Him.

Believers are indeed the dwelling place of the Spirit. But, unfortunately, they are often lacking in the fruit of the Spirit. They need to be quickened and given new life. This was brought home to me forcefully by Bishop Festo Kivengere. In an article on the remarkable revivals that have swept East Africa, he said: "I want to share with you . . . the glorious work of the Holy Spirit in bringing new life to a dead church. . . . You can call it renewal, coming to life or whatever you choose. . . . The Lord Jesus in his risen power through the power of the Holy Spirit began to visit a church which was scattered like bones. . . . It may surprise some of you . . . that you can be evangelical and dry, but you can. And then Jesus Christ came. . . . The attraction, the growing power came through a simple presentation of the New Testament and the Holy Spirit took men and women, including myself, from our isolation and drew us to the center, the Cross. The theme of East African revival was the Cross and we needed it. . . . The Holy Spirit drew men and women from their isolation, and changed us—sins were sins in the glare of God's love and hearts were melted."[2]

For example, I have a pastor friend in Florida. His various degrees came from one of America's most prestigious eastern universities. He pastored a church in New England. Through his much learning, he had become almost an "agnostic," though deep in his heart he still believed. He said he watched his church in New England dwindle around him. There was no authority or power in his ministry. Then through a series of events he came to accept the Bible as the infallible Word of God. He began to live and speak with power. The fruit of the Spirit was evident in his life and spiritual power was evident in his ministry. He saw his church blossom like a rose. People began to come from all around to hear him preach.

Third, the Holy Spirit gives gifts to specific people in the Church "for the equipping of the saints for the work of service, to the building up of the body of Christ" (Eph. 4:12). Since we will examine these gifts more closely in later chapters, it is enough to say here that the Holy Spirit gives every Christian some gift the moment he receives Christ. No Christian can say, "I have no gift." Every believer has at least one gift from the Holy Spirit. A weakness in today's churches is the failure to recognize, cultivate, and use fully the gifts God has given people in the pews.

I have a pastor friend on the west coast of the United States. One Sunday he passed out blank slips of paper to his congregation. He said, "I want you to spend a week studying, thinking, and praying about what gift you have from the Holy Spirit. Write it on this slip of paper. Then we will collect the slips next Sunday morning." More than 400 slips of paper were turned in the following Sunday. Some listed only one gift—some listed two or three—and some said they were not certain about their gift. However, as a result the entire congregation was mobilized. All the gifts began to be used. It transformed the church into a "growth" church and a spiritually revitalized membership. Until then the people were expecting the pastor to have all the gifts and to do all the work. They were simply spectators. Now they realized that they had as great a responsibility to use their gifts as the pastor has to use his gifts.

The Holy Spirit's Work in the Believer's Life

Having considered the Holy Spirit's work in the world and the Church, we must now consider each believer. *First,* the Holy Spirit illumines (enlightens) the Christian's mind: "For to us God revealed them through the Spirit; for the Spirit searches all things, even the depths of God" (1 Cor. 2:10); "And do not be conformed to this world, but be transformed by the renewing of your mind" (Rom. 12:2); "And that you be renewed in the spirit of your mind" (Eph. 4:23).

In a small book stressing the importance of allowing God to develop and use our converted minds, John R. W. Stott says: "Nobody wants a cold, joyless, intellectual Christianity. But does this mean we should avoid 'intellectualism' at all costs? . . . Heaven forbid that knowledge without zeal should replace zeal without knowledge! God's purpose is both, zeal directed by knowledge, knowledge fired with zeal. As I once heard Dr. John Mackay say, when he was President of Princeton Seminary, 'Commitment without reflection is fanaticism in action. But reflection without commitment is the paralysis of all action.' "[3]

Dr. Stott stresses how mistaken are those who say that what matters in the end is "not doctrine but experience." In rebuttal he says, "This is tantamount to putting our subjective experience above the revealed truth of God."[4] It is the business of the Holy Spirit to lift the veil Satan has put over our minds, and to illuminate them so that we can understand the things of God. He does this especially as we read and study the Word of God, which the Holy Spirit has inspired.

Second, the Holy Spirit not only illumines the Christian's mind, but also indwells his body. "Do you not know that your body is a temple of the Holy Spirit who is in you, whom you have from God, and that you are not your own?" (1 Cor. 6:19).

If we Christians realized that God Himself in the person of the Holy Spirit really dwells within our bodies, we would be far more careful about what we eat, drink, look at, or read. No wonder Paul said, "But I buffet my body and make it my slave, lest possibly, after I have preached to others, I myself should be disqualified" (1 Cor. 9:27). Paul disciplined his body for fear of God's disapproval. This should drive us to our knees in confession.

In other ways I need not enlarge upon now the Holy Spirit works in the lives of believers. For example, He comforts them (Acts 9:31); He guides them (John 16:13); He sanctifies them (Rom. 15:16); He tells His servants what to preach (1 Cor. 2:13); He directs missionaries where to go (Acts 13:2); He helps us in our infirmities (Rom. 8:26); and He even tells believers where they are not to go (Acts 16:6,7).

In summation, broadly speaking, the operations of the Holy Spirit among men in the three periods of human history may be defined by three words: "upon," "with," "in." In the Old Testament He came *upon* selected persons and remained for a season (Judg. 14:19). In the Gospels He is represented as dwelling *with* the disciples in the person of Christ (John 14:17). From the second chapter of Acts onward He is spoken of as being *in* the people of God (1 Cor. 6:19).

3. The Holy Spirit and the Bible

"Some time ago a man took his worn New Testament to a bookbinder to bind it with a fine Morocco leather cover and to print *The New Testament* on the edge in gold leaf letters.

"At the appointed time he returned to find his New Testament beautifully bound. The bookbinder had one apology, however: 'I did not have small enough type in my shop to print out fully the words on the edge so I abbreviated them.' Looking on the edge of his Book, the man saw—T.N.T.

"This is true! It is God's dynamite."[1]

In the New Testament Paul declares that all Scripture comes from God. In fact, he says: "All Scripture is inspired by God and profitable for teaching, for reproof, for correction, for training in righteousness" (2 Tim. 3:16). He used a Greek word for "inspired" that literally means "God-breathed." Somewhat as God breathed life into man and made him a living soul, so also He breathed life and wisdom into the written Word of God. This makes the Bible the world's most important book, especially to everyone who believes in Christ. The Bible is the constant fountain for faith, conduct, and inspiration from which we drink daily.

The Holy Spirit Was the Inspirer of Scripture

Hundreds of passages indicate—either directly or indirectly —that God the Holy Spirit inspired the men who wrote the Bible. We do not know exactly how He imprinted His message on the minds of those He chose to write His Word, but we know

He did lead them to write what He wanted. "For no prophecy was ever made by an act of human will, but men moved by the Holy Spirit spoke from God" (2 Peter 1:21).

It seems that each book of the Bible came into being because of a special need at that time. Yet even as God was meeting a particular need, He was looking into the distant future too. He designed the Bible to meet the needs of all people in all ages. For this reason, biblical writers sometimes wrote about future events they did not understand fully but saw only dimly. Isaiah may not have fully understood the fifty-third chapter of his book as he detailed the suffering of Jesus Christ more than 700 years before it took place. "As to this salvation, the prophets who prophesied of the grace that would come to you made careful search and inquiry, seeking to know what person or time the Spirit of Christ within them was indicating as He predicted the sufferings of Christ and the glories to follow" (1 Peter 1:10, 11).

Throughout both the Old and New Testaments we find constant references to the Spirit of God inspiring the men of God who would write the Scriptures. For example, the Bible teaches that the Spirit spoke through David, who wrote many of the Psalms: "The Spirit of the Lord spoke by me, and His word was on my tongue" (2 Sam. 23:2).

He also spoke through the great prophet Jeremiah: "I will put My law within them, and on their heart I will write it; and I will be their God, and they shall be My people. And they shall not teach again, each man his neighbor and each man his brother, saying, 'Know the Lord,' for they shall all know Me, from the least of them to the greatest of them," declares the Lord, "for I will forgive their iniquity, and their sin I will remember no more" (Jer. 31:33, 34).

Ezekiel said: "The Spirit then entered me and made me stand on my feet, and He spoke with me and said to me, 'Go, shut yourself up in your house'" (Ezek. 3:24).

The apostle Peter spoke of "all things, about which God spoke by the mouth of His holy prophets from ancient time" (Acts 3:21).

The Book of Hebrews quotes from the Law (Heb. 9:6–8), the prophets (Heb. 10:15–17), and the Psalms (Heb. 3:7–10), in each case attributing authorship to the Holy Spirit.

Jesus assured the disciples in advance that the Holy Spirit would inspire the writers of the New Testament: "The Holy Spirit . . . will teach you all things, and bring to your remembrance all that I said to you" (John 14:26). This embraces the four Gospels, Matthew to John. Jesus' statement, "He will guide you into all the truth" (John 16:13), takes in the books from Acts to Jude. "He will disclose to you what is to come" (John 16:13), covers the Book of Revelation as well as many other passages throughout the New Testament. Thus, as someone has said, Scripture is literature indwelt by the Spirit of God.

Just as God the Holy Spirit inspired the writing of the Scriptures, so He was instrumental in the selection of the sixty-six books that comprise the canon of the Bible. Contrary to the opinion of many, the question of what books were included in the Bible was not settled simply by the human choice of any church council. The Holy Spirit was at work in Spirit-filled believers who selected the sixty-six books we have in our Bibles. And at last, after years and even centuries of discussion, prayer, and heartsearching, the canon of Scripture was closed. The Holy Spirit in His work did not bypass the human processes, but instead, He worked through them.

"Inspiration by the Spirit" Defined

When discussing the inspiration of the Bible, we immediately touch one of the most controversial questions of the ages. Ever since Satan questioned Eve in the Garden of Eden, "Indeed, has God said . . . ?" men have attacked the Word of God. But every time in history they have doubted it, dire consequences have resulted—whether in the life of an individual, a nation (ancient Israel), or the Church. Without exception the individual, the nation, or the Church went into a period of spiritual decline. Often idolatry and immorality followed.

Competent scholars agree that the Holy Spirit did not merely use the biblical writers as secretaries to whom He dictated the Scriptures, although some sincere Christians think He did this. The Bible itself does not state in detail just *how* the Holy Spirit accomplished His purpose in getting the Scripture written. However, we do know that He used living human minds and guided their thoughts according to His divine purposes. Moreover, it has always been clear to me that we cannot have inspired ideas without inspired words.

It would be helpful if we define the important words associated with God-breathed Scripture. The first is *inspiration*.

When we speak of the *total* (or *plenary*) *inspiration* of the Bible, we mean that all of the Bible, not just some parts of it, are inspired. Dr. B. H. Carroll, founder of the largest theological seminary in the world (Southwestern Baptist Theological Seminary of Fort Worth, Texas), spoke and wrote at length on this subject:

. . . the Bible is called holy because it is that infallible, *theopneustos* [God-breathed-out], product of the Holy Spirit. . . .

A great many people say, "I think the Word of God is in the Bible, but I don't believe that all of the Bible is the Word of God; it contains the Word of God, but it is not the Word of God."

My objection to this is that it would require inspiration to tell the spots in it that were inspired. It would call for an inspiration more difficult than the kind that I talk about, in order to turn the pages of the Bible and find out which part is the Word of God. . . .

In other words, with reference to the Scriptures, inspiration is plenary, which means full and complete, hence my question is, "Do you believe in the plenary inspiration of the Bible?" If the inspiration is complete, it must be plenary.

My next question is this: "Do you believe in plenary verbal inspiration?"

I do, for the simple reason that the words are mere signs of ideas, and I don't know how to get at the idea except through the words. If the words don't tell me, how shall I know? Sometimes the word is a very small one, maybe only one letter or a mere element. The word with one letter—the smallest letter—shows the inspiration of the Old Testament. The man that put that there was inspired.

Take the words of Jesus. He says, "Not one jot or tittle of that law shall ever fail."

The "jot" is the smallest letter in the Hebrew alphabet and the "tittle" is a small turn or projection of a Hebrew letter. He says the heavens may fall, but not one jot or tittle of that law shall fail. Then He says that the Scriptures cannot be broken.

What is it that cannot be broken? Whatever is written cannot be broken if it is *theopneustos*. But the word is not inspired if it is not *theopneustos*, which means God-breathed, or God-inspired.[2]

We could say much more about the complete trustworthiness of the Bible. By way of illustration, hundreds of times the Bible uses phrases like "God said," or "The word of the Lord came unto me saying." It is also interesting that Jesus never once told us to doubt the difficult passages of the Old Testament Scriptures. For example, He accepted as fact, not fiction, the stories of Jonah and the fish, Noah and the ark, and the creation of Adam and Eve. If these stories had not been literally true, He surely would have told us so. But time after time Jesus (and the New Testament writers) quoted the Scriptures as authoritative and as the very Word of God.

Of course, inspiration by the Holy Spirit does not refer to the many English translations, but to the original languages. No modern language, whether English, French, or Spanish, has in it the exact equivalent for every Greek or Hebrew word. However, numerous scholars agree that most of the translations, even with their variations, do not alter or misrepresent the basic theological teachings of the Scriptures—especially those dealing with salvation and Christian living.

My wife has more than twenty different translations available at all times. By the time she has compared the various wordings of all these, she can be reasonably sure that she has a good idea of the meaning the Holy Spirit intended to convey in any passage of Scripture.

It is also interesting that some words could not be translated into other languages so it was necessary to lift them from the original tongue. The Greek word for "baptism" had no English equivalent, so it came to *be* the English word. The Holy Spirit has seen to it that the Bible is not a dead book but a living vehicle for Him to use as He wishes.

There is a second word we should discuss when we talk about the Bible. Not only is the Bible inspired, but it is also *authoritative*. When we say the Bible is *authoritative*, we mean that it is God's binding revelation to us. We submit to it because it has come from God. Suppose we ask: What is the source of our religious knowledge? The answer is, the Bible, and it is authoritative for us. As Dr. John R. W. Stott has written,

"To reject the authority of either the Old Testament or the New Testament is to reject the authority of Christ. It is supremely because we are determined to submit to the authority of Jesus Christ as Lord that we submit to the authority of Scripture. . . . submission to Scripture is fundamental to everyday Christian living, for without it Christian discipleship, Christian integrity, Christian freedom and Christian witness are all seriously damaged if not actually destroyed."[3]

Yes, every area of our lives is to be under the Lordship of Jesus Christ. And that means the searchlight of God's Word must penetrate every corner of our lives. We are not free to pick and choose the parts of the Bible we want to believe or obey. God has given us all of it, and we should be obedient to all of it.

Having declared what I believe about the authority, inspiration, and infallibility of the Bible, I must still answer one further question. On what basis have I come to believe all of this about the Bible? There are various reasons for having confidence in the Bible as God's Word, but it is at this point that the work of the Holy Spirit is most plainly manifested. The truth of the matter is that the same Holy Spirit who was the author of the Scriptures through the use of human personalities also works in each of us to convince us the Bible is the Word of God to be trusted in all its parts.

In his *Institutes of the Christian Religion,* John Calvin has a word about the testimony of the Holy Spirit that I like:

"The same Spirit, therefore, who has spoken through the mouths of the prophets must penetrate into our hearts to persuade us that they faithfully proclaimed what had been divinely commanded. . . . Until he illumines their minds, they ever waver among many doubts! . . . Let this point therefore stand: that those whom the Holy Spirit has inwardly taught truly rest upon Scripture, and that Scripture indeed is self-authenticated; hence, it is not right to subject it to proof and reasoning. And the certainty it deserves with us, it attains by the testimony of the Spirit. For even if it wins reverence for itself by its own majesty, it seriously affects us only when it is sealed upon our hearts through the Spirit."

Calvin continues, "Therefore, illumined by his power, we believe neither by our own nor by anyone else's judgment that Scripture is from God; but above human judgment we affirm with utter certainty (just as if we were gazing upon the majesty of God himself) that it has flowed to us from the very mouth of God by the ministry of men. We seek no proofs, no marks of genuineness upon which our judgment may lean; but we subject our judgment and wit to it as to a thing far beyond any guesswork! This we do, not as persons accustomed to seize upon some unknown thing, which, under closer scrutiny, displeases them, but fully conscious that we hold the unassailable truth!"[4]

The Illumination of the Spirit

That the writers of the Old and New Testaments were inspired by the Holy Spirit is one part of the story. In addition, He illumines the minds and opens the hearts of its readers. We find spiritual response to the Word of God described in scores of ways. Jeremiah said, "Thy words were found and I ate them, And Thy words became for me a joy and the delight of my heart; For I have been called by Thy name, O Lord God of hosts" (Jer. 15:16). Furthermore, Isaiah said, "The grass withers, the flower fades, But the word of our God stands forever" (Isa. 40:8).

Jesus warned the Sadducees of His day that they entertained many errors in their teachings because they did not know the Scriptures or the power of God (Matt. 22:29). This links the Scriptures to the power of the Holy Spirit, who effects change through the Bible. Moreover, John records Jesus' words, "the Scripture cannot be broken" (John 10:35). Jesus also said, "You are already clean because of the word which I have spoken to you" (John 15:3).

So through the Bible the Holy Spirit not only gives us doctrinal and historical truth; He also uses it as the vehicle for speaking to our hearts. This is why I constantly urge people to study the Scriptures—whether they fully understand what they are reading or not. The reading of Scripture itself enables the Holy Spirit to enlighten us and to do His work in us. While we read the Word, its message saturates our hearts, whether we are conscious of what is happening or not. The Word with all its mysterious power touches our lives and gives us its power.

This is seen, for example, in a statement Paul made: "Eye hath not seen, nor ear heard, neither have entered into the heart of man, the things which God hath prepared for them that love him. But God hath revealed them unto us by his Spirit . . ." (1 Cor. 2:9, 10 KJV).

Note that Paul does not say God reveals these wonderful things to us by His *Word* (although it is there that we find them), but rather He does it by His *Spirit* through His Word. "We have received, not the spirit of the world, but the Spirit who is from God, that we might know the things freely given to us by God" (1 Cor. 2:12).

As the Reverend Gottfried Osei-Mensah of Kenya said at the Lausanne Congress on Evangelization in 1974: "It is the work of the Holy Spirit to reveal truths previously hidden from human search and understanding, and to enlighten men's minds to know and understand them (1 Cor. 2:9, 10). . . . If the role of the Holy Spirit is to teach, ours is to be diligent students of the Word."[5]

This has been my experience as I have studied the Scriptures. Things I may have known intellectually for years have come alive to me in their fuller spiritual significance almost miraculously. As I have studied the Scriptures, I have also learned that the Spirit always lets more light shine from the Word. Almost every time I read an old, familiar passage I see something new. This happens because the written Word of God is a living Word. I always come to the Scriptures with the Psalmist's prayer, "Open my eyes, that I may behold wonderful things from Thy law" (Ps. 119:18).

The Unity of the Spirit and the Word

A glorious unity exists between the Holy Spirit and the Word of God. On the day of Pentecost Peter illustrated this in quoting from the Old Testament, "This is that which was spoken by the prophet Joel" (Acts 2:16 KJV). "This" refers to the promised Spirit. "That" refers to the written Word. "This is that" shows the wonderful unity that exists between the Spirit and the Word.

"Where the word of a king is, there is power" (Eccl. 8:4 KJV), and "where the Spirit of the Lord is, there is liberty" (2 Cor. 3:17). These two things—power and liberty—will characterize the utterances of that man who, filled with the Spirit, proclaims the Word of God. James Hervey describes the change that took place in Wesley when he was controlled by the Spirit. "Wesley's preaching," he says, "once was like the firing of an arrow—all the speed and force depended on the strength of his arm in bending the bow; now it was like the fire of a rifle ball—the force depending upon the power, needing only a finger touch to let it off."

I believe effective preaching must be biblical preaching, whether it is the exposition of a single word in the Bible, a text, or a chapter. The Word is what the Spirit uses. So the important element is that the Word of God be proclaimed. Thousands of pastors, Sunday school teachers and Christian workers are powerless because they do not make the Word the source of their preaching or teaching. When we preach or teach the Scriptures, we open the door for the Holy Spirit to do His work. God has not promised to bless oratory or clever preaching. He has promised to bless His Word. He has said that it will not return to Him "empty" (Isa. 55:11).

It is the Word of God which changes our lives also. Remember, God has given us His Word "for teaching, for reproof, for correction, for training in righteousness; that the man of God may be adequate, equipped for every good work" (2 Tim. 3:16, 17). Are these things happening in our lives? Are we learning God's truth? Jesus said, "Thy word is truth" (John 17:17). Are we being convicted of sin in our lives, and our need of God's correction and God's righteousness, as we read the Word of God? The Bible says, "For the word of God is living and active and sharper than any two-edged sword, and piercing as far as the division of soul and spirit, of both joints and marrow, and able to judge the thoughts and intentions of the heart. And there is no creature hidden from His sight, but all things are open and laid bare to the eyes of Him with whom we have to do." (Heb. 4:12, 13). Let the study of the Bible become central in your life—not just so you will know it, but that you will obey it. Let Job's statement be yours: "I have not departed from the command of His lips; I have treasured the words of His mouth more than my necessary food" (Job 23:12).

George Muller (the great founder of the Bristol Orphanage in the last century) once said, "The vigor of our Spiritual Life will be in exact proportion to the place held by the Bible in our life and thoughts. . . . I have read the Bible through one hundred times, and always with increasing delight. Each time it seems like a new book to me. Great has been the blessing from consecutive, diligent, daily study. I look upon it as a lost day when I have not had a good time over the Word of God."[6]

The Spirit Is Using the Word Today

The Spirit has the power to transform and inspire lives today through the Bible. Here are some situations where He has recently touched people:

A former surgeon-general of Portugal was out walking one rainy day. When he returned to his home, he found a piece of paper sticking to his shoe. When he pulled it off, he discovered it to be a tract that presented the Gospel by using Scripture. On reading it, he was soundly converted to Jesus Christ.

Dr. J. B. Phillips writes in the preface to his *Letters to Young Churches* that he was "continually struck by the living quality of the material" on which he worked; often he "felt rather like 'an electrician rewiring an ancient house without being able to turn the mains off'."[7]

Many prisoners in the "Hanoi Hilton" during the Vietnam war were gloriously sustained by the Spirit through the Word of God. These men testified to the strength they received from the Word of God. Howard Rutledge, in his book *In the Presence of Mine Enemies,* tells how the prisoners developed a code system that the enemy was never able to break. By it they communicated with one another, sharing names and serial numbers of every prisoner. They also passed along other messages as well, including Scripture verses that they knew.

Geoffrey Bull, a missionary on the borders of Tibet, said in his book, *When Iron Gates Yield,* that during his three years of imprisonment he was relentlessly brainwashed and would have succumbed had it not been for Scriptures he had committed to memory. He repeated them over and over to himself when he was in solitary confinement. Through them God strengthened him to face the torture designed to break him down.

I have written here mainly of those who were imprisoned or in desperate circumstances. Yet much could be said about the daily nourishment and reinforcement of faith we all receive from studying the Word of God, and the wisdom it provides us for day-to-day living. It reminds me of Hebrews 11:32, "And what more shall I say? For time would fail me to tell of Gideon, Barak, Samson, Jephthah . . ." (RSV). Tens of thousands of God's saints and sufferers through the ages have found their dark nights lightened and tortured souls strengthened because they found help from the Spirit in the Word of God.

As we approach the end of the age, persecution is going to be intensified. We are already seeing evidences in many parts of the world. The Scriptures you memorize now and the teachings of the Word of God you learn now will sustain you in that hour!—if you are called on to suffer physically and mentally for the name of Christ!

4. The Holy Spirit and Salvation

During one of our London Crusades, a Russian nobleman came one evening. He spoke no English. Yet when the invitation was given to receive Christ he responded. The trained Russian-speaking counselor asked him how, knowing no English, he had understood enough of the message to respond so intelligently. "When I entered this place," the nobleman replied, "I was overwhelmed with a longing for God. Tell me, how can I find Him?"

This is but one of hundreds of similar stories that have come to my attention during my years of ministry. In our Crusades we have counselors who speak various languages. For example, in our recent Crusade in Toronto, trained counselors were available to help in twenty-eight languages. It is amazing that in almost every service people respond to the "invitation" who understand little or no English. To me, this is clearly the work of the Holy Spirit drawing people to the Savior in spite of the language barrier.

When a person comes to Christ, the Bible tells us the Holy Spirit has been at work in a number of ways. Some of these we may not fully understand, and yet this does not alter the fact that the Holy Spirit is deeply involved in our salvation. In this chapter we will look at some of the ways the Spirit works to bring us to Christ.

The Need for Spiritual Rebirth

We live in a revolutionary, changing world. Man's moral capacities lag far behind his technological skills and discoveries.

This could mean disaster for the human race. In light of this, the greatest need in the world is to bring about the transformation of human nature. Many of our technologists are saying there is a great need for a new breed of man. Even the political radicals and the humanists talk about the "new man." From this it is clear that they acknowledge that man, as he is, is not good enough. So they also look for the arrival of the new man who, they say, will come into being when society has been changed so that a new environment can produce him.

There are also the technocrats who believe that technology is now advancing so rapidly that we will soon be able to create an entirely new human race. We have genetic engineers who believe that by the end of this century they will be able to create any type of person they want.

But there is only one ultimate answer to the need of man to be changed. Science and technology cannot change man's basic nature. Economic restructuring cannot change man's basic nature. No amount of self-improvement or wishful thinking can change man's basic nature. Only God—the One who created us— can re-create us. And that is precisely what He does when we give ourselves to Jesus Christ. The Bible says, "Therefore if any man is in Christ, he is a new creature; the old things passed away; behold, new things have come" (2 Cor. 5:17). What a tremendous statement!

The Bible speaks of this change in various ways. One of the most vivid is the term "born again." Just as we have been born physically, so we can be born again—spiritually. "For you have been born again not of seed which is perishable but imperishable, that is, through the living and abiding word of God" (1 Peter 1:23).

Certainly few passages in the New Testament speak as directly about the Holy Spirit's role in our salvation as the third chapter of John. In it, John recounts for us an interview Jesus had with a very influential religious leader named Nicodemus. Nicodemus was wealthy, and a member of the Sanhedrin, the ruling council of the Jewish nation. He probably fasted several times a week, and spent time each day in the Temple in prayer. He tithed his income, and was apparently a noted religious teacher. He would have been considered a model Christian in some circles today. But Jesus said all his goodness was not enough. Instead, Jesus said, "You must be born again" (John 3:7).

Jesus went on to explain that this new birth—this spiritual regeneration—is accomplished by the Holy Spirit. "The wind blows where it wishes and you hear the sound of it, but do not know where it comes from and where it is going; so is every one who is born of the Spirit" (John 3:8). There is something mysterious about this; we cannot fully understand how the new birth comes to us. It is from above, not from the earth or from within our human nature. It comes because of the love and grace of God. It comes because of the death and resurrection of Jesus Christ. It comes because of the action of the Holy Spirit.

In its notes on John 3 the *Open Bible* describes the encounter between Jesus and Nicodemus this way: "What a shock it must have been [to Nicodemus] to learn that his religion was not enough! It never is. He came to Jesus, addressing Him as 'a teacher come from God.' Jesus knew Nicodemus, as He knows all men [John 2:24, 25], and Jesus knew that he needed more than a teacher—he needed a Saviour. He needed more than religion—he needed regeneration. He needed more than law—he needed life. Jesus began by going right to the point when He said, 'Ye must be born again.' Nicodemus asked, 'How can a man be born when he is old?' [This was a very natural question for Nicodemus to ask.] Then Jesus pointed out the dissimilarity in the two births: 'That which is born of flesh is flesh' (the flesh will never change); and 'that which is born of the Spirit is spirit' (the Spirit will never change). [John 3:6]"[1]

Jesus knew what lies in the hearts of all men—the fatal disease that causes lying, cheating, hate, prejudice, greed, and lust. He said, "For out of the heart come evil thoughts, murders, adulteries, fornications, thefts, false witness, slanders. These are the things which defile the man" (Matt. 15:19, 20). Psychologists realize something is wrong with the human race, but they disagree as to the problem. The Bible says man's problem is the direct result of his decision as an intelligent, moral, responsible being to revolt against the will of his Maker. Man's disease is called S-I-N in the Bible.

Sin is a transgression of the law (1 John 3:4). It is falling short of doing one's duty, a failure to do what one knows he ought to do in God's sight. It is iniquity—a turning aside from a straight path. Isaiah said, "All of us like sheep have gone astray, each of us has turned to his own way" (Isa. 53:6). The Bible teaches that the sinner is "dead" before God when it says that "through one man sin entered into the world, and death through sin, and so death spread to all men, because all sinned" (Rom. 5:12). Thus a radical change is needed in the inner being of every man. This is a change man cannot earn, nor is it something he can do for himself. It is a change science cannot accomplish for him; it is something God alone can and must do.

The Holy Spirit Convicts Us and Calls Us

One of the most devastating effects of sin is that it has blinded us to our own sin. "The god of this world has blinded the minds of the unbelieving, that they might not see the light of the gospel of the glory of Christ, who is the image of God" (2 Cor. 4:4). Only the Holy Spirit can open our eyes. Only He can convict us of the depth of our sin, and only He can convince us of the truth of the gospel. That is one reason the Holy Spirit is called "the Spirit of truth" in John 14:17. In speaking of the Holy Spirit, Jesus said, "And He, when He comes, will convict the world concerning sin, and righteousness, and judgment; concerning sin, because they do not believe in Me; and concerning righteousness, because I go to the Father, and you no longer behold Me; and concerning judgment, because the ruler of this world has been judged" (John 16:8–11).

J. Gresham Machen wrote: "There must be the mysterious work of the Spirit of God in the new birth. Without that, all our arguments are quite useless. . . . What the Holy Spirit does in the new birth is not to make a man a Christian regardless of the evidence, but on the contrary to clear away the mists from his eyes and enable him to attend to the evidence."[2]

We should also remember that it is the truth of the Word of God which is used by the Holy Spirit to bring conviction to our hearts. The Bible tells us, "So faith comes from hearing, and hearing by the word of Christ" (Rom. 10:17). Or again we read that, "The word of God is living and active and sharper than any two-edged sword, and piercing as far as the division of soul and spirit, of both joints and marrow, and able to judge the thoughts and intentions of the heart" (Heb. 4:12). God the Holy Spirit can take the humblest preaching or the feeblest words of our witness to Christ, and transform them by His power into a convicting word in the lives of others.

Apart from the ministry of the Holy Spirit we would never clearly see the truth of God concerning our sin, or the truth of God about our Savior. I believe this is what Jesus meant in John 6:44: "No one can come to Me, unless the Father who sent Me draws him; and I will raise him up on the last day."

However, the Bible also gives us a solemn warning about resisting the calling of the Holy Spirit. In Genesis 6:3 we read: "My Spirit shall not strive with man forever." Without the "striving" of the Spirit it would be impossible for a person to come to Christ. Yet, there is also the danger that we will pass the point of no return, and that our hearts will be so calloused and hardened by sin that we will no longer hear the voice of the Spirit.

Again, there is much we may not understand fully about this, and it is not our place to say when that point has been reached in another person's life. No man could have been more hardened, seemingly, than King Manasseh in the Old Testament, and yet he eventually repented of his sin and was forgiven by God in His grace (2 Chron. 33). But we dare not neglect the warning of the Bible that tells us, "Now is the time of God's favor, now is the day of salvation" (2 Cor. 6:2 NIV). The writer of Proverbs said, "A man who hardens his neck after much reproof will suddenly be broken beyond remedy" (Prov. 29:1).

The Holy Spirit Regenerates Us

Along with repentance and faith, one of the works of the Spirit of God in the heart of man is regeneration. "Regeneration" is another term for renewal or rebirth. "He saved us, not on the basis of deeds which we have done in righteousness, but according to His mercy, by the washing of regeneration and renewing by the Holy Spirit" (Titus 3:5). Actually the Greek word translated "regeneration" here is a compound of two Greek words; it literally means "birth again" or new birth.

This is a once-for-all change, though it has continuing effects. In John 3:3 the Bible speaks of one being "born again," and the Amplified Version suggests "born anew" or "born from above" to clarify the meaning. The sinner in his natural state is spiritually dead in trespasses and sins. In regeneration that which is dead is made alive. He is justified by God from the guilt of a broken law, and he is forgiven of every sin. Further, by the new birth the justified sinner becomes a new creation—a new creature (2 Cor. 5:17; Gal. 6:15 RSV). Moreover, regeneration, like justification, is immediate and constitutes a one-time act of the Holy Spirit, though the person who is "born again" might, or might not, be conscious of the exact time. Theologians have long debated exactly when regeneration actually takes place in a person's life. In spite of some disagreements, the central issue is clear: it is the Holy Spirit who regenerates us within.

The gift of new or divine life to the regenerated person comes to the soul from Christ through the Holy Spirit. Jesus said that the new birth is "a mystery." He uses the illustration of the wind blowing: we sense its effects but we cannot see where it comes from or where it is going. Thus regeneration is a hidden transaction in the same sense that it is something which takes place within the individual heart and may or may not be known to the one who receives it—and often it is not immediately visible to people around him. The results that flow from the new birth are so incalculably significant that they deserve to be called "a miracle"—the greatest of all miracles! Even as unbelieving men did not know Jesus on earth, and failed to realize that God incarnate was standing before them, so it is possible for "the new man" in Christ to go unrecognized for at least a while. Yet, known or unknown to the world, the new man exists within. Sooner or later the new birth will manifest itself in godly living. But the divine life, which will abide forever, is there, and the "new man" who possesses the kingdom of God is there (2 Cor. 5:17)—a new creature.

This is not to deny the importance of personal faith and decision. We do not passively sit back and wait for the Spirit to do His work before we come to Christ. We are commanded to "Ask, and it shall be given to you; seek, and you shall find; knock, and it shall be opened to you" (Matt. 7:7). We have the promise of God: "And you will seek Me and find Me, when you search for Me with all your heart" (Jer. 29:13). Furthermore, the Scripture tells us that even faith itself is a gift of God's grace. "Because of his kindness you have been saved through trusting Christ. And even trusting is not of yourselves; it too is a gift from God" (Eph. 2:8 LB). We therefore have everything we need to decide for Christ, but we still have a responsibility to respond to the call and conviction of the Holy Spirit.

When a person is born again, the process is uncomplicated from the divine perspective. The Spirit of God takes the Word of God and makes the child of God. We are born again through the operation of the Holy Spirit, who in turn uses the divinely inspired Word of God. God's Spirit brings life to men. At this point the Holy Spirit indwells a person for life. He receives *eternal* life.

As an evangelist for over thirty-five years, I have watched hundreds of thousands of people come down aisles in auditoriums, stadiums, churches, tents, and brush arbors, to make what has often been referred to as a "decision" for Christ. Years ago I tried to change the terminology to "inquirers." Walking down an aisle in an evangelistic meeting does not necessarily mean a person has been or will be regenerated. Going forward to make some kind of public commitment to Christ is only a visible, though an important, act. It may or may not reflect what is going on or has already taken place in the human heart. Regeneration is *not* the work of the evangelist; it is the work of God's Spirit. The indispensable condition of the new birth is repentance and faith, but repentance and faith itself does not save. Genuine faith is God's gift to a person—as I have said, even helping us to repent. When a person displays that kind of repentance and faith, we may be sure that God the Holy Spirit accompanies it with regeneration. In this we see the love and grace of God shed abroad toward judgment-bound sinners through Jesus Christ.

Thus, to be born again means that "as the Father raises the dead and gives them life, even so the Son also gives life to whom He wishes" (John 5:21). In Acts, Peter called it "repenting" or "being converted." In Romans 6:13, Paul spoke of it as being "alive from the dead." To the Colossians, Paul said, ". . . you laid aside the old self with its evil practices, and have put on the new self who is being renewed to a true knowledge according to the image of the One who created him" (Col. 3:9, 10).

You and I cannot inherit regeneration: Rather, "as many as received Him [Jesus], to them He gave the right to become children of God, even to those who believe in His name" (John 1:12). A person may have been baptized, as Hitler and Stalin were, but that is no guarantee that he has been regenerated. Simon the Sorcerer was baptized by Philip after having "believed" in some fuzzy mental sense, but Peter told him, "Your heart is not right before God" (Acts 8:21).

A person may be confirmed in one of the more liturgical churches, but that does not necessarily mean he has been regenerated. In the Book of Acts we read, "The Lord was adding to their number day by day those who were being saved" (Acts 2:47). The one indispensable condition for admission to the fellowship of the early church was that each one first had to have been regenerated.

Nor can one be regenerated by doing good works: "He saved us, not on the basis of deeds which we have done in righteousness, but according to His mercy, by the washing of regeneration and renewing by the Holy Spirit" (Titus 3:5). A man can join every club in town and become involved in every charitable event and be a "good," "moral" person all his life, and still not know what it means to be regenerated.

Others try to be regenerated by reformation. They do their best to reform by making new resolutions. But the Bible says, "All our righteous deeds are like a filthy garment" in the sight of God (Isa. 64:6).

Some well-meaning people even try to find salvation through imitating Christ in their lives. But this is not acceptable to God, because no one can really imitate Christ. Christ was pure. Men are sinners, *dead* in sin. What they need is life, and this can be supplied only by the Holy Spirit through regeneration.

Have you been regenerated by the power of the Spirit of God? Nothing less can bring true spiritual rebirth to your life. But God sent His Son into the world to give us new life. God has given us His Word, and the power of the Holy Spirit can take it and bring regeneration—spiritual rebirth—to us.

The new birth will bring about a change in your relationship with God, a change in your relationship with your family, a change in your relationship with yourself, a change in your relationship with your neighbors. Gradually, if you are an obedient believer, it will bring about a change in disposition, affection, aims, principles, and dimensions.

The Holy Spirit Assures Us

After we receive Christ as Savior we may be confused sometimes because many of the old temptations have not disappeared. We still sin. Sometimes we lose our tempers. Pride and jealousy may still crop up from time to time. This is not only confusing, it is discouraging and sometimes leads to spiritual depression. We may even have some particular "besetting sin" which plagues us, and which we do not seem to be able to conquer.

But the moment you and I received Christ and were regenerated by the Holy Spirit we were given a new nature. Thus, those of us who are born again have two natures. The old nature is from our first birth; the new is from our new birth. By the old birth we are children of the flesh; by the new birth we are children of God. This is why Jesus told Nicodemus that he "must be born again."

Whatever the problem, whenever the old nature within us asserts itself, a new believer may begin to doubt whether or not he has really been born again. Satan would want us to doubt the reality of our salvation—which is really doubting God's Word to us. We will write more fully about the assurance of our salvation in a later chapter, but at this point we need to remind ourselves that the Holy Spirit also gives us assurance that we have been born again and have become members of the family of God. "And the Holy Spirit also bears witness to us" (Heb. 10:15). By the written Word of God, and by the quiet work of the Spirit in our hearts, we know we have been born again—regardless of the accusations of Satan. "The Spirit Himself bears witness with our spirit that we are children of God" (Rom. 8:16).

How to Become Born Again

First, realize that you are a sinner in God's eyes. You may not consider yourself a bad person, because you know you have lived a fairly decent life. On the other hand, you may be carrying a burden of guilt over some sins committed in the past. Whatever your background, the Bible tells us "there is none righteous, no, not one" (Rom. 3:10 KJV). We have all broken the Law of God, and we all deserve nothing but God's judgment and wrath.

Second, realize that God loves you and sent His Son to die for you. You deserve to die for your sins, but Christ died in your place. "For Christ also died for sins once for all, the just for the unjust, in order that He might bring us to God" (1 Peter 3:18). That is the wonder of the gospel—that God loves us! He loves you, in spite of the fact you are a sinner.

Third, repent of your sins. Repentance comes from a Greek word meaning "a change of mind." It means that I admit I am a sinner, and that I feel sorry for the fact I have sinned. But repentance also means I actually turn my back on my sins—I reject them—and determine by God's grace to live as He wants me to live. Jesus said, "unless you repent, you will all likewise perish" (Luke 13:3). Repentance involves a willingness to leave sin behind, and turn my life over to Jesus Christ as Lord of my life. We see ourselves as God sees us and we pray, "God, be merciful to me, the sinner!" (Luke 18:13).

Fourth, come by faith and trust to Christ. Salvation, the Bible tells us, is a free gift. God has done everything possible to make salvation available to us, but we must respond and make that gift our own. "For the wages of sin is death, but the free gift of God is eternal life in Christ Jesus our Lord" (Rom. 6:23).

How do you accept this gift? By a simple act of faith in which you say "yes" to Christ. If you have never accepted Christ into your life, I invite you to do it right now before another minute passes. Simply tell God you know you are a sinner, and you are sorry for your sins. Tell Him you believe Jesus Christ died for you, and that you want to give your life to Him right now, to follow Him as Lord the rest of your life. "For God so loved the world, that He gave His only begotten Son, that whoever believes in Him should not perish, but have eternal life" (John 3:16).

If you have done that, God has forgiven all your sins. What a wonderful thing to know that every sin you ever committed—even the things you did not realize were sins—are all washed away by the blood of Jesus Christ, "in whom we have redemption, the forgiveness of sins" (Col. 1:14). More than that—you can accept by faith now that you are a new creation in Christ.

In their conversation Jesus reminded Nicodemus of an incident in the wilderness journey of the ancient Israelites. God had judged His sinning people by sending among them serpents whose bites were fatal. Many Israelites were suffering and dying. Then God told Moses to fashion a serpent of brass and lift it high on a pole. All who looked upon that serpent by faith after they had been bitten would be saved. That sounded like an insult to their intelligence. There was no healing quality in brass. And they knew that rubbing medicine on their bites would not heal them. Fighting the serpents was of no avail. Making an offering to the serpent on the pole wouldn't help. Prayer to the serpent would not save them from death. Even Moses the prophet of God could not help them.

Rather, *all* they had to do was look at the serpent of brass in childlike faith that God would save them totally by His grace. When they looked at the serpent of brass, they were looking beyond the serpent to God Himself. So it is as if Jesus said, "I am going to be lifted up—look unto me and be saved." Of course, His "lifting up" was to take place at His forthcoming death on the cross. No one can come to Christ unless the Holy Spirit draws him to the cross, where Jesus by His blood cleanses away the sin of each person who places his faith in Him.

As with the Israelites in the wilderness, God does not mean to insult our intelligence. But if you have not believed in Christ, your mind has been blinded spiritually by the devil and affected by sin. That is why the apostle Paul said, "For since in the wisdom of God the world through its wisdom did not come to know God, God was well-pleased through the foolishness of the message preached to save those who believe" (1 Cor. 1:21).

At first it looks foolish to believe that Jesus Christ, who died on a cross and rose again 2,000 years ago, can transform your life radically today by the Holy Spirit. Yet millions of Christians on every continent would rise at this moment to testify that He *has* transformed their lives. It happened to me many years ago. It could happen to you—today!

5. Baptism with the Spirit

Many years ago when I was attending a small Bible school in Florida, I visited what was called a "brush arbor revival meeting." The speaker was an old-fashioned Southern revival preacher. The little place seated about two hundred people and was filled. The speaker made up in thunder what he lacked in logic, and the people loved it.

"Have you been baptized with the Holy Spirit?" he asked the audience during the sermon.

Apparently he knew a great many in the audience because he would point to someone and ask, "Brother, have you been baptized with the Spirit?" And the man would answer, "Yes, bless God."

"Young man," he said, spotting me, "have you been baptized with the Holy Spirit?" "Yes, sir," I replied.

"When were you baptized with the Holy Spirit?" he asked. He had not questioned the others on this.

"The moment I received Jesus Christ as my Savior," I replied. He looked at me with a puzzled expression, but before going to the next person he said, "That couldn't be."

But it could! It was.

I do not doubt the sincerity of this preacher. However, in my own study of the Scriptures through the years I have become convinced that there is only one baptism with the Holy Spirit in the life of every believer, and that takes place at the moment of conversion. This baptism with the Holy Spirit was initiated at Pentecost, and all who come to know Jesus Christ as Savior share in that experience and are baptized with the Spirit the moment they are regenerated. In addition, they may be filled with the Holy Spirit; if not, they need to be.

The scriptural usage of the word *baptism* shows that it is something initiatory both in the case of water baptism and Spirit baptism, and that it is *not repeated.* I can find no biblical data to show that the baptism with the Spirit would ever be repeated.

"For by one Spirit we were all baptized into one body" (1 Cor. 12:13). The original Greek of this passage makes it clear that this baptism of the Spirit is a completed past action. (The King James Version incorrectly translates it into the present tense rather than the past.)

Two things stand out in that verse: first, the baptism with the Spirit is a collective operation of the Spirit of God; second, it includes every believer. Dr. W. Graham Scroggie once said at Keswick, "Observe carefully to whom the Apostle is writing and of whom he is speaking." He uses the word *"all"*—"It is not to the faithful Thessalonians, nor to the liberal Philippians, nor to the spiritual Ephesians, but to the carnal Corinthians (1 Cor. 3:1)," Scroggie went on. The clear indication is that baptism with the Spirit is connected with our *standing* before God, not our current subjective *state;* with our *position* and not our *experience.*

This becomes still clearer if we examine the experiences of the Israelites described in 1 Corinthians 10:1–5. In these verses there are five *alls.* "All under the cloud," "all passed through the sea," "all were baptized," "all ate," "all drank." It was after all these things happened to all the people that the differences came: "Nevertheless, with most of them God was not well-pleased" (1 Cor. 10:5).

In other words, they were all part of the people of God. This did not mean, however, that all lived up to their calling as God's holy people. In like manner, all believers are baptized with the Holy Spirit. This does not mean, however, that they are filled or controlled by the Spirit. The important thing is the great central truth—when I come to Christ, God gives His Spirit to me.

Differences That Divide Us

I realize that baptism with the Holy Spirit has been differently understood by some of my fellow believers. We should not shrink from stating specific differences of opinion. But we should also try to understand each other, pray for each other, and be willing to learn from each other as we seek to know what the Bible teaches. The differences of opinion on this matter are somewhat similar to differences of opinion about water baptism and church government. Some baptize babies; others do not. Some sprinkle or pour; others only immerse. Some have congregational church polity; others have presbyterian or representative democracy; still others have the episcopal form. In no way should these differences be divisive. I can have wonderful Christian fellowship, especially in the work of evangelism, with those who hold various views.

On the other hand, the question of the baptism with the Holy Spirit, in my judgment, is often more important than these other issues, especially when the doctrine of the baptism with the Spirit is distorted. For example, some Christians hold that the Spirit's baptism only comes at some time subsequent to conversion. Others say that this later Spirit baptism is necessary before a person can be fully used of God. Still others contend that the baptism with the Spirit is always accompanied with the outward sign of a particular gift, and that unless this sign is present the person has not been baptized with the Spirit.

I must admit that at times I have really wanted to believe this distinctive teaching. I, too, have wanted an "experience." But I want every experience to be biblically based. The biblical truth, it seems to me, is that we are baptized into the body of Christ by the Spirit at conversion. This is the only Spirit baptism. At this time we can and should be filled with the Holy Spirit, and afterward, be refilled, and even filled unto all fullness. As has often been said, "One baptism, but many fillings." I do not see from Scripture that this filling by the Holy Spirit constitutes a second baptism, nor do I see that speaking in tongues is a necessary accompaniment of being filled with the Spirit.

Sometimes these different opinions are really only differences in semantics. As we shall see in the next chapter, what some people call the baptism of the Spirit may really be what the Scripture calls the filling of the Spirit, which may take place many times in our lives after our conversion.

There are, incidentally, only seven passages in the New Testament which speak directly of the baptism with the Spirit. Five of these passages refer to the baptism with the Spirit as a future event; four were spoken by John the Baptist (Matt. 3:11; Mark 1:7, 8; Luke 3:16; and John 1:33) and one was spoken by Jesus after His resurrection (Acts 1:4, 5). A sixth passage looks back to the events and experiences of the day of Pentecost (Acts 11:15–17) as fulfilling the promises spoken by John the Baptist and Jesus. Only one passage—1 Corinthians 12:13—speaks about the wider experience of all believers.

During my ministry I have known many Christians who agonized, labored, struggled, and prayed to "get the Spirit." I used to wonder if I had been wrong in thinking that having been baptized by the Spirit into the body of Christ on the day of my conversion I needed no other baptism. But the longer I have studied the Scriptures the more I have become convinced that I was right. Let's trace out what God did in Christ's passion week, and fifty days later at Pentecost, to see that we need not seek what God has already given every believer.

Calvary and Pentecost

When Jesus died on the cross, He bore our sins: "God sending his own Son in the likeness of sinful flesh, and for sin, condemned sin in the flesh" (Rom. 8:3 KJV).

Isaiah prophesied, "The Lord hath laid on him the iniquity of us all" (Isa. 53:6 KJV). Paul said, "He hath made him to be sin for us, who knew no sin" (2 Cor. 5:21 KJV). This made the holy Jesus represent sin for the whole world.

Quite clearly Jesus did not say that His death on the cross would mark the cessation of His ministry. The night before His death He repeatedly told the disciples that He would send the Holy Spirit.

The night before He was to die, He told His disciples, "It is expedient for you that I go away: for if I go not away, the Comforter will not come unto you; but if I depart, I will send him unto you" (John 16:7 KJV). Before He could send the Holy Spirit, who is the Comforter, Jesus had to go away: first, to the death of the cross; then to the resurrection; then, to the ascension into heaven. Only then could He send the Holy Spirit on the day of Pentecost. And after His death and resurrection He commanded them to remain in Jerusalem to await the gift of the

Spirit, "Tarry ye in the city . . . until ye be endued with power from on high" (Luke 24:49 KJV). Before He ascended He told them to stay in Jerusalem until they were "baptized with the Holy Spirit not many days hence" (Acts 1:5 KJV).

That's why John the Baptist proclaimed the twofold mission of Christ: first, he proclaimed the ministry of Christ as "the Lamb of God, which taketh away the sin of the world" (John 1:29 KJV); second, he predicted that Christ's ministry at Calvary would be followed by His ministry through baptism with the Holy Spirit (John 1:33).

When Christ rose from the dead this baptism with the Spirit that was to signify the new age still lay in the future; but it was to occur fifty days after the resurrection.

Ten days after the ascension, Pentecost dawned. The promise was fulfilled. The Holy Spirit came on 120 disciples. A little later when Peter was explaining it to a much larger crowd, he referred to the gift as "the gift of the Holy Spirit." He urged his audience, "Repent, and be baptized . . . and ye shall receive the gift of the Holy Spirit" (Acts 2:38 KJV).

John Stott reminds us, "The 3,000 do not seem to have experienced the same miraculous phenomena (the rushing mighty wind, the tongues of flame, or the speech in foreign languages). At least nothing is said about these things. Yet because of God's assurance through Peter they must have inherited the same promise and received the same gift (verses 33, 39). Nevertheless, there was this difference between them: the 120 were regenerate already, and received the baptism of the Spirit only after waiting upon God for ten days. The 3,000 on the other hand were unbelievers, and received the forgiveness of their sins and the gift of the Spirit simultaneously—and it happened immediately they repented and believed, without any need to wait.

"This distinction between the two companies, the 120 and the 3,000, is of great importance, because the *norm* for today must surely be the second group, the 3,000, and not (as is often supposed) the first. The fact that the experience of the 120 was in two distinct stages was due simply to historical circumstances. They could not have received the Pentecostal gift before Pentecost. But those historical circumstances have long since ceased to exist. We live after the event of Pentecost, like the 3,000. With us, therefore, as with them, the forgiveness of sins and the 'gift' or 'baptism' of the Spirit are received together."[1]

From that day onward, the Holy Spirit has lived in the hearts of all true believers, beginning with the 120 disciples who received Him at Pentecost. When they received the Holy Spirit, He united them by His indwelling presence into one body—the mystical body of Christ, which is the Church. That is why when I hear terms like "ecumenicity," or "ecumenical movement," I say to myself: an ecumenicity already exists if we have been born again. We are all united by the Holy Spirit who dwells within our hearts whether we are Presbyterian, Methodist, Baptist, Pentecostal, Catholic, Lutheran, or Anglican.

There were, it is true, several other occasions recorded in the Book of Acts which were similar to Pentecost, such as the so-called "Samaritan Pentecost" (Acts 8:14–17) and the conversion of Cornelius (Acts 10:44–48). Each of these, however, marked a new stage in the expansion of the Church. Samaritans were a mixed race, scorned by many as unworthy of the love of God. Their baptism by the Spirit was a clear sign that they too could be part of God's people by faith in Jesus Christ. Cornelius was a Gentile, and his conversion marked still another step in the spread of the Gospel. The baptism of the Spirit which came to him and his household showed conclusively that God's love extended to the Gentiles as well.

In view of all this, no Christian need strive, wait, or "pray through to get the Spirit." He has received Him already, not as a result of struggle and work, agonizing and prayer, but as an unmerited and unearned gift of grace.

W. Graham Scroggie once said something like this at Keswick, "On the day of Pentecost all believers were, by the baptism of the Spirit, constituted the body of Christ, and since then every separate believer, every soul accepting Christ in simple faith, has in that moment and by that act been made partaker of the blessing of the baptism. It is not therefore a blessing which the believer is to seek and receive subsequent to the hour of his conversion."

Three Possible Exceptions Explained

I have just suggested that all believers have the Holy Spirit, who comes to dwell within them at the time of their regeneration or conversion. However, some have urged that the Book of Acts gives us several examples of people who did not receive the Holy

Spirit when they first believed. Instead, some contend, these incidents indicate that a baptism with the Spirit occurs subsequent to our incorporation into the body of Christ. Three passages are of particular interest at this point. Personally I found these passages difficult to understand when I was a young Christian (and to some extent I still do) and I know many people have had the same experience. I would not pretend to have all the answers to the questions raised by these passages, but my own study has led me to some observations which might be helpful.

The first passage is found in Acts 8 where Philip's trip to Samaria is recounted. He preached Christ and performed a number of miracles. The Samaritans were emotionally stirred. Many of them professed faith and were baptized. The apostles in Jerusalem were so concerned about what was happening in Samaria that they sent two of their leaders, Peter and John, to investigate. They found a great stir and a readiness to receive the Holy Spirit. "Then they began laying their hands on them, and they were receiving the Holy Spirit" (Acts 8:17).

As we compare Scripture with Scripture, we immediately discover one extraordinary feature in this passage: When Philip preached in Samaria, it was the first time the gospel had been proclaimed outside Jerusalem, evidently because Samaritans and Jews had always been bitter enemies. This gives us the clue to the reason the Spirit was withheld till Peter and John came: It was so they might see for themselves that God received even hated Samaritans who believed in Christ. There could now be no question of it.

Notice too what happened when the Spirit of the Lord suddenly removed Philip, taking him down to Gaza where he witnessed to the Ethiopian eunuch. When the Ethiopian believed and received Christ, he was baptized with water. But at no time did Philip lay hands on him and pray for him to receive the Holy Spirit, nor was anything said about a second baptism. Thus the situation in Samaria as recounted in Acts 8 was unique and does not fit with other passages of Scripture as we compare Scripture with Scripture.

A second passage that gives some people difficulty deals with the conversion of Saul on the road to Damascus as recorded in Acts 9. Some say that when he was later filled with the Spirit in the presence of Ananias (v. 17), he experienced a second baptism of the Spirit.

Here again the situation is unique. God had chosen this persecutor of the Christians "to bear My name before the Gentiles and kings and the sons of Israel" (v. 15). When Saul called Jesus "Lord," he used a term that can mean "my very own lord," signifying his conversion, or simply "Sir," a title of respect rather than a confession of faith. We do know that later Ananias called Paul "brother," as most of our English translations phrase it (v. 17). But here again, most of the Jews of that day called each other "brother." He might have been calling Saul a brother in the sense that American black people often refer to each other as "brother."

In other words, when did Saul's regeneration take place? Was it on the Damascus road, or could it have been over a period of three days of witnessing by Ananias (which would cover the period of Saul's blindness)? I am convinced that the new birth is often like natural birth: the moment of conception, nine months of gestation, and then birth. Sometimes it takes weeks of conviction by the Holy Spirit. I've seen people in our crusades come forward more than once, and not experience the assurance of their salvation until the third or fourth time. When were they regenerated? Only God the Holy Spirit knows; it might have been at baptism or confirmation and they came forward for assurance. It may be that some are coming (as I sometimes have said) to "re-confirm their confirmation."

Furthermore, Acts 9:17 says Paul is to be filled with the Holy Spirit. The verse does not use the word baptism, and when he was filled it does not say he spoke in other tongues. My point is that even if Paul was regenerated on the Damascus road, his later filling is not presented as a second baptism. And possibly his regeneration did not occur until Ananias came to him. So the passage does not teach that Paul was baptized twice with the Spirit.

A third text that has given rise to some controversy is Acts 19:1–7. Paul visited Ephesus and found twelve professing disciples who had not received the Holy Spirit. On reading this passage the question immediately arises: Were these twelve people true Christians before their meeting with Paul? They seemed to be ignorant about the Holy Spirit and Jesus. Also they talked about John's baptism. Certainly, Paul did not reckon their earlier baptism sufficient grounds for calling them believers. He had them undergo water baptism in the name of Christ.

Probably thousands of people had heard John or Jesus during the previous few years. John's baptism had made a deep impression on them, but during the intervening period of time they probably had lost all contact with the teachings of both John and Jesus. Thus, again we have a unique situation. The very fact that the apostle asked such searching questions would indicate that he doubted the genuineness of their conversion experience.

However, we must still deal with Acts 19:6: "And when Paul had laid his hands upon them, the Holy Spirit came on them; and they began speaking with tongues and prophesying." Dr. Merrill Tenney calls them "belated believers." The interesting thing is that all these events took place simultaneously. Whether the tongues spoken of here were the tongues to which Paul refers in 1 Corinthians 14, or Luke speaks about at Pentecost, we are not told. The word "prophesying" here carries with it the idea of testimony or proclamation. Apparently they went about telling their friends how they had come to believe in Jesus Christ. In my thinking, this does not suggest a second baptism with the Spirit subsequent to a baptism with the Spirit at regeneration. Rather, it appears that they were regenerated and baptized with the Spirit at the same time.

To summarize, it is my belief that Pentecost instituted the Church. Then all that remained was for Samaritans, Gentiles and "belated believers" to be brought into the Church representatively. This occurred in Acts 8 for Samaritans, Acts 10 for Gentiles (according to Acts 11:15), and Acts 19 for belated believers from John's baptism. Once this representative baptism with the Spirit had occurred, the normal pattern applied—baptism with the Spirit at the time each person (of whatever background) believed on Jesus Christ.

Our Share in Pentecost

Pentecost was an event then which included not only those who participated at that moment but also those who would participate in the centuries ahead. Perhaps we can use the atonement here by way of analogy. Christ died once for all; He died for members of His body who were not yet born or regenerated. Thus, you and I became members of His body by regeneration through the one-time shedding of His blood. So also you and I in similar fashion now participate in the new reality, the Church. What was formed by the baptism with the Spirit at Pentecost is, on our part, entered into when we were made to "drink of one Spirit" (1 Cor. 12:13) so that each believer comes into the benefits of it at the moment of his regeneration even as, at the same time, he comes into the benefits of the shed blood of Jesus for justification. So the Lord adds to the Church those who are being saved (Acts 2:47).

It may sound strange to speak of present-day believers as sharing in an event that took place 2,000 years ago. However, the Bible offers many examples similar to those of the atonement and the baptism with the Spirit. In Amos 2:10 (KJV), God said to His erring people, "I brought *you* up from the land of Egypt, and led you forty years through the wilderness" (italics mine), although the people whom the prophet addressed lived hundreds of years after the Exodus. The fact is that the nation was regarded as one and continuous; and so it is with the Church.

One Baptism and Regeneration

Since the baptism with the Spirit occurs at the time of regeneration, Christians are never told in Scripture to seek it. I am convinced that many of the things some teachers have joined to baptism with the Holy Spirit really belong to the fullness of the Spirit. Thus, the purpose of the baptism with the Holy Spirit is to bring the new Christian into the body of Christ. No interval of time falls between regeneration and baptism with the Spirit. The moment we received Jesus Christ as Lord and Savior we received the Holy Spirit. He came to live in our hearts. "Any one who does not have the Spirit of Christ does not belong to him," said Paul in Romans 8:9 (RSV). It is not a second blessing, or third, or fourth. There are and will be and should be *new fillings*—but not *new baptisms*.

Nowhere in the New Testament is there a command to be baptized with the Holy Spirit. Surely if baptism with the Spirit were a necessary step in our Christian lives, the New Testament would be full of it. Christ Himself would have commanded it. But we are not commanded as Christians to seek something that has already taken place. Thus, when I was asked as a young Bible school student in Florida if I had received the baptism of the Spirit, it was correct for me to respond that I had already received it at the moment of my conversion.

The Unity of the Spirit

In 1 Corinthians 12:13, the apostle Paul writes, "For by one Spirit we were all baptized into one body—Jews or Greeks, slaves or free—and all were made to drink of one Spirit" (RSV). Paul has been talking about the need for *unity* in the disobedient and carnal Corinthian church. David Howard says: "Notice the emphasis in these phrases: 'the same Spirit' (vv. 4, 8, 9); 'one Spirit' (vv. 9, 13 . . .); 'one and the same Spirit' (v. 11); 'the same Lord' (v. 5); . . . 'the body is one' (v. 12); 'one body' (v. 12, 13); 'there are many parts, yet one body' (v. 20); 'that there may be no discord in the body' (v. 25)."[2]

Howard later continues, "In this context of unity Paul says, 'For by one Spirit we were all baptized into one body—Jews or Greeks, slaves or free—and all were made to drink of one Spirit.' John R. W. Stott [*The Baptism and Fullness of the Holy Spirit,* p. 22] points out in this connection, 'So the baptism of the Spirit in this verse, far from being a dividing factor . . . is the great uniting factor.' "[3]

The Conclusion of the Matter

This much all Christians are agreed upon: Every true believer must be baptized by the Spirit into the body of Christ. Beyond that opinions differ significantly, however. But even here we should never forget a crucial area of agreement.

To see it, we must first recall that we all believe salvation is past, present, and future: We *have been saved* (justification), we *are being saved* (sanctification), and we *will be saved* (glorification). Between the time we are justified and the time when we shall be glorified falls that period in our pilgrim journey we call sanctification.

This has to do with holiness. And holiness proceeds from the work of the Spirit in our hearts. Whatever may be our differences about a second Spirit baptism, tongues, and Spirit-filling, all Christians are agreed that we should seek after *holiness*—without which no man shall see the Lord. Let us, therefore, seek ardently the kind of life that reflects the beauty of Jesus and marks us as being what saints (in the best sense of that word) ought to be!

How does this kind of life come? It comes as we are filled with the Holy Spirit—as He works in and through us as we are yielded to God and His will. It is to this subject of the filling of the Spirit that we must now turn in the next chapter.

6. The Seal, the Pledge, and the Witness of the Holy Spirit

An English missionary died in India in the early part of this century. Immediately after his death his former neighbors broke into his house and started carrying away his possessions. The English Consul was notified, and since there was no lock on the door of the missionary's house, he pasted a piece of paper across it and affixed the seal of England on it. The looters did not dare break the seal because the world's most powerful nation stood behind it.

The sealing of the Holy Spirit is one of a series of events that take place simultaneously, of which we may not even be aware, the moment we repent of our sins and receive Christ as Savior. First, of course, God regenerated and justified us. Second, the Holy Spirit baptized us into the body of Christ. Third, the Holy Spirit took up His abode in our hearts immediately. Several other events accompanying our salvation, together with His continuing work in us, are the focus of this and the next chapters.

The Seal

The fourth event is what the Bible calls "the Seal." It translates a Greek word that means to confirm or to impress. This word is used three times in the New Testament in connection with believers. It is also mentioned in the life of Jesus. John says that "on Him [Jesus] the Father, even God, has set His seal" (John 6:27). Here we see that the Father sealed the Son.

At the moment of conversion, however, believers are sealed with the Spirit for the day of redemption: "Having also believed,

74

you were sealed in Him with the Holy Spirit of promise" (Eph. 1:13; cf. 4:30).

It seems to me that Paul had two main thoughts in mind concerning our sealing by the Holy Spirit. One concerns security, and the other, ownership. Sealing in the sense of security is illustrated in the Old Testament when the king sealed Daniel into the lion's den so that he could not get out. Also, in ancient times, as when Esther was queen (Esth. 8:8), the king often used his own ring to affix his mark or seal to letters and documents written in his name. Once he had done this, no one could reverse or countermand what he had written.

Pilate did much the same when he ordered the soldiers to secure the tomb of Jesus. He said, " 'You have a guard; go, make it as secure as you know how.' And they went and made the grave secure, and along with the guard they set a seal on the stone" (Matt. 27:65, 66). "Seal" in this passage is the same Greek word used in passages which speak of the sealing of the Holy Spirit. A. T. Robertson says that the sealing of the stone was "probably by a cord stretched across the stone and sealed at each end as in Dan. 6:17. The sealing was done in the presence of the Roman guard who were left in charge to protect this stamp of Roman authority and power."[1] In an even more meaningful way, when the Holy Spirit seals us or puts His mark on us, we are secure in Christ.

One of the most thrilling thoughts that has ever crossed my mind is that the Holy Spirit sealed me. And He has sealed you— if you are a believer.

Nothing can touch you. "For I am convinced that neither death, nor life, nor angels, nor principalities, nor things present, nor things to come, nor powers, nor height, nor depth, nor any other created thing, shall be able to separate us from the love of God, which is in Christ Jesus our Lord" (Rom. 8:38, 39).

Yet this sealing with the Holy Spirit signifies more than security. It also means ownership. In the Old Testament we read that Jeremiah bought a piece of property, paid for it in front of witnesses, and sealed the purchase according to the Law and custom (Jer. 32:10). He was now the owner.

The allusion to the seal as the proof of purchase would have been especially significant to the Ephesians. The city of Ephesus was a seaport, and the shipmasters of the neighboring ports carried on an extensive trade in timber. The method of purchase was this: the merchant, after selecting his timber, stamped it with his own signet—an acknowledged sign of ownership. In due time the merchant would send a trusted agent with the signet; he would locate all the timbers that bore the corresponding impress, and claim them. Matthew Henry sums it up: "By him [the Holy Spirit] believers are sealed; that is, separated and set apart for God, and distinguished and marked as belonging to him."[2] You and I are God's property forever!

The Pledge

As we trust in Christ, God gives us the Spirit not only as a seal, however. He is also our pledge, or, as some translations read, "earnest," according to such passages as 2 Corinthians 1:22 and Ephesians 1:14.

"Now He who establishes us with you in Christ and anointed us is God, who also sealed us and gave us the Spirit in our hearts as a pledge" (2 Cor. 1:21, 22).

In the apostle Paul's day, businessmen considered a pledge to do three things: it was a down payment that sealed a bargain, it represented an obligation to buy, and it was a sample of what was to come.

Suppose you were to decide to buy a car. The pledge would first be a down payment sealing the transaction. It would also represent an obligation to buy the car. And it would be a sample of what was to come—the remaining portion of the selling price.

The Holy Spirit likewise seals God's purchase of us. And His presence shows God's sense of obligation to redeem us completely. Perhaps best of all, the presence of the Holy Spirit, living in fellowship with us, provides us with a foretaste, a sample, of our coming life and inheritance in God's presence.

In Numbers 13 when the spies of Israel set out to scout the land of Canaan, they reached it at the time of the first ripe grapes. They came to "the valley of Eshcol and from there cut down a branch with a single cluster of grapes" (Num. 13:23). This they brought back with them for the people of Israel to see. The cluster of grapes was the pledge of their inheritance. It was a small foretaste of what lay before them in the Promised Land. This was God's pledge that as they moved forward in faith, they would receive in full what they now had only in part.

Recently, one of New York's leading grocery stores exhibited a basket of choice and beautiful grapes in the window. A notice appeared above the basket announcing: "A whole carload like this sample basket is expected in a few days." The grapes were a "pledge" of what was to come. The firstfruits are but a handful compared with the whole harvest; so, reasoning from the known to the unknown, we ask with the hymnwriter:

"What will Thy presence be,
If such a life of joy can crown
Our walk on earth with Thee?"

The New Testament refers to the pledge of the Spirit three times:

1. "[God] also sealed us and gave us the Spirit in our hearts as a pledge" (2 Cor. 1:22). Here the Spirit's presence in our lives is God's pledge that He will fulfill His promise.

2. "Now He who prepared us for this very purpose is God, who gave to us the Spirit as a pledge" (2 Cor. 5:5). The context here suggests that the Spirit in our lives is God's pledge that we shall receive spiritual bodies at Christ's coming.

3. "[The Holy Spirit] is given as a pledge of our inheritance, with a view to the redemption of God's own possession, to the praise of His glory" (Eph. 1:14). Here the Spirit is God's pledge guaranteeing our inheritance until the future brings the total redemption of those who are God's possession.

In summary, we can say that when we are baptized into the body of Christ, the Spirit enters our lives and by His presence seals us. He is God's pledge assuring us of our inheritance to come.

The conclusion of the matter has been graphically expressed by Matthew Henry: "The earnest [this is the King James version's word for 'pledge'] is part of payment, and it secures the full sum: so is the gift of the Holy Ghost; all his influences and operations, both as a sanctifier and a comforter, are heaven begun, glory in the seed and bud. The Spirit's illumination is an earnest [pledge] of everlasting light; sanctification is an earnest of perfect holiness; and his comforts are earnests of everlasting joys. He is said to be the earnest, *until the redemption of the purchased possession.* It may be called here the possession, because this earnest makes it as sure to the heirs as though they were already possessed of it; and it is purchased for them by the blood of Christ. The redemption of it is mentioned because it was mortgaged and forfeited by sin; and Christ restores it to us, and so is said to redeem it, in allusion to the law of redemption."[3]

The Witness of the Spirit

Not only is the Holy Spirit our seal and our pledge, but He is also our witness within, assuring us of the reality of our salvation in Jesus Christ.

Jesus personally spoke to His disciples and provided them with assurance when He was with them. In like manner the Holy Spirit witnesses to and in the hearts of all true believers. Several passages in the New Testament touch on this subject.

First, the Scripture teaches us the Holy Spirit is a witness to the finality and sufficiency of Jesus Christ's atonement for us. We find this in Hebrews 10:15–17, where the writer contrasts the ineffectiveness of the oft-repeated Levitical sacrifices with the sacrifice of Christ, which was offered *one* for all and *once* for all. Our conscience could never be finally relieved of its burden of sin by the continual animal sacrifices. But on the other hand, "by one offering He [Jesus Christ] has perfected for all time those who are sanctified. And the Holy Spirit also bears witness to us" (Heb. 10:14, 15). It is a witness linked to Jeremiah 31, "I will forgive their iniquity, and their sin I will remember no more" (v. 34). Since this witness to us is engraved in the written Word of God that never varies, its comfort relieves us of our fears through all the changing scenes of time.

Second, the Scripture also teaches us the Holy Spirit witnesses that we have become, by faith in Jesus Christ and His work on the cross, the children of God. "The Spirit Himself bears witness with our spirit that we are children of God" (Rom. 8:16). We have not only been saved and baptized into the body of Christ, but we have been adopted into the family of God. "And because you are sons, God has sent forth the Spirit of His Son into our hearts, crying, 'Abba! Father!' Therefore you are no longer a slave, but a son; and if a son, then an heir through God" (Gal. 4:6, 7). Because we are declared sons of God by the Spirit's witness we can cry out from our hearts, "Abba, Father." This is the Magna Charta of the Christian's liberation from the power of sin to the privileges and wealth of Christ. The fact of our sonship is repeatedly declared. Each day you and I should sing, "I am a child of the King."

C. S. Lewis wrote this about the Christian's personal relationship with God: "To put ourselves thus on a personal footing with God could, in itself and without warrant, be nothing but presumption and illusion. But we are taught that it is not; that it is God who gives us that footing. For it is by the Holy Spirit that we cry 'Father.' By unveiling, by confessing our sins and 'making known' our requests, we assume the high rank of persons before Him. And He, descending, becomes a Person to us."[4]

Thus, by the Holy Spirit the Christian has a witness within himself. "The one who believes in the Son of God has the witness in himself" (1 John 5:10). Our sins and iniquities are remembered against us no more. We have been adopted into the heavenly family. The Spirit bears witness that as believers in the Lord Jesus Christ we have eternal life.

Finally, the Scripture teaches us the Holy Spirit witnesses to the truth of every promise God has given us in His Word. The Spirit, who inspired the written Word of God, also works in our hearts to assure us that its promises are true, and that they are for us. We know Christ is our Savior, because the Bible tells us this and the Spirit assures us it is true. We know we have become children of God because the Bible tells us this and the Spirit again assures us it is true. "But when He, the Spirit of truth, comes, He will guide you into all the truth" (John 16:13). "Thy word is truth" (John 17:17). Some times I speak with people who tell me they are lacking the assurance of their salvation. When I inquire further, I often find they have been neglecting the Word of God. "And the witness is this, that God has given us eternal life, and this life is in His Son. He who has the Son has the life; he who does not have the Son of God does not have the life. These things I have *written* to you who believe in the name of the Son of God, in order *that you may know that you have eternal life*" (1 John 5:11–13, italics mine).

The Spirit therefore witnesses in our hearts, convincing us of the truth of God's presence and assurance. This is something often difficult to explain to an unbeliever, but countless believers know of the Spirit's assurance in their hearts.

John Wesley, the founder of the Methodist church, once observed, "It is hard to find words in the language of men, to explain the deep things of God. Indeed, there are none that will adequately express what the Spirit of God works in His children. But . . . by the testimony of the Spirit, I mean, an inward impression on the soul, whereby the Spirit of God immediately and directly witnesses to my spirit, that I am a child of God; that Jesus Christ hath loved me, and given Himself for me; that all my sins are blotted out, and I, even I, am reconciled to God."[5]

We can see then that God places a *seal* on us when we receive Christ. And that seal is a person—the Holy Spirit. By the Spirit's presence God gives us security and establishes His ownership over us.

Further, the Spirit is God's *pledge*. He not only seals the arrangement, but He represents God's voluntary obligation to see us through. And fellowship with the Spirit is a sample of what we can expect when we come into our inheritance in heaven.

Finally, the Spirit *witnesses* to us by His Word and within our hearts that Christ died for us, and by faith in Him we have become God's children. What a wonderful thing to know the Holy Spirit has been given to us as a seal—a pledge—and a witness! May each of these give us new assurance of God's love for us, and give us confidence as we seek to live for Christ. And with the apostle Paul may we say, "Thanks be to God for His indescribable gift!" (2 Cor. 9:15).

7. The Christian's Inner Struggle

An Eskimo fisherman came to town every Saturday afternoon. He always brought his two dogs with him. One was white and the other was black. He had taught them to fight on command. Every Saturday afternoon in the town square the people would gather and these two dogs would fight and the fisherman would take bets. On one Saturday the black dog would win; another Saturday, the white dog would win—but the fisherman always won! His friends began to ask him how he did it. He said, "I starve one and feed the other. The one I feed always wins because he is stronger."

One or Two Natures?

This story about the two dogs is apt because it tells us something about the inner warfare that comes into the life of a person who is born again.

We have two natures within us, both struggling for mastery. Which one will dominate us? It depends on which one we feed. If we feed our spiritual lives and allow the Holy Spirit to empower us, He will have rule over us. If we starve our spiritual natures and instead feed the old, sinful nature, the flesh will dominate.

Every Christian can identify with the apostle Paul when he said, "For that which I am doing, I do not understand; for I am not practicing what I would like to do, but I am doing the very thing I hate. . . . I find then the principle that evil is present in me . . . but I see a different law in the members of my body, waging war against the law of my mind, and making me a prisoner of the law of sin which is in my members" (Rom. 7:15, 21, 23).

Many young Christians have said things like this to me from time to time: "Since I became a Christian, I have had struggles within that I never had before. I didn't know I was such a sinner! I never wanted to sin like this before. I thought God had saved me from my sins!"

Actually, strange as it may seem, this condition is something to be thankful for. It is an evidence that the Holy Spirit has come into your life, illuminating the darkness of sin, sensitizing your conscience to sin, awakening in you a new desire to be clean and free from sin before God. Those old sins were there before. Those old temptations were there strongly before, but they didn't appear evil to you then. But now the Holy Spirit has come into your life. You are a new person, born again by this same Spirit. And everything looks different now.

The Struggle within

Now you have become keenly aware of the basic problem in a Christian's life, the struggle with sin. In the New Testament the apostle Paul talks of every Christian being in an intense spiritual battle: "For our struggle is not against flesh and blood, but against the rulers, against the powers, against the world forces of this darkness, against the spiritual forces of wickedness in the heavenly places" (Eph. 6:12). So there are external spiritual forces which are at work in this world, seeking to keep us from God and His will. But we must not always blame Satan for everything that goes wrong or every sin we commit. Often it is our own sinful nature which is at work within us. "For the flesh sets its desire against the Spirit, and the Spirit against the flesh; for these are in opposition to one another, so that you may not do the things that you please" (Gal. 5:17).

And this is not just external to us. This battle goes on inside of us. And that's the theme of Romans 7, especially verses 7 through 25. Look at Romans 7:7 and 8, for example. (Read it in a good modern translation of the Bible.) Let me paraphrase what Paul is saying:

Before I heard the law of God and the good news of salvation, I didn't know covetousness was sin, but then I heard the tenth commandment, "Thou shalt not covet." God's law showed me this sin in my heart, and I suddenly became keenly aware how much covetousness was a live, writhing evil within me. And I realized how great a sinner I was, doomed to die—but for Christ! As a Christian I began to fight this evil desire in me. And what a struggle! I tried to stop coveting and envying, but I couldn't.

That's the picture, and I'm sure you have often felt just as Paul did. Maybe your sin is wrong sexual desires, pride, gluttony, laziness, or anger, or some other besetting sin (Heb. 12:1 KJV). But you feel the same inner struggle. Sometimes you conclude just as Paul did in Romans 7:22–24 which I quoted above.

But don't stop there! Note Paul's glorious conclusion in verse 25 and 8:2 (there were no chapter divisions in Paul's original letter!): "Thanks be to God through Jesus Christ our Lord! . . . For the law of the Spirit of life in Christ Jesus has set you free from the law of sin and of death." As a great saint said many years ago, "Sin no longer reigns, but it still fights!"

Horatius Bonar was a brilliant theologian, a great saint, and a compassionate pastor. He died at the age of 33, but not before a great revival had taken place in his church in Scotland. His sermons and books have blessed God's people for the last 150 years. He spoke honestly for all of us when he said: "While conversion calms one kind of storm it raises another, which is to be lifelong."[1] Efforts to explain this struggle by theologians have gone on for centuries. Some have taken Paul's words and spoken of the "two natures" in the Christian—the "old man" and the "new man." This terminology comes from such passages as Ephesians 4:22–24 where Paul says, "That, in reference to your former manner of life, you lay aside the *old self,* which is being corrupted in accordance with the lusts of deceit . . . and put on the *new self,* which in the likeness of God has been created in righteousness and holiness of the truth" (italics mine).

Speaking of this in the footnote on that passage, *The New Scofield Reference Bible* says, "The 'new man' is the regenerate man as distinguished from the old man . . . and is a new man as having become a partaker of the divine nature and life . . . in no sense the old man made over, or improved."[2] In a footnote on Romans 7:15, Scofield continues, "The apostle personifies the struggle of the two natures within the believer —the old or Adamic nature, and the divine nature received through the new birth."[3]

How can we visualize and understand what is going on inside of us? I think Romans 8:1–13 describes it best. Let me try to paraphrase what Paul is saying here, and let me put it in the first person—this is how it applies to me:

I was born in sin. For years I was controlled by sin and didn't know it. I was literally "dead in trespasses and sin" (Eph. 2:1). Then I heard the Word of God, the law and the Gospel. I was ' convicted. I saw my sins for the first time. I accepted Christ. And now the law of God is speaking to me every day through the Word of God.

Now I have become conscious of sins I didn't know I had. Sometimes I despair (like Paul in Romans 7:24: "Wretched man that I am!"), but, praise the Lord, I know now there is no condemnation anybody can bring against me because I am in Christ (Rom. 8:1). Christ has set me free from the law of sin and death (Rom. 8:2). I am still me—with my old sinful personality and nature, sinful habits that have grown strong in the many years before I was a Christian. But now the Holy Spirit has come into my life. He shows me my sin. He actually condemns the sin in me (Rom. 8:3). And by His power He helps me to meet the requirements of God's law (Rom. 8:4).

If I keep thinking about my old life and my sins, I will go back to that life. The old "me" will continue to sin. But if I put my mind on Christ and try to listen and obey the Holy Spirit (Rom. 8:5), the Holy Spirit will give me life and peace (Rom. 8:6). If a man is a Christian, he has the Holy Spirit (Rom. 8:9). His spirit has been made alive (Rom. 8:10). The Holy Spirit is giving life to his body, bringing it back from the deadness of sin (Rom. 8:11) and bringing abundant new life in Christ.

The Two Natures

God uses many strong figures of speech to describe what the Holy Spirit does for us throughout the Bible. We have already noticed this in John 3. He says we are "born again" by the Holy Spirit. This is clearly an illustration to describe, in physical terms, a great spiritual truth. And here in regard to our Christian life in Romans 7 and 8 and in Ephesians 4, God uses psychological terms—"new nature . . . old nature" or "new man and old man"—to try to make us understand the radical change that takes place in our Christian life when we are controlled by the Holy Spirit.

We consciously feel that we are just one person. When I have sinned, deep down I know that I did it. I felt the pull of temptation. I responded and at some point willed to sin. At some point I said "Yes" to the devil as he tempted me through my old habits, my old desires, my old motives, or appealed to my old goals in life. This is what Paul means in talking about the "old nature" or the sin principle. But it is really me. I am one person before God. I am responsible for my sins. I can't blame the sin principle that still lives within. I have a choice either to yield to the Spirit—the new impetus in my life—or the old force of sin.

But now the Holy Spirit has come into my heart. He has given me new life—God's quality of eternal life. And He Himself is in me to break the old habits, to purify my motives, to set my eyes on new goals, especially the goal of becoming like the Lord Jesus Christ (Rom. 8:29).

So for the rest of my Christian life until Christ comes and calls me home, I am being sanctified (growing more and more into spiritual maturity) by the Holy Spirit through the Word of God. Best of all, the Holy Spirit is daily, quietly making me to be conformed more and more to the Lord Jesus Christ if I am cooperating with Him: "But we all, with unveiled face beholding as in a mirror the glory of the Lord, are being transformed into the same image from glory to glory, just as from the Lord, the Spirit" (2 Cor. 3:18).

But never forget there will always be a struggle, both without and within. The devil is an implacable enemy. He never gives up. Through "the world" and the flesh, he appeals to the old force within me to reassert itself. He appeals to my lusts, my covetousness, and my pride, just as he did to Eve and Adam (Gen. 3). I will always feel the pull of temptation. My old tendencies will be awakened and will want to sin. *But* I have the Holy Spirit within me, a more powerful principle or force: "Greater is He who is in you than he who is in the world" (1 John 4:4). If I cooperate with Him and turn to Him for help, He will give me the power to resist temptation. He will make me stronger as a result of every test.

Perhaps the next time the devil will appeal to a different weakness in *"the flesh."* I have a different set of temptations. But the Holy Spirit is always in my heart to give me victory over this new struggle, and as I win victory after victory I get stronger. Dr. Bonar says that God recognizes the saint's inner conflict "as an indispensable process of discipline, as a development of the contrast between light and darkness, as an exhibition of the way in which God is glorified in the infirmities of His saints, and in their contests with the powers of evil."[4]

In Romans 7 Paul is not saying he cannot help but sin because of his old nature which he can't control. Rather, Paul is describing the struggle all of us are going to have and telling us we can have victory in Christ by the power of His Holy Spirit that lives within us (Rom. 8:4).

Sanctification

The word sanctification comes from the Greek word which means "to be separate" or "set apart for a purpose." Paul speaks of the believer as having been "sanctified by the Holy Spirit" (Rom. 15:16). He wrote to the Corinthians saying that they, *having been sanctified,* are called to be saints (1 Cor. 1:2). We Christians are to be "progressively sanctified" or "made righteous" in holiness as we daily abide in Christ—and obey His Word. Abiding and obedience are the keys to a successful Spirit-dominated life. We are as much sanctified as we are possessed by the Holy Spirit. It is never a question of how much you and I have of the Spirit, but how much He has of us.

The Scriptures teach that "sanctification" has *three parts* to it. *First,* the moment you receive Christ there is an immediate sanctification. *Second,* as we progress in the Christian life there is a "progressive sanctification." *Third,* when we go to heaven there will be total and "complete" sanctification, which is called "glorification."

We have a friend on one of the Caribbean islands who purchased the ruins of an old mansion. In his eyes he sees it as it will someday be, beautiful, restored, perfect. It is "sanctified." In the meantime, he is working on it with his limited resources, his ingenuity, and his love. To the average beholder it may look like something out of a horror movie, with its scraps of lumber, patched tin roof, fabulous tile floor. But to our friend it is special. Loved. He sees it as it will be someday. Perhaps the world sees the body of Christ (the true Church) as others see this mansion. But God sees it as it will eventually be. Perfect, complete. It is being sanctified. In our friend's eyes, the mansion is already beautiful, because he sees in his mind's eye the finished product. When he begins work on it, it will be in the process of being restored. And someday our friend will complete his work, and the mansion will be in reality what he always hoped it would be.

In a far greater way, God looks on us in Jesus Christ. He sees us now as fully sanctified, because He knows what we will be some day. Also He is at work in us restoring us—we are being sanctified. And some day that process will be complete when we go to be with Him throughout all eternity. We will be fully sanctified.

J. B. Phillips says that God predestinates us "to bear the family likeness of his Son" (Rom. 8:29). That is what is happening to us now as believers. We are being progressively sanctified—to spiritual maturity—to bear the family likeness of His Son. Remember that Jesus Christ was perfect—and we are to strive for perfection. While this will be complete only in heaven, it should be our goal right now. This is what the Bible means when it commands us, "Like the Holy One who called you, be holy yourselves also in all your behavior; because it is written, 'You shall be holy, for I am Holy' " (1 Peter 1:15, 16). Whether we realize it or not we are growing spiritually through the conflicts, turbulence, troubles, temptations, testings, and so on that afflict all Christians slowly or rapidly. But there is coming a day when all of this will be past, and we will be completely sanctified, "We know that, when He appears, we shall be like Him, because we shall see Him just as He is" (1 John 3:2).

In the meantime, Christians, day by day, week by week, and month by month, are told to walk in the Spirit. Walking in the Spirit means being led and directed by the Holy Spirit. This comes as we progressively yield various areas of our lives to the Spirit's control. Paul said, "Walk by the Spirit, and you will not carry out the desire of the flesh" (Gal. 5:16). Now desire in itself is not wrong, it's *what* we desire or lust for that is wrong— and *when* we yield.

The Old Self-Life

When Eve had a desire to "know" (but based on self)—Satan turned healthy desire into unhealthy. And Eve disobeyed God.

Flesh is the Bible's word for unperfected human nature. Leaving off the "h" and spelling it in reverse we have the word *self*. Flesh is the self-life: it is what we are when we are left to our own devices. At times our *self* behaves itself very well. It can do good things, it can be moral, and it can have extremely high ethical standards. But sooner or later your self and mine will show itself to be *selfish*.

We try to educate self, to train and discipline it. We pass laws to compel it to behave. But Paul said that the flesh has a mind of its own and that "the natural mind" is not subject to the law of God. God clearly says He has no confidence in our flesh. Paul declared, "I know that nothing good dwells in me, that is, in my flesh" (Rom. 7:18). The moment we realize this and yield to the dictates of the Holy Spirit in our lives, greater victory, greater spiritual maturity, greater love, joy, peace and other fruits will manifest themselves.

Recently, a friend of ours was converted to Christ. He had previously led a wild life. One of his old friends said to him, "I feel sorry for you. You now go to church, pray, and read the Bible all the time. You no longer go to the nightclubs, get drunk, or enjoy your beautiful women." Our friend gave a strange reply. He said, "I do get drunk every time I want to. I do go to nightclubs every time I want to. I do go with the girls when I want to." His worldly friend looked puzzled. Our friend laughed and said, "Jim, you see, the Lord took the *want* out when I was converted and He made me a new person in Christ Jesus."

St. Augustine once said, "Love God and live as you please." If we truly love God we will want to do what pleases Him. It is as the Psalmist says in Psalm 37, "Delight yourself in the Lord; And He will give you the desires of your heart" (v. 4). Delighting in the Lord alters the desires.

The Battle with the Flesh

If we as Christians try to make ourselves better or good or even acceptable to God by some human effort, we will fail. Everything we have and are and do comes through the Holy Spirit. The Holy Spirit has come to dwell in us, and God does His works in us by the Holy Spirit. What we have to do is yield ourselves to the Spirit of God so that He may empower us to put off the old and put on the new.

Paul makes all of this clear in Galatians 5:17, "For the flesh sets its desire against the Spirit, and the Spirit against the flesh; for these are in opposition to one another." This indicates what the real conflict is in the heart of every true believer. The flesh wants one thing and the Spirit wants another. The black dog and the white dog are often fighting. As long as there is not the surrender of mind and body every moment of the day, the old nature will assert itself.

Conscious of my own weakness, sometimes on rising in the morning I have said, "Lord, I'm not going to allow this or that thing to assert itself in my life today." Then the devil sends something unexpected to tempt me, or God allows me to be tested at that exact point. Many times in my life the thing I never meant to do in my mind I did in the flesh. I have wept many a bitter tear of confession and asked God the Spirit to give me strength at that point. But this lets me know that I am engaged in a spiritual warfare every day. I must never let down my guard—I must keep armed.

Many of the young people I meet are living defeated, disillusioned, and disappointed lives even after coming to Christ. They are walking after the flesh because they have not had proper teaching at this precise point. The old man, the old self, the old principle, the old force, is not yet dead or wholly renewed: it is still there. It fights every inch of the way against the new man, the new force, that God made us when we received Christ. Only as we yield and obey the new principle in Christ do we win the victory.

"Yielding" is the secret! Paul said, "I appeal to you therefore, brethren, and beg of you in view of [all] the mercies of God, to make a decisive dedication of your bodies—presenting all your members and faculties—as a living sacrifice, holy (devoted, consecrated) and well pleasing to God, which is your reasonable (rational, intelligent) service and spiritual worship" (Rom. 12:1, *Amplified*). When total surrender occurs, there is another "experience." For most Christians it is not just a second experience—but it comes many times throughout our lives.

The Works of the Flesh

Thus, we see that there is a continuing conflict going on in every one of us between the flesh on the one hand and the Spirit on the other. When Paul uses the word "flesh," he really means human nature in all its weakness, its impotence, and its helplessness. The flesh is the lower side of man's nature. The flesh is all that man is without God and without Christ. Paul lists the works of the flesh in Galatians 5:19–21. When we read this terrible list, we should also read Romans 1:17–32. In these passages the depravity of human nature is pictured for us. We see it for what it is.

Every day we read about this depravity in our newspapers. We watch it on the newscasts on our television screens daily. Everywhere, unregenerate human nature calls the signals and produces the works of the flesh. The sins of the flesh are flaunted shamelessly. They are committed blatantly and without repentance by unregenerate men. However, the Christian can sometimes temporarily yield to one or more of these terrible things. He is immediately convicted by the Holy Spirit and quickly repents and finds forgiveness.

In Galatians 5 there is a catalog of fifteen *works of the flesh* which range from sexual sins to drunkenness and include idolatry and sorcery. What strikes terror in every Christian heart is the knowledge that these sins can easily creep into our lives unless we are spiritually vigilant and strong. "Therefore let him who thinks he stands take heed lest he fall" (1 Cor. 10:12). With this in mind, let us look at the list of sins Paul lists in Galatians 5, so we will be better prepared to fight against the flesh.

Some have suggested that these can be divided into three categories, or sets. The first set are sexual immorality, impurity, and sensuality (Gal. 5:19).

1. Immorality. The Greek word here is broad enough to cover all kinds of sexual wickedness and is, incidentally, the word (*porneia*) from which the word "pornography" comes. Premarital sex, extramarital sex, abnormal sex, incest, prostitution, and surely sex sins in the heart are part of what the apostle has in mind here.

2. Impurity. Here the Greek word suggests any kind of impurity, whether in thought or deed. It might even include unnatural lust as described by Paul in Romans 1:24. It surely would cover some of the modern films, pornographic literature, and "evil imaginations." William Barclay describes it as the pus of an unclean wound; a tree that has never been pruned; material that has never been sifted.

3. Sensuality. This Greek word can be thought of as wantonness or debauchery. But there may be more to it than that. It has in it the notion of reckless shamelessness, or even an open indulgence in impurity. The same word is used in 2 Peter 2:7 when the apostle speaks of the licentiousness of Sodom and Gomorrah. It can be no less than lewdness and sensuality of any kind.

The second set of the works of the flesh enumerated by Paul are these:

1. Idolatry. The Greek word for idolatry is the worship of false gods of which there are many today. By implication we think of it as including anything that comes between us and God. Money can become an idol if we worship it above our worship of God. Pleasure can become an idol, even a relationship to another person can become an idol if it takes the place of God.

2. Sorcery. The Greek word here can be translated witchcraft; the idea especially is the administering of magical potions and drugs. Thus it is related also to the use of drugs; we get our word "pharmacy" from this Greek word, *pharmakia.* Throughout Scripture, witchcraft and sorcery are condemned. This evil is spreading rapidly in Western societies at an alarming rate.

3. Enmities. The Greek word for enmities has to do with hatred. Hatred contains within it the idea of something latent, like an animal ready to spring on its prey. Hostility, antipathy, antagonism, animosity, rancor, and intense dislike are all comparable terms for what is translated here as hatred.

4. Strife. The Greek word refers to variance, contentions, strife, fighting, discord, wrangling, and quarreling. Many churches are hard hit by internal discord that divides laymen from pastors, and laymen from laymen. When members of a congregation do not speak to each other and when they fight with one another, this sin is at work and the Spirit of God is quenched. Numerous families are infected by this spirit. Many marriages, even Christian ones, are being destroyed by this sin.

5. Jealousy—a very common sin. It involves envy when someone gets an honor we wanted, or it can mar a marriage relationship when a husband or a wife is jealous of his or her partner. We read of murders being committed because of jealousy, of friends who have not spoken for years. On the other hand, there is the beautiful example of Jonathan who was *not* jealous of David (1 Sam. 20).

6. Outbursts of anger. The Greek word for wrath means unrighteous fits of rage, passionate outbursts of anger and hostile feelings. John uses the same root word in the Apocalypse about the righteous wrath of God. Man's wrath can be righteous or unrighteous, but God's wrath is always righteous for He cannot sin. There is a righteous wrath, but it is not a fit of anger. Here anger or wrath is a sin we must cast out of our lives. Someone has well said, "Righteous indignation is usually one part righteous and nine parts indignation."

7. Disputes. This Greek word for disputes or strife means selfish ambition, self-seeking, and selfishness. This violates both parts of the Ten Commandments (Exod. 20). First it is a sin against God when selfish ambition replaces the will of God for our lives. Then it violates the command to love our neighbors, for acts of self-seeking are always committed at someone else's expense.

8. Dissensions. The Greek word means seditions, dissensions, or divisions. Believers are to be of one mind. "He is the God that maketh men to be of one mind in an house" is the Prayer Book version of Psalm 68:6.[5] Unless principles are at stake or the Word of God is threatened, then discord can become sinful. We are to contend for the faith, but even when doing so we are not to be contentious. Truth often divides, but when truth is not at stake, God's people should be able to live together in love by the grace of the Holy Spirit.

9. Factions. The Greek word for factions, or heresies, has to do with sects and sectarianism. It means to choose that which is bad, or to form an opinion contrary to the revelation of God in Scripture. This is the same word found in 2 Peter 2:1 (NIV): "But there were also false prophets among the people, just as there will be false teachers among you. They will secretly introduce destructive heresies, even denying the sovereign Lord who bought them—bringing swift destruction on themselves." Thus this is a serious sin. As Alexander said, "Error is often plausibly dressed in the outer garb of truth."

10. Envyings. This Greek word means resentment at the

excellence or good fortune of another, a jealous spirit. We may envy someone his beautiful voice, his great wealth, his superior position, or his athletic attainments. Or we may begrudge a girl her beauty, a person his position in public office. Envy has been the downfall of many a Christian. Normally, there can be no envy that does not involve covetousness.

11. Drunkenness. This Greek word means overindulgence in alcohol. Alcohol may be used for medicine, but it can also become a terrible drug. The way it is used in our world is probably one of the great evils of our day. It is a self-inflicted impediment that springs from "a man taking a drink, a drink taking a drink, and drink taking the man." Distilled liquors as we have them today were unknown in Bible times. This modern use of alcohol is far more dangerous than the use of wine, which was also condemned when taken to excess. Teetotalism or nonteetotalism cannot be proven from Scriptures. Whatever we do, we should do it to the glory of God (1 Cor. 10:31).

I had a wonderful Christian friend in England many years ago. He was a godly man with a great knowledge of the Scriptures and a deep and holy walk with God. Once when we had a meal with him he said, "I serve wine at my table to the glory of God. I know you don't take wine, to the glory of God, so we have provided ginger ale for you." He continued, "We are taught to respect each other's liberty and each other's conscience."

12. Carousings. In the Greek this means orgies. In Romans 13:13 and 1 Peter 4:3 it is associated with illicit sex, drunkenness, and other evils in which no Christian should indulge.

There may be someone reading this who has been guilty of one, or even all of the sins listed here. Does this mean you can never enter the kingdom of Heaven; that the door is forever closed to you? Certainly not. The Bible says that by repentance and faith anyone can be forgiven (1 John 1:9).

However, Galatians 5:21 constitutes the most serious warning to those who may think they can sin that grace may abound. The apostle sternly says, "Those who practice such things [i.e. those things just enumerated] shall not inherit the kingdom of God." Paul's whole terrible list when practiced by men violates God's will for them. God hates these things so much that He will judge those who do them. People whose lives are characterized by such deviations from the will of God will be separated from

Him and lost in outer darkness. The reason I have listed all this is because millions of professing Christians are only just that—"professing." They have never possessed Christ. They live lives characterized by the flesh. Tens of thousands have never been born again. They will go into eternity lost—while thinking they are saved because they belong to the church, or were baptized, and so on.

But there is another truth we should not forget. Today people do many of these forbidden things in the name of freedom. What they fail to see is that such activities actually enslave those who become involved in them. And when liberty becomes license, liberty not only is misconstrued—those who misconstrue are themselves shackled so that they lose the liberty of which Scripture speaks. True freedom consists not in the freedom to sin, but the freedom *not* to sin.

Another truth is that those who live in the flesh can be changed only by the Spirit of God. This is why a deep spiritual awakening is so desperately needed today. You cannot legislate successfully against these problems. No matter how many laws are passed, or how many good intentions there may be, in those persons outside of Christ the old nature is in control. It may be subdued at times; it may be controlled by sheer discipline on other occasions, but there will come times when these works of the flesh will manifest themselves by boiling over in strife and eventually war.

However, the Christian has become a new creation. He can come under the control of the Holy Spirit and produce the fruit of the Spirit, which is a whole new set of principles that develop a new man and could eventually produce a new society.

Paul says, "Now those who belong to Christ Jesus have crucified the flesh with its passions and desires" (Gal. 5:24). During the lifetime of our Lord Jesus Christ, He lived as a man, He was tempted as a man, yet He kept the whole law of God and had victory over the flesh. Those of us who are bound to Him by faith are, in principle at least, finished with all that belongs to the flesh. Yet Paul recognizes that these old fleshly tendencies still lurk within us and that we must almost hourly yield to the Holy Spirit to have total and complete victory.

The Scripture does not say, "They that are Christ's *should* crucify the flesh." This took place positionally and legally when

Jesus Christ hung on the cross. Galatians 2:20 reads, "I *have been* crucified with Christ" (italics mine). Romans 6:6 says, "Knowing this, that our old self *was crucified* with Him" (italics mine). It is a completed action, a settled matter. Since we believers have already been crucified even as we have already been saved, we are now called upon to work out that crucifixion in the flesh so that we do not make provision for the works of the flesh. We have been buried with Christ and now are raised from the dead unto the new life in Him.

Many people say, "I cannot live a life like this. I cannot hold out." If it were up to you and me, we could not. The apostle Paul says, "Consider yourselves to be dead to sin" (Rom. 6:11). He also said sin shall no longer reign in our mortal bodies. This means that "by faith" we accept what Jesus Christ has done for us at the cross. By faith we turn over our lives totally and completely and without reservation to the Holy Spirit. Christ sits on the throne of our hearts. No one, or anything, is going to push Him off. The Holy Spirit produces the "fruit of the Spirit." While the works of the flesh would like very much to manifest themselves—and sometimes do—they no longer reign, they are no longer in control. It is no longer a practice; it is no longer a habit; we are transformed by His grace and live the new life in Christ. But this is only possible as we are filled with the Holy Spirit. It is to this important topic that we now turn.

8. The Fullness of the Spirit

Our home is supplied by a reservoir fed by two mountain springs. These two springs on the mountain above the house, according to the mountain people who lived here before we did, never fluctuate. Rainy season or dry, they remain the same. We draw on the water as we need it, and the springs continually flowing into the reservoir keep it filled to overflowing. That is literally what it means to "be being filled with the Spirit."

All Christians are committed to be filled with the Spirit. Anything short of a Spirit-filled life is less than God's plan for each believer.

What does the Bible mean when it speaks of the fullness of the Holy Spirit? Let's define the fullness of the Spirit. To be Spirit-filled is to be controlled or dominated by the Spirit's presence and power. In Ephesians 5:18 Paul says, "And do not get drunk with wine, for that is dissipation, but be filled with the Spirit." Here he draws a contrast between two things. A person who is filled with alcohol is controlled or dominated by alcohol. Its presence and power have overridden his normal abilities and actions.

It is interesting that we often say someone is "under the influence" of alcohol. Now that is somewhat the meaning of being filled with the Spirit. We are "under the influence" of the Spirit. Instead of doing things only with our own strength or ability, He empowers us. Instead of doing only what we want to do, we now are guided by Him. Unfortunately millions of God's people do not enjoy the unlimited spiritual wealth at their disposal because they are not filled with the Holy Spirit.

I remember a great woman Bible teacher by the name of Ruth

Paxson whom I heard speak on this theme many times. She was a guest in our home, and I still have some of the notes I made from her lectures.

As she reminded us, the lives of many reflect the practices and standards of this present world. True, they have been baptized with the Holy Spirit into the body of Christ, and they are going to heaven. But they are missing so much of what God wants them to have in this life. Consciously or unconsciously they are more interested in imitating the world system dominated by Satan than in imitating Christ. They do not really want to share the reproach of Christ outside the camp (Heb. 13:13). Their gifts are often unused, and spiritual fruit is absent from their lives. Nor do they have any great concern to evangelize the spiritually needy in their own community. Their zeal to walk in obedience to the commandments of Christ grows weak. Their devotional life is uneven, if not totally neglected, and they anticipate reading the newspaper more than reading the Word of God. If they do pray, it is a cheerless duty and a tedious task rather than a joy. As with Lot in Sodom, sin for them has lost some of its sinfulness; their sensitivity to sin has been numbed and the edge of conscience blunted. Known sins remain unconfessed.

Christians have more equipment and technology for evangelizing the world than ever before. And there are better trained personnel. But one of the great tragedies of the present hour is this: Christians so often lack the fullness of the Spirit with its true dependence on God's power for their ministry. Illustrations of the kind of spiritual power they need but lack abounded in the first century. It was said of the Christians in one city, "These men who have turned the world upside down have come here also" (Acts 17:6 RSV). And from time to time in later centuries this same Holy Spirit power was unleashed upon the world. Isolated instances of it exist right now. But what if the *full* power of the Holy Spirit were to be loosed today through all true believers? The world could again be turned upside down.

The Biblical Basis for Being Filled with the Spirit

I think it proper to say that anyone who is not Spirit-filled is a defective Christian. Paul's command to the Ephesian Christians, "Be filled with the Spirit," is binding on all of us Christians everywhere in every age. There are no exceptions. We must conclude that since we are ordered to be filled with the Spirit, we are sinning if we are not filled. And our failure to be filled with the Spirit constitutes one of the greatest sins against the Holy Spirit.

It is interesting to note that the command to "Be filled with the Spirit" actually has the idea of continuously being filled in the original Greek language which Paul used. We are not filled once for all, like a bucket. Instead, we are to be filled constantly. It might be translated, "Be filled and keep on being filled," or "Be being filled."

Ephesians 5:18 literally says, "Keep on being filled with the Spirit." Dr. Merrill C. Tenney has compared this to the situation of an old-time farmhouse kitchen. In one corner was a sink; above it was a pipe through which came a continuous stream of water from the spring outside. The water, by running constantly, kept the sink brimful of good water. In like manner the Christian is not to let himself be emptied of the Spirit that he may later become full again; rather he is constantly to accept the direction and energy of the Spirit so he is always overflowing.

The overflowing rivers and the abundant life are available blessings for all Christians. Rivers of living water fail to flow in our lives not because God denies them to us, but because we do not want them or we refuse to meet the conditions to get them.

This continuous filling by the Holy Spirit is also what Jesus was teaching in John 4, in speaking to the Samaritan woman at Jacob's well: "Everyone who drinks of this water shall thirst again; but whoever drinks of the water that I shall give him shall never thirst; but the water that I shall give him shall become in him a well of water springing up to eternal life" (John 4:13, 14). Jesus spoke of the Holy Spirit in the same way in John 7:38: "He who believes in Me, as the Scripture said, 'From his innermost being shall flow rivers of living water.'" The overflowing spring and the continual river speak of the constant supply of the Holy Spirit's blessing available to all Christians. This living water of which Jesus speaks—this continual filling by the Holy Spirit—fails to flow in our lives not because God denies it to us, but because we do not want it or we refuse to meet the conditions God sets up to get it.

In reading John 7:38 one day, I was stopped short and struck with awe by the grandeur of Jesus' words. He did not speak of drops of blessings, few and far between, as in a light shower on a spring day. He spoke of rivers of living water. Consider the Mississippi, the Amazon, the Danube, or the Yangtze Rivers: However much may be taken from them, they do not run dry but continue to flow generously. The sources from which they come keep sending water down their course. These rivers illustrate the life of the Spirit-filled Christian. The supply is never exhausted because it has its source in the Holy Spirit who is inexhaustible.

Bishop Moule once said, "Never shall I forget the gain to conscious faith and peace which came to my own soul not long after a first decisive and appropriating view of the crucified Lord as the sinner's sacrifice of peace." What was the cause of this gain? He says it was "a more intelligent and conscious hold upon the living and more gracious personality of the Spirit through whose mercy the soul had got that blessed view. It was a new contact as it were with the inner and eternal movements of redeeming goodness and power. A new discovery in divine resources."

One of the prayers of the great Welsh revival was:
"Fill me, Holy Spirit, fill me,
More than fulness I would know:
I am smallest of Thy vessels,
Yet, I much can overflow."[1]

We must make ourselves available to the Holy Spirit so that when He fills us we will become vessels of blessing to the world, whether large and beautiful in great service, or small and unnoticed by men. To me the Corinthian church was one of the saddest and most tragic churches in the New Testament. Its members had been baptized with the Spirit; they had been given many of the gifts of the Spirit; and therefore they had much to commend them. Yet Paul said they were fleshly and unspiritual. "And I, brethren, could not speak to you as to spiritual men, but as to men of flesh, as to babes in Christ. . . . for you are still fleshly" (1 Cor. 3:1, 3). This means that you and I may have one or more gifts of the Spirit and still be unspiritual, lacking in "the fullness of the Spirit." To say that having the gift of evangelism, or the gift of a pastor, or of a teacher, or the gift of tongues, or the gift of healing (or any other gift), is proof that we have the fullness of the Spirit is misleading. Furthermore, any gift we may have will never be used to its fullest potential for God unless it is brought under the control of, and empowered by, the Holy Spirit. There is nothing more tragic than a gift of God which is misused for selfish or unspiritual purposes.

So it is critical that we be filled with the Spirit. In considering this, however, we must not be confused by mere terminology. Some Christians have used terms like "the second baptism" or "the second blessing" or "a second work of grace." None of these terms are used in the Bible, but I realize that for many people they are simply semantic equivalents for the fullness of the Spirit. The name we give the experience is less important than that we actually *be* filled with the Spirit.

I prefer not to use these terms, however, since they can lead to confusion in some people's minds. Personally I believe the Bible teaches there is one baptism in the Spirit—when we come to faith in Christ. The Bible teaches there are many fillings—in fact, we are to be continuously filled by the Holy Spirit. One baptism—many fillings! I do not personally find anything in Scripture which indicates there must be some later "baptism of the Spirit" into our lives after conversion. He is already there, and we are called to yield to Him continually, but never do I condemn those who hold a different view. Many of those holding a different view are among my closest friends. Differences at this point do not constitute a basis for division of Christian fellowship.

Maybe we need to reverse the figure we use. When we are filled with the Spirit, it is not a question of there being more of Him, as though His work in us is quantitative. It is not how much of the Spirit *we* have, but how much the Spirit has of *us*. He is in us in all His fullness, whether we see this exhibited in our lives or not. When we receive Christ as Savior and Lord, you and I receive Him in full, not just in part. Then as we come to understand more and more of Christ's lordship, we surrender and yield more and more. So, seeking the fullness of the Spirit, we receive and enjoy His filling and His fullness more and more.

When we receive Christ as Savior, our spiritual capacities are extremely small. At that moment we have surrendered to Him as Savior and Lord as best we know how. It may even be proper to say we are filled with the Spirit at that time, in the sense that we are under His influence and control. However, there are still many areas of our lives which need to be yielded to His control, and we may not even be aware of them at that moment. As we grow in the grace and knowledge of Christ, our spiritual capacities enlarge. We soon discover in our Christian life that we are not yet "perfect." We often stumble and fall into sins—including sins of which we may not be conscious at the time. There are many sins of omission also—things we should be doing or attitudes we should be having, but they have not become part of us yet. Part of the work of the Holy Spirit is to convict us of these sins and bring us to true repentance. At such a time we need a new filling of the Holy Spirit, that He might control and dominate us. There also may be new tasks or challenges that God gives us, and this should always cause us to seek afresh the power and presence—the filling—of the Holy Spirit.

It is also common for a young Christian to believe that he must rely on his own wisdom and strength to fight sin in his life, or to undertake some task God has given him. Such a person may realize that his salvation is based totally on what God has done in Christ, but at the same time be unaware that he is just as dependent on God the Holy Spirit for his Christian growth. Often he will fight bravely and struggle against temptations, or zealously seek to witness for Christ, and yet see little or no real progress. Why? It is because he is doing everything in the energy of the flesh, not in the power of the Spirit. Such a person needs to understand God's provision of the Holy Spirit and be yielded to His control. He needs to be filled with the Spirit.

Sometimes in this situation the Holy Spirit may fill such a person in deeply moving and memorable ways. Other Christians who may be more mature may still have an overwhelming spiritual experience in which the Holy Spirit fills them in fresh and wonderful ways. Some people call this a "baptism of the Spirit," but I think it is more Scriptural to speak of it as "a new filling of the Holy Spirit." This experience may come at a critical point in one's life when he is facing some crucial decision or some particularly difficult problem or challenge. Or this experience may come very quietly. In fact, there can even be times in which the filling of the Holy Spirit is very real, and yet we may be almost completely unaware of it.

Both of these experiences have been true in my own life. There have been times of deep awareness of the Holy Spirit's presence. There have been other times in which I have felt weak and inadequate, and yet in retrospect I know the Holy Spirit was in control of my life.

In my own life there have been times when I have also had the sense of being filled with the Spirit, knowing that some special strength was added for some task I was being called upon to perform.

We sailed for England in 1954 for a crusade that was to last for three months. While on the ship, I experienced a definite sense of oppression. Satan seemed to have assembled a formidable array of his artillery against me. Not only was I oppressed, I was overtaken by a sense of depression, accompanied by a frightening feeling of inadequacy for the task that lay ahead. Almost night and day I prayed. I knew in a new way what Paul was telling us when he spoke about "praying without ceasing." Then one day in a prayer meeting with my wife and colleagues, a break came. As I wept before the Lord, I was filled with deep assurance that power belonged to God and He was faithful. I had been baptized by the Spirit into the body of Christ when I was saved, but I believe God gave me a special anointing on the way to England. From that moment on I was confident that God the Holy Spirit was in control for the task of the 1954 Crusade in London.

That proved true.

Experiences of this kind had happened to me before, and they have happened to me many times since. Sometimes no tears are shed. Sometimes as I have lain awake at night the quiet assurance has come that I was being filled with the Spirit for the task that lay ahead.

However there have been many more occasions when I would have to say as the apostle Paul did in 1 Corinthians 2:3: "I was with you in weakness and in fear and in much trembling." Frequently various members of my team have assured me that when I have had the least liberty in preaching, or the greatest feeling of failure, God's power has been most evident.

In other words it is still true, as Paul continued in his letter to the church at Corinth, "My message and my preaching were not in persuasive words of wisdom, but in demonstration of the Spirit and of power, that your faith should not rest on the wisdom of men, but on the power of God" (1 Cor. 2:4, 5).

But note, those who *heard* the word sensed the power, not necessarily the one who proclaimed it. Filling does not necessarily imply "feeling."

Full and Filled

Two words used in the New Testament sometimes puzzle Christians: the words are *full* and *filled*. Some people make a distinction between them. I agree that there may be some distinction, but it is only minor. For instance, to be *full* of the Spirit seems to me to refer to the "state of being" of the believer. I think that John the Baptist and the apostle Paul were full of the Spirit all the time; that is, it was a continuous state. However, for them to be "filled with the Spirit" might also refer to a particular and occasional empowering or "anointing" for special purposes and special tasks. On occasion some of the New Testament saints God used for special assignments were said to be "filled with the Spirit." They might not have been able to bear it if that surcharge of power filled them all the time. But in moments of great need they could bear it for a season.

I believe God gives us the strength of the Holy Spirit commensurate with the tasks He gives us.

We have a friend who is a retired Presbyterian clergyman. His father operated a pile driver. He once told of watching the great pile drivers driving the posts into the river bed of the Mississippi in the process of building a bridge. Each pole was lifted into place and then with a mighty pounding of the pile driver each pole was driven securely into the riverbed.

That evening the little boy, Grier Davis, was playing in his sandpile and trying to reenact what he had seen earlier. But try as he would, he could not drive the sticks into the sand as he had seen the pile driver drive the poles into the Mississippi River bottom. Then he had a bright idea. Running to his father he asked if he might have permission to borrow one of the pile

drivers. With a chuckle the father explained that the pile driver
was much too powerful for the small job he was attempting to
accomplish, and that a hammer would be more like it.

So it is with the power of the Holy Spirit. When God calls us
to any task He also supplies the power for that task.

Thus it should be the normal situation of the Christian to be
filled with the Spirit because we keep on being filled. But, then,
what are we to make of the repeated, specific times of filling
mentioned in the Book of Acts? Dr. Merrill C. Tenney uses a
city house to illustrate this:

Most homes are connected to a water main. This supplies the
house with adequate water for normal life. But suppose a fire
breaks out. Then firemen tap a nearby hydrant to secure a much
greater flow of water to meet the emergency. To be "full" of
the Spirit is like a house supplied continuously with adequate
water. But to be "filled" on occasion, as the apostles were in
Acts 4:31, is to be given extra energy and power for special
service. "And when they had prayed, . . . they were all filled
with the Holy Spirit, and began to speak the word of God with
boldness" (Acts 4:31). For the special task of persisting in
evangelism, even when the religious leadership violently opposed them, the apostles needed a special filling of God's power.
They had been "full of the Spirit" all along. Now they needed
"extra filling" to meet the extra demands on them.

Filled for a Purpose

Of course, God has a purpose in wanting us to be filled with
the Spirit. We saw this in Acts 4:31, "And they were all filled
with the Holy Spirit, and began to speak the word of God with
boldness." In other words, the disciples were filled *for a purpose*
—to proclaim the Word of God. The great question every believer must face is, "What is my motivation in wanting to be
filled with the Spirit? Do I desire this fullness merely in the
interest of self-enjoyment and self-glorification, or in order that
Christ might be glorified?"

Often a Christian may sincerely seek the power of the Holy
Spirit, and yet—either by ignorance or design—seek it for the
wrong reasons. Some look for some type of emotional experience
and want the fullness of the Spirit simply to give them a new (and

even spectacular) experience. Some seek certain sensations because they see other Christians who may have had a particular form of experience which they believe has come from the Holy Spirit. Perhaps out of a misguided desire to be spiritually like others, or even spiritually superior, a person seeks the Spirit's fullness. Or again, a person may seek the Spirit's fullness only because he is encountering some particular problem, and he is hoping he can get out of the difficulty by having an experience of the Spirit's power. In short, people may yearn for the Spirit's power for all kinds of reasons.

It is true that the Spirit may bring some of these happenings into our lives. On occasion He may give us a deeply emotional sense of His presence, or make us particularly happy, or help us overcome a particularly troublesome difficulty. But we must be very careful that we do not seek His fullness for selfish reasons. He has come that we might glorify Christ.

The purpose of filling is that those who are filled may glorify Christ. The Holy Spirit came for this purpose. Jesus said, "He shall glorify Me; for He shall take of Mine, and shall disclose it to you" (John 16:14). That is, the Holy Spirit does not draw attention to Himself, but to Christ. Jesus said, "When the Helper comes, whom I will send to you from the Father, that is the Spirit of truth, who proceeds from the Father, He will bear witness of Me" (John 15:26). I believe this is one of the tests of a Spirit-filled life. Is Christ becoming more and more evident in my life? Are people seeing more of Him, and less of me?

For this reason I was hesitant about writing a book like this. I am a bit suspicious of people who make a fetish of talking about Him: "The Holy Spirit . . . this," and "the Holy Spirit . . . that." The Holy Spirit did not come to glorify Himself; He came to glorify Christ.

One other point—a person who is filled with the Spirit may not even be conscious of it. Not one biblical character said, "I am filled with the Spirit." Others said it about them, but they did not claim it for themselves. Some of the most godly people I have known were not conscious that they were filled with the Spirit. Someone has said that the nearer to heaven we get, the more conscious of hell we feel.

We've been considering power for use, but what about its abuse? What about those who want the Spirit's power for wrong reasons? One example in the New Testament of a person wanting the power of the Spirit for selfish reasons is found in Acts 8. Simon the sorcerer "believed," was baptized, and then was amazed by the signs and great miracles performed by the apostles. He was particularly interested when he noted how the converts received the Holy Spirit. Offering Peter and his fellow workers money, he said, "Give me also this power, that any one on whom I lay my hands may receive the Holy Spirit" (Acts 8:19 RSV). Peter immediately rebuked him, saying "your heart is not right before God" (v. 21). The Holy Spirit's power is for a purpose—but that purpose is always for the glory of God, not personal advantage or advancement.

Power for a Holy Life

Ultimately we need the filling of the Holy Spirit so that we may glorify Christ. But how do we glorify Christ? We glorify Christ when we live for God—trusting, loving, and obeying Him. Jesus said, "Let your light shine before men in such a way that they may see your good works, and glorify your Father who is in heaven" (Matt. 5:16). Paul said, "Whether, then, you eat or drink or whatever you do, do all to the glory of God" (1 Cor. 10:31). What a concept—everything we do should glorify God!

And yet this brings us to the heart of the problem. Why do we need the fullness of the Holy Spirit? *Because only in the power of the Spirit can we live a life that glorifies God.* We cannot glorify God in the energy of the flesh. This was Paul's cry in Romans 7: "I do not understand my own actions. For I do not do what I want, but I do the very thing I hate. . . . I can will what is right, but I cannot do it. For I do not do the good I want, but the evil I do not want is what I do" (Rom. 7:15, 18, 19 RSV). But in the power of the Holy Spirit we can live a life that increasingly glorifies God. God the Holy Spirit gives us power for a purpose—power to help us glorify God in every dimension of our lives.

In the Christian life, power is dynamically related to a Person. This Person is the Holy Spirit Himself, indwelling the Christian and filling him with the fullness of His power. As we said earlier, He supplies His power for a purpose; it is to be used. Although His limitless resources are available to us, He will permit us to have only as much power as He knows we will use or need. Unfortunately, many Christians are disobedient and, having prayed for power, have no intention of using it, or else neglect to follow through in active obedience. I think it is a waste of time for us Christians to look for power we do not intend to use: for might in prayer, unless we pray; for strength to testify, without witnessing; for power unto holiness, without attempting to live a holy life; for grace to suffer, unless we take up the cross; for power in service, unless we serve. Someone has said, "God gives dying grace only to the dying."

Power for Service

We glorify God by living lives that honor Him, and we can only do this in the power of the Holy Spirit. But we also glorify God as we serve Him, and we can only do that in the power of the Holy Spirit also. We are filled by the Spirit to serve.

Peter was so filled with the Holy Spirit that when he preached, 3,000 people were saved in one day at Pentecost. It is interesting that the Bible is full of statistics; this is one of them. Someone must have counted the number who were converted on that day, and Luke, inspired by the Holy Spirit, wrote down the number. In Acts 4:4 he says the number of men who believed "came to be about five thousand." And the same Spirit who inspired this keeping of statistics, saw to it that they were kept accurately.

In Acts 4:8 Peter and John, who had been arrested for preaching, were brought before the religious leaders. Then Scripture says Peter, "filled with the Holy Spirit," fearlessly proclaimed the death and resurrection of Christ. This same Peter, now full of the Holy Spirit, was so bold he was ready to face death for Christ. Yet only a few weeks earlier he had denied Him with curses. The fullness of the Holy Spirit made the difference.

Shortly afterward, Peter and his companions went to a prayer meeting. As we have already seen, when they prayed "they were all filled with the Holy Spirit, and began to speak the word of God with boldness" (Acts 4:31). The filling was given to them to serve Christ by boldly proclaiming the gospel. It is significant to me that here Peter had two fillings. He was filled before he preached (v. 8), and he was filled again after he and his fellow workers prayed (v. 31).

But the filling of the Spirit for power was not limited to preaching. The apostles became so tied down with the daily ministrations to the multiplied new believers that they were unable to devote themselves fully to the ministry of the Word. So they asked for seven men to be appointed for this practical job —a job of administration.

They laid down three qualifications for the officeholders: they were to be "of good reputation, full of the Spirit and of wisdom" (Acts 6:3).

This admonition tells us something important. If all the believers were "of good reputation, full of the Spirit and of wisdom," then the instructions make no sense. Some must have lacked some vital requirement. A good reputation, being full of the Holy Spirit, and wisdom were all required.

No man should be an officer in the church today who does not possess these qualifications. Of how many church members today can it be said they are "of good reputation, full of the Spirit and of wisdom"? Yet these requirements were for a practical, not a spiritual, ministry.

Does this not show us that to carry out the most practical job to the glory of God (be it as a craftsman, an administrator, a housekeeper, or secretary) we need to be filled with God's Holy Spirit—as well as of good reputation and wisdom?

We could go on and on because the early Church was empowered for every form of service by the filling of the Holy Spirit.

I am convinced that to be filled with the Spirit is not an option, but a necessity. It is indispensable for the abundant life and for fruitful service. The Spirit-filled life is not abnormal; it is the normal Christian life. Anything less is subnormal; it is less than what God wants and provides for His children. Therefore, to be filled with the Spirit should never be thought of as an unusual or unique experience for, or known by, only a select few. It is intended for all, needed by all, and available to all. That is why the Scripture commands all of us, "Be filled with the Spirit."

9. How to Be Filled with the Holy Spirit

In my ministry I am frequently asked, "How can I be filled with the Spirit?" We have been commanded to be filled, but how do we obey? How does the presence and power of the Holy Spirit become a reality in each of our lives? This is the heart of the matter. Everything I have said so far about the filling of the Spirit will only be an intellectual curiosity, unrelated to our lives, unless we learn in our own experience what it means to be filled with the Spirit.

It is interesting that the Bible nowhere gives us a neat, concise formula for being filled with the Spirit. I believe that may be because most believers in the first century did not need to be told how to be filled. They knew that the Spirit-filled life was the normal Christian life. It is a sad commentary on the low level of our spiritual lives today that we are so confused about the filling of the Spirit.

And yet the Bible does say a great deal about this subject, and when we look at the New Testament as a whole there can be little doubt in our minds either about the meaning of the Spirit-filled life, or how the Spirit-filled life becomes a reality in our lives. *I believe the New Testament's teaching on how to be filled with the Holy Spirit can be summarized in three terms: Understanding, Submission, and Walking by Faith.*

Understanding

The first step in being filled with the Spirit is *understanding*. That is, there are certain things we must know and *understand*—

certain truths God has revealed to us in His Word, the Bible. Some of these we have already mentioned, but let us be sure we have them clearly in our minds. What are these truths?

The first truth we must understand is that God has given us His Holy Spirit, and that He dwells within us. If I have accepted Christ as my Savior, the Spirit of God dwells within me. Remember—I may not necessarily *feel* His presence, but that does not mean He is absent. It is the *fact* of His presence that we must understand. God has promised that the Spirit lives within you if you belong to Christ, and God cannot lie. *We accept this fact by faith.*

We also must understand that God *commands* us to be filled with the Spirit. That means it is His will for you to be filled— and to refuse to be filled with the Spirit is to act contrary to the will of God. It is His command, and therefore it is His will. Just to make it even clearer—God *wants* to fill us with His Spirit. That is a wonderful truth to me. God does not give us a full measure of the Spirit grudgingly or unwillingly. No, He wants us to live our lives controlled and guided by the Holy Spirit. "If you then, being evil, know how to give good gifts to your children, how much more shall your heavenly Father give the Holy Spirit to those who ask Him?" (Luke 11:13). If I fail to be filled with the Spirit, remember that it is not because of God's reluctance. The fault is entirely on my side.

This leads to a further point we must understand, and that is the presence of sin in our lives. What is it that blocks the work of the Holy Spirit in our lives? It is sin. *Before we can be filled with the Holy Spirit we must deal honestly and completely with every known sin in our lives.* This may be very painful for us, as we face up to things that we have hidden or not even realized about our lives. But there will be no filling by the Holy Spirit apart from cleansing from sin, and the first step in cleansing from sin is awareness of its presence.

Most of us have had the experience at one time or another of having pipes clogged in our homes so that the water came through only in a trickle, or perhaps was stopped entirely. Where I live in North Carolina we rarely have extremely cold weather, but once in a while I have seen the temperature go below zero. Even though the pipes are buried quite deep coming from the spring into our house in a natural flow, I have seen them completely frozen. On one occasion we had to dig up the hard frozen ground and use blowtorches to melt the ice at an elbow in the pipe. So it is with sin in our lives. Sin is like the ice in our pipes— our spiritual lives have been "frozen" by a hostile world. There is only one solution, and that is repentance to clear the blockage and restore the flow of the Holy Spirit.

We are all familiar with "hardening of the arteries" as being one of the dangerous diseases to which a large percentage of the population is subject. The arteries become clogged with substances that still baffle medical experts. They still do not know how to unclog these arteries so that the blood can have free flow. Frequently bypass surgery is used, but medical opinion is divided even over this method in some instances. Vast amounts of money are being spent on medical research in many countries of the world trying to discover a chemical that will unclog arteries and save millions from death every year.

In the same way, our lives need that chemical provided by the blood of Christ to unclog the pipes, or arteries, of our lives so that the vital sap of the vine may flow. Sin is the great clogger, and the blood of Christ is the great cleanser when applied by repentance and faith.

Sometimes new believers are startled to find they are still sinners, and they not only continue to be tempted but they can still yield to temptation. Actually this should be no surprise, because the old sin nature is still within us. Before a person comes to Christ there is only one force at work in him—the old carnal nature. But when we accept Christ into our lives the Holy Spirit comes to dwell within us. Now there are two natures at work in our lives—the old sinful nature that wants us to live for self, and the new spiritual nature that wants us to live for God. The question is—which of these two natures will rule over our actions? This is why being filled with the Holy Spirit is so important. Unless the Spirit controls our lives, we will be dominated by our old sinful nature. The Spirit's work will be blocked, however, as long as we allow sin to remain.

So we must deal completely with sin in our lives if we are to know the infilling of the Holy Spirit. This is not easy for several reasons. For one thing, it may be extremely painful for us to face the reality of sin in our lives. Pride is often at the root of our sins, and our pride is often deeply wounded when we honestly admit

112 △ THE HOLY SPIRIT

before God and before men that we are not as good as we had
thought we were.

Dealing with sin in our lives is also hard because (as we shall
see) we must not only know our sin, but we must repent of it.
And some of us may be harboring sin and tolerating it, unwilling
to give it up. Like the rich young ruler in Mark 10, we want what
Jesus has for us, but we want to cling to our sin even more.

There is a further reason it is difficult for us to deal with sin
in our lives, and it is simply this: sin blinds us spiritually, and
one of the things about which we are blinded often is the awe-
some depth of sin. We do not see how much it has invaded every
area of our lives, and just how much it has infected everything
we say and think and do. It is all too easy to confess the sins
which we see in our lives, and yet fail to see the many other sins
possibly hindering even more directly our walk with the Lord.

That is why the Bible is so vital in this matter. We must not
be content with a casual examination of our lives, thinking that
only the sins which seem to give us the most trouble are worthy
of being confessed. Instead, as we prayerfully study the Word of
God, the Holy Spirit—who is, remember, the author of Scripture
—will convict us of other areas of sin which need confessing to
God. We must confess not only what we think is sin, but what
the Holy Spirit labels as sin when we really listen to His voice
from the Word of God. "All Scripture is inspired by God and
profitable for teaching, for reproof, for correction, for training
in righteousness" (2 Tim. 3:16).

Confession should be as broad as sin. The Song of Solomon
warns us about "the little foxes, that spoil the vines" (2:15 KJV).
This is a picture of the way "little" sins can destroy our fruitfulness for the Lord. There may be pride, jealousy, or bitterness in
our lives. There may be backbiting, impatience, unkindness, or
an uncontrolled temper—any one of which can make life miserable for those around us. Unclean thoughts may need to be
brought to God for cleansing. Gluttony or laziness may need to
be faced. Or the Holy Spirit may speak to us about our use of
time, our use of money, or our life style, or our use (or abuse) of
some gift He has given us. Perhaps our treatment of someone
near to us has become cold and indifferent. In other words, every
sin that we can identify we should bring to God for confession.

Sin takes all sorts of forms, and the Holy Spirit must guide us as we prayerfully examine our lives.

A young man came to me recently and said that he had lost the Holy Spirit. I replied that he had not lost the Holy Spirit, but he might well have grieved the Spirit through some particular sin. He replied that he could not think of a single thing in his life that stood between him and God. I asked him, "What about your relationship with your parents?" In response he said, "Well, it's not the best." I dug deeper and asked him, "Do you honor your father?" He agreed that he had sinned in this area. I said, "Why don't you go and have a straight, frank talk with him, and confess your sin, if you have been wrong?" He did that, and a few days later he came to me with a broad smile and said, "Fellowship restored!"

There is one other point we need to make about confession of our sins. We must not only be honest about the various sins in our lives, but we must get down to the deepest sin of all—our failure to let Christ rule our lives. *The most basic question any Christian can ask is this: Who is ruling my life, self or Christ?*

Sin will always be a continuing problem—our lives will always be marked by defeat and discouragement—as long as we try to keep "self" at the center of our lives. It is amazing how many Christians never really face this issue of Christ's Lordship, and yet the New Testament is full of statements about Christ's demand for our full commitment. "If anyone wishes to come after Me, let him deny himself, and take up his cross daily, and follow Me" (Luke 9:23). How easy it is for us to set up our own goals, operate by our own motives, and seek our own desires, without ever asking God for His will above all else. He calls us to renounce our plans and practices, and seek His way. He asks us to step off the throne of our lives, and let Him rule in every area of everything we are and do. "And He died for all, that they who live should no longer live for themselves, but for Him who died and rose again on their behalf" (2 Cor. 5:15). Have you seen how completely—and tragically—sin has dominated your life, and are you willing to yield to Christ's authority and rule in everything?

We also need to understand that the Holy Spirit is in us, and God wants our lives to be controlled by Him. But we must understand our sin in all its dimensions. Most of all we need to face the crucial question of who is controlling our lives—we or Christ? Only when we understand these matters can we move to the second step.

Submission

The second step in being filled by the Holy Spirit is what we might term *submission*. What do I mean by this? By submission I mean that we renounce our own way and seek above all else to submit to Christ as Lord and be ruled by Him in every area of our lives.

The importance of this will be seen from what we said above about the way sin blocks the control of the Spirit in our lives. The essence of sin is self-will—placing ourselves at the center of our lives instead of Christ. The way to be filled—controlled and dominated—by the Spirit is to place Christ at the center of our lives, instead of self. This only happens as we submit to Him—as we allow Him to become Lord of our lives.

How does submission become a reality in our lives? There are, I believe, two steps.

First, there is the step of confession and repentance. We have just seen that one of the things we must understand is the depth of our sin. But we must move beyond understanding. Sin must be confessed to God and we must repent of it. There are many people who know they are sinners, and they can tell you what particular sins are a problem to them. They may even feel sorry for their sins and wish things were different. But there is never any change. Why? Because they have never confessed their sins to God and repented of them.

There is actually a difference between confession and repentance, although I believe the Bible sees them as being intimately related, like two sides of the same coin. Confession is acknowledgment of sin. It is admitting before God that I know I am a sinner, because I have committed certain sins which are known to me. The wonderful thing is that God has promised to forgive us when we turn to Him in humble confession. One of the great promises of the Bible is 1 John 1:9: "If we confess our sins, He is faithful and righteous to forgive us our sins and to cleanse us from all unrighteousness."

To repent means to *renounce* sin. In the Greek (the language in which the New Testament was originally written) the word "repent" meant a complete and total change of mind. To repent is not only to feel sorry for my sin, or even just to confess it to God. To repent of my sin is to turn from it, and to turn to Christ and His will.

If I have been guilty of evil thoughts, I renounce them when I repent of them and determine by God's grace to fill my mind with things that honor Him. If I have mistreated someone and acted in an unloving way toward him, I determine to do whatever is necessary to replace my mistreatment with loving acts toward that person. If my life style is not pleasing to God, I will change it to bring it more in line with God's will. Repentance is a conscious turning from my sins. "Remember therefore from where you have fallen, and repent" (Rev. 2:5).

If the first step in our submission is confession and repentance of every known sin in our lives, *the second step is yielding ourselves to God and His will.* Confession and repentance might be described as the negative side of submission; this involves getting rid of everything which hinders God's control over our lives. Yielding to God might be described as the positive side; this involves placing ourselves totally and completely (as best we know how) into the hands of God in complete submission to His will for our lives.

This step of yielding ourselves to God is clearly presented in the sixth chapter of Romans. In that passage Paul talks vividly about the way sin has ruled our lives in the past. But now we belong to Christ—we are no longer living for our old master, sin—we are now living for Christ, our new Master. Therefore we should not yield to sin, but yield ourselves to God. "Neither yield ye your members as instruments of unrighteousness unto sin: but yield yourselves unto God, as those that are alive from the dead" (Rom. 6:13 KJV). Paul then goes on to tell us that we have been set free from our slavery to sin—we no longer belong to sin. We have changed masters. Just as a slave in the first century might be sold and come under the ownership of a new master, so we have been purchased with the blood of Christ, and we belong now to God. "Having been freed from sin, you became slaves of righteousness" (Rom. 6:18).

In the original Greek language the words which are translated "yield yourselves to God" in the King James Version have a beautiful meaning. The thought has been translated in various ways by other versions: "Put yourselves in God's hands" (Phillips); "offer yourselves to God" (NIV); "present yourselves to God" (New American Standard Version). However, the fullest meaning of the word "yield" is "to place yourself at the disposal of someone." In other words, when we yield ourselves to Christ, we do not simply sit back and hope that God will somehow work through us. No, instead we place ourselves at His disposal—we say, in effect, "Lord, I am Yours, to be used in whatever way You want to use me. I am at Your disposal, and You may do with me whatever You will. I seek Your will for my life, not my own will." "Put yourselves at the disposal of God" (Rom. 6:13 NEB).

The same term is used in Romans 12:1: "I urge you therefore, brethren, by the mercies of God, to present your bodies a living and holy sacrifice, acceptable to God." This includes every area of our lives. It includes our abilities, our gifts, our possessions, and our families—our minds, wills, and emotions. Nothing is excluded. We can hold nothing back. In principle He must control and dominate us in the whole and the part. This verse reminds us of the sacrifices in the Old Testament, which the worshiper presented wholly to God. He could keep back no part of it, and it was all consumed on the altar. In the same way our surrender —our submission and yielding—must be total. It is a surrender without any conditions attached.

More and more I am coming to see that this *surrender* is a definite and conscious act on our part in obedience to the Word of God. It should, in fact, occur at the time of our conversion when we repent and receive Christ not only as our Savior but as our Lord. But for many people it may well be a crisis event which comes after conversion.

Perhaps we have not understood fully what it means to follow Christ as Lord, but later we begin to see that Jesus Christ calls us not simply to believe in Him but to follow Him without reserve as His disciples. If we find ourselves fuzzy and confused about Christ's Lordship, we should take action immediately. Our intention should be a complete and final act of submission in principle, even though in months ahead the Holy Spirit may well show us other areas of our lives that need to be surrendered. This is, in fact, one of the signs of our yieldedness—as we place ourselves at God's disposal, He leads us into new areas of commitment.

The Holy Spirit may test us many times to see if we really mean business. He may even call on us to surrender something in principle that He really does not want us to surrender in fact, but which He wants us to be willing to surrender. We must be open to everything He wants to do in and through our lives.

Perhaps several illustrations will help us understand more clearly this matter of yielding ourselves to God's will. In Romans 6, Paul (as we have seen) uses the illustration of a slave who has a new master. Professor William Barclay reminds us about the real meaning of Paul's analogy:

"When we think of a servant, in our sense of the word, we think of a man who gives a certain agreed part of his time to his master, and who receives a certain agreed wage for doing so. Within that agreed time he is at the disposal and in the command of his master. But, when that time ends, he is free to do exactly as he likes. . . . But, in Paul's time, the status of the slave was quite different. Quite literally he had no time which belonged to himself. He had no moment when he was free. Every single moment of his time belonged to his master. He was the absolutely exclusive possession of his master, and there was not one single moment of his life when he could do as he liked. In Paul's time a slave could never do what he liked; it was impossible for him to serve two masters, because he was the exclusive possession of one master. That is the picture that is in Paul's mind."[1]

Now the parallel between the slave of Paul's time and the Christian is not exact (as Paul himself says) because there is a sense in which the Christian is the freest person in the world since he knows the spiritual freedom Christ brings. But on the other hand, you and I are called to belong to God, and to be His people. We are called to be at His disposal, ready and eager to do His will. Paul told Titus that Christ "gave himself for us to redeem us from all wickedness and to purify for himself a people that are his very own, eager to do what is good" (Titus 2:14 NIV).

Perhaps another illustration will help me make my point. The principle of yielding to Christ is like the commitment a bride and groom make when they are linked together in marriage. A new situation is created that becomes an enduring reality. In principle it is a complete and final act once they have repeated the vows and consummated the marriage. They are married, in fact and in principle, but—and this is a crucial thing—in practice husband and wife discover that their lives have to be constantly surrendered to each other in line with the new fact of their mutual commitment to each other in marriage.

Two people are not less married because there are defects in their lives and problems in the everyday details of living. Instead, they each grow, learning more of what it means to love each other and adjust to each other as a result of that love. Likewise in our spiritual pilgrimage we see sins which mar our relationship with God, but beneath it is a commitment which seeks to move beyond to a higher life, based on wholehearted surrender to God.

Have you ever submitted your life to God? Have you ever confessed your sin to Him, and repented of your sin as best you know how? Are there particular sins that are obstacles to your full commitment? Are there other sins, which you have not even begun to admit? Most of all, have you ever really told God—as fully and as simply as you know how—that you want His will in your life, whatever it may be?

There are people who suggest we should pray for God to fill us with His Holy Spirit. While this may be a valid prayer, I personally see little or no example of this in the New Testament. Instead, I believe we should pray that God will take possession of our lives totally and completely. We should pray that we will be emptied of self—self-love, self-will, self-ambition—and be placed completely at His disposal.

If you have never taken the step of submission to God and His will, I urge you to get on your knees before you read another page of this book, and give your life without reserve to your Master and Lord. "Therefore, shake off your complacency and repent. See, I stand knocking at the door. If anyone listens to my voice and opens the door, I will go into his house and dine with him, and he with me" (Rev. 3:19, 20 *Phillips*).

Faith

We now come to the last step in the infilling of the Holy Spirit, which I like to call "Walking in Faith." We must first *understand* certain things—then we must *submit* and yield ourselves to God —and then we must learn the secret of *walking in faith.*

The main point is this: When we are yielded to God and His will, we are filled with the Holy Spirit. The Holy Spirit controls and dominates us. Now we are to *act* on that truth and *walk* or live with full assurance that God has already filled us, and we are under His control.

The Apostle Paul puts it this way: "Likewise reckon ye also yourselves to be dead indeed unto sin, but alive unto God through Jesus Christ our Lord" (Rom. 6:11 KJV). The word in Greek which we translate "reckon ye" was sometimes used in accounting or mathematics. After a business transaction, for example, the amount of money would be computed and entered in the books. The entry in the accounting books demonstrated that the transaction had already taken place and payment had been made. Now when we yield ourselves to Christ and follow Him as Lord of our lives, we know that something has happened. The Holy Spirit has taken over our lives, to guide and empower us. We are now to walk in faith, reckoning ourselves to be dead to sin and alive to God. We *are* filled with the Holy Spirit; now we *are to live* in light of this truth. This is not pretending; it is acting on God's promise. Dr. John Stott puts it this way:

"Now 'reckoning' is not make-believe. It is not screwing up our faith to believe something we do not believe. We are not to pretend that our old nature has died when we know perfectly well that it has not. . . . We are simply called to 'reckon' this—not to pretend it, but to realize it. It is a fact. And we have to lay hold of it. We have to let our minds play upon these truths. We have to meditate upon them until we grasp them firmly."

Dr. Stott then continues: "Can a married woman live as though she were still a single girl? Well, yes, I suppose she can. It is not impossible. But let her feel that ring on the fourth finger of her left hand, the symbol of her new life, the symbol of her identification with her husband, let her remember who she is, and let her live accordingly. . . . Our minds are so to grasp the fact and the significance of our death and resurrection with Christ, that a return to the old life is unthinkable. A born-again Christian should no more think of going back to the old life than an adult to his childhood, a married man to his bachelor-hood, or a discharged prisoner to his prison cell."²

If you have fulfilled the Scriptural requirements for being filled with the Holy Spirit—especially the repentance and submission we have considered—then you and I can privately say to ourselves, "By faith I know I am filled with the Holy Spirit." I've never known a person whom I thought was truly filled with the Holy Spirit who went out and bragged about it, or sought to draw attention to himself. If we are filled with the Holy Spirit others will soon notice it, because the filled person produces the fruit of the Spirit. But we may not even be aware of this. In fact, some of God's greatest saints have indicated that the closer they came to Christ the more sinful they felt. My friend and associate, Roy Gustafson, once said, "The Holy Spirit didn't come to make us Holy-Spirit-conscious, but Christ-conscious." Thus, when we say to ourselves that we are filled with the Spirit it means that every known sin and hindrance is out of the way and then we claim by faith that we are filled.

There are, I believe, several things we should remember at this point.

First, we must remember that the filling of the Spirit is not a matter of feeling, but of faith. We may feel strongly the closeness of God when we are filled, or we may not. Instead of trusting in our feelings, we must trust God's promises. We must reckon ourselves to be filled by His Spirit. James McConkey put it this way:

"Nothing is more hurtful than to be constantly inspecting our own inner lives to see if God is fulfilling His promise in our experience. It is like the child constantly digging up the seed to see if it has sprouted. The question of the experience of fullness of the Spirit belongs to the Lord."³

Also, we must remember that the filling of the Spirit does not mean we are perfect and without sin. It means we are controlled by the Spirit, but sin is still a reality, lurking around the corner ready to lunge at the first opportunity. We may be blameless in our desire to serve Christ, but that does not make us without fault. A Scottish preacher of another generation explained it this way:

"I have lying on the table beside me a letter, which will illustrate the point at issue. I received it when I was away in New Zealand on a mission tour, in 1891. It was from my eldest daughter, then a child of five years of age. It reads: 'Dear father, I wrote all this myself. I send you a kiss from Elsie.' The fact of the matter is, that it is not writing at all, but an attempt at printing in large capitals, and not one of the letters is properly formed; there is not as much as one straight stroke on the page. . . . Now, this letter which I prize so dearly is certainly not a 'faultless' production; it is as full of faults as it is full of letters, but most assuredly it is 'blameless.' I did not blame my child for her crooked strokes, and answer with a scold, for I judged her work by its motive. I knew it was the best she could do, and that she had put all the love of her little heart into it. She wanted to do something to please me, and she succeeded. By the grace of the indwelling Christ . . . this is what our daily life, our daily life-work may be, viz., 'blameless.' "[4]

This brings me to the last truth about the filling of the Holy Spirit: *the filling of the Holy Spirit should not be a once-for-all event, but a continuous reality every day of our lives.* It is a process. We must surrender ourselves to Him daily, and every day we must choose to remain surrendered. In every situation involving conflict between self and God's will, we must make our decisions on the basis of our constant submission to Christ.

As we have seen, the Greek verb used by Paul in his command in Ephesians 5:18, "Be filled with the Spirit," carries with it the idea that we should keep on being filled with the Spirit. We are already the temple of God, indwelt by the Holy Spirit, but He wants to fill us. However, He can fill only those who wish to be emptied of self and yielded to Him. Therefore, this active surrender must continue day by day, concerning little things as well as big ones. If we sin we need to repent so that He can fill us again. And if on occasion we face exceptional pressure, we need to pray for His additional help.

And so the four steps we have outlined above are not only a beginning, but a process. Each day we should seek to understand more from God's Word. We should pray that God will help us see our sin each day. Each day we should confess and repent. And each day we should submit our wills to His will. We should so walk in faith that He is continually filling us as we submit to Him. Each day we should walk in obedience to His Word.

Personally I find it helpful to begin each day by silently committing that day into God's hands. I thank Him that I belong to Him, and I thank Him that He knows what the day holds for me. I ask Him to take my life that day and use it for His glory. I ask Him to cleanse me from anything which would hinder His work in my life. And then I step out in faith, knowing that His Holy Spirit is filling me continually as I trust in Him and obey His Word. Sometimes during the day I may not be aware of His presence; sometimes I am. But at the end of the day, I can look back and thank Him, because I see His hand at work. He promised to be with me that day—and He has been!

This can be your experience also as you daily yield to the Lordship of Jesus Christ in your life. May you yield each day to Him. And may you be able to look back at the end of each day and know that His Holy Spirit has been your guide and your strength as you have yielded to Him.

10. Sins against the Holy Spirit

One of the most solemn themes in all Scripture concerns sins against the Third Person of the Trinity, the Holy Spirit. Believers and unbelievers alike can and do sin against Him. What is the nature of these sins, and how can we guard ourselves against committing them?

Blaspheming the Holy Spirit

Of all the sins men commit against the Holy Spirit none is worse than that of blaspheming Him. The reason for this is clear: It is the one sin for which there is no forgiveness. All other sins against the Holy Spirit are committed by *believers*. We can repent of them, be forgiven, and make a new start.

Not so with blaspheming the Spirit. This sin is committed by *unbelievers* and is often called "the unpardonable sin." It was committed by the enemies of Jesus when they accused Him of casting out devils by the power of Satan after Jesus had clearly stated that they were cast out by the power of the "Spirit of God." He then continued: "Therefore I say to you, any sin and blasphemy shall be forgiven men, but blasphemy against the Spirit shall not be forgiven. And whoever shall speak a word against the Son of Man, it shall be forgiven him; but whoever shall speak against the Holy Spirit, it shall not be forgiven him, either in this age, or in the age to come" (Matt. 12:31, 32).

When my father was a young man, he attended a revival meeting in North Carolina and became convinced through a sermon on this subject that he had committed the unpardonable sin.

And he lived with this awful thought for many years. He agonized over it, was frightened by it, and thought of himself as a doomed man who could never repent of his sin. In time he discovered that his sin was not one which excluded him from the mercy and grace of God. He came to know that the Holy Spirit would not be convicting and wrestling with him and drawing him to Christ if he had really committed this unpardonable sin.

Perhaps I can venture a definition of what I understand the unpardonable sin to be. It seems to me, negatively, that no one has committed this sin who continues to be under the disturbing, convicting, and drawing power of the Holy Spirit. So long as the Spirit strives with a person he has not committed the unpardonable sin. But when a person has so resisted the Holy Spirit that He strives with him no more, then there is eternal danger. In other words, the unpardonable sin involves the total and irrevocable rejection of Jesus Christ.

I believe this is what Stephen was talking about in the sermon he preached just prior to his martyrdom. In that message he said, "You . . . who are stiff-necked . . . are always resisting the Holy Spirit" (Acts 7:51).

The context makes it clear that Stephen was saying, first of all, that just as their fathers had refused to take seriously the proclamations of the prophets and messengers of God, or to believe them, so his listeners were guilty of like sins. In the Old Testament we read that some opposed, maligned, persecuted, and ridiculed the prophets. Since the prophets were inspired by the Holy Spirit, these people were in fact resisting the Spirit. So Stephen says that when the people to whom he was speaking refused to hear Christ's apostles and chosen ones, who were speaking through the Holy Spirit, they were in effect resisting the Holy Spirit.

Now the fatal infection of sin in the hearts of unregenerate people will always cause them to resist the Holy Spirit. The flesh and the reprobate mind always fight Him. When people do this, they will not receive the Word of God in its power unless the Holy Spirit gains victory over them.

But Stephen was saying something more, too. He was telling them and us that just as God the Spirit strove in vain with people in the Old Testament and they were doomed, so his listeners would be doomed if they did not heed the work of the Spirit in

their hearts. Resisting the Spirit is a sin committed only by unbelievers. But it is a sin that, when carried on long enough, leads
to eternal doom. Only certain judgment remains for those who
so resist the Spirit.

The only way any sinner can be forgiven for resisting the
Holy Spirit is to cease resisting and to embrace Jesus Christ, to
whom the Spirit bears witness. That person has hope only if
he repents immediately and allows the Spirit to work in his heart.

I think pastors, teachers, evangelists, and all Christian workers should handle this subject very carefully. For the most part
Christian workers should be extremely hesitant to draw their
own conclusions dogmatically as to when someone has committed the unpardonable sin. Let the Holy Spirit and God the
Father make that decision. We should always urge men everywhere to repent and turn to Jesus since we do not know when
the Spirit has stopped dealing with them. And let us pray that
those about whom we are most uncertain may yet respond to the
good news that Jesus saves.

Are you perhaps one of those who worries about having committed the unpardonable sin? If so, you should face squarely
what the Bible says on this subject, not what you may have
heard from others. The unpardonable sin is rejecting the truth
about Christ. It is rejecting, completely and finally, the witness
of the Holy Spirit, which declares that Jesus Christ is the Son of
God who alone can save us from our sins. Have you rejected
Christ in your own life, and said in your heart that what the
Bible teaches about Him is a lie? Then I tell you as solemnly
and as sincerely as I know how that you are in a very dangerous
position. I urge you without delay to accept the truth about
Christ, and come to Him in humble confession and repentance
and faith. It would be tragic for you to persist in your unbelief,
and eventually go into eternity without hope and without God.

On the other hand you may be a believer, but you have committed some sin which you have thought might keep you from
being saved. No matter what it is, remember that God loves you,
and He wants to forgive you of that sin. Right now you need to
confess that sin to Him and seek His forgiveness. You need
to be freed from the burden of guilt and doubt that has oppressed
you. Christ died to free you from it. If you have come to Christ,
you know on the basis of God's Word that this sin—whatever it

is—is not the unpardonable sin. It will not send you to hell, because you are saved by faith in the shed blood of Christ. But you need to put it out of your life by casting it on Christ. Remember the words of the Psalmist, "As far as the east is from the west, so far has He removed our transgressions from us" (Ps. 103:12).

Grieving the Spirit

We now come to two sins against the Holy Spirit which can be committed by *Christians*. One is to grieve the Holy Spirit, and the other is to quench the Spirit. These are inclusive terms, for almost any wrong action we take can be included under one of these two headings. Let us look first at grieving the Spirit.

Paul warns his readers that they are not to "grieve the Holy Spirit of God, by whom you were sealed for the day of redemption" (Eph. 4:30). It is important and consoling to hear Paul say that we are "sealed for the day of redemption." This means we are and will remain Christians. So he is not speaking of judgment in the sense that what we do here will separate us from the love of God and cause us to go to hell. He is speaking rather of things we do that are inconsistent with the nature of the Holy Spirit and thus hurt His heart and wound Him in His own selfhood. We can bring pain to the Spirit by what we do.

"Grieve" is a "love" word. The Holy Spirit loves us just as Christ did, "Now I urge you, brethren, by our Lord Jesus Christ and by the love of the Spirit, to strive together with me in your prayers to God for me" (Rom. 15:30). We may hurt or anger one who has no affection for us, but we can grieve only a person who loves us.

I once heard a father tell his son, "Unless you are good, I won't love you any more." This was unfortunate. He had every right to tell the boy to be good, but he had no reason to tell him that he would withdraw his love. A father should always love his son—whether he is good or bad. But when he is bad, his father's love for him is mixed with pain and even sorrow and anguish.

How do Christians grieve the Holy Spirit? In Ephesians 4:20–32 Paul says that whatever is unlike Christ in conduct, speech, or disposition grieves the Spirit of grace. In one of her books, Ruth Paxson suggests that we can know what hurts the Spirit when we consider our conduct in light of the words Scripture uses to depict the Spirit. The Holy Spirit is the Spirit of:

1. *Truth* (John 14:17); so anything false, deceitful, or hypocritical grieves Him.

2. *Faith* (2 Cor. 4:13); so doubt, distrust, anxiety, worry, grieve Him.

3. *Grace* (Heb. 10:29); so whatever in us is hard, bitter, malicious, ungracious, unforgiving, or unloving grieves Him.

4. *Holiness* (Rom. 1:4); so anything unclean, defiling or degrading grieves Him.

What happens when we grieve the Holy Spirit? Ordinarily He delights to take the things of Christ and reveal them to us. He also imparts to us joy, peace, and gladness of heart. But when we grieve Him this ministry is suspended.

I come from that region of the United States where the textile industry is prominent. Some years ago I walked through a very large factory where hundreds of looms were spinning cloth made of very fine linen threads. The manager of the mill said, "This machinery is so delicate that if a single thread out of the whole thirty thousand which are weaving at this moment should break, all of these looms would stop instantly." To demonstrate it he stepped to one of the machines and broke a single thread. Instantly every loom stopped until the thread had been fixed; then they went on automatically.

This mechanical wonder provides a rough analogy of "that which is spiritual." When I commit one sin, one disobedient act, one departure from the clearly seen pathway of the will and the fear of God, then the ministry of the Spirit in my life is impaired. While the ministry of the Spirit in my life is withdrawn it is not stopped. Unlike the machinery, it is impaired. As soon as the broken thread has been repaired the full ministry of the Spirit commences again as He illuminates my mind, satisfies my heart needs, and makes the ministry of Christ effective to me.

There is one glorious and gracious aspect to this, however. To grieve the Holy Spirit is not to lose Him in my life. He does not cease to seal me; He does not remove Himself from me. Indeed a believer cannot grieve Him so that He goes away totally. I have been singularly blessed by the hymns of William Cowper, who was an associate of John Newton. But these lines have always troubled me:

> Return, O holy Dove! return,
> Sweet messenger of rest!
> I hate the sins that made Thee mourn,
> And drove Thee from my breast.[1]

I have the uneasy impression that these words suggest more than just causing the Spirit within me to stop His wonderful work. They imply that I lose Him. If that is what Cowper meant, I think he was mistaken.

It is possible that the sense of the Holy Spirit's presence may be taken away or withdrawn from men. Psalm 51 makes this clear when David cried, "Do not take Thy Holy Spirit from me" (v. 11). But remember that the Holy Spirit has sealed every believer for the day of redemption, that is, the redemption of our bodies (Eph. 1:13; 4:30; Rom. 8:23). You and I may backslide, but this is quite different from falling from grace, or having the Holy Spirit totally withdrawn from us.

If the Spirit were to withdraw Himself from a believer He has sealed, would He not be denying the whole scheme of salvation? But when He is grieved, He does bring about an absence of joy and power in our lives until we can renounce and confess the sin. Though we may appear happy, we are inwardly wretched when we are out of communion with the Holy Spirit. This is not because the Spirit has abandoned us, but because He deliberately makes us wretched until we return to Christ in brokenness, contrition, and confession. Psalm 32—which many think was written by David after his sin with Bathsheba—is an excellent example of this: "When I kept silent about my sin, my body wasted away through my groaning all day long. For day and night Thy hand was heavy upon me; My vitality was drained away as with the fever-heat of summer. I acknowledged my sin to Thee, and my iniquity I did not hide; I said, 'I will confess my transgressions to the Lord'; and Thou didst forgive the guilt of my sin. . . . Be glad in the Lord and rejoice you righteous ones, and shout for joy all you who are upright in heart" (Ps. 32:3–5, 11).

I believe that once we have been baptized into the body of Christ and indwelt by the Holy Spirit we will never be abandoned by the Spirit again. We are sealed forever. And He is the earnest, the pledge, of what is to come. I realize that many of my brethren in the faith hold a different view, but as far as I have light at this moment, I believe we are kept by the Holy Spirit.

On the one hand the Holy Spirit who indwells us secures us for God. He does this on the basis of Christ's blood in which we have trusted and by which we know we have been redeemed. On the other hand, He gives us continuous enjoyment in the knowledge that we belong to God; that enjoyment is interrupted only when some work of the flesh grieves the One who has sealed us. As translated by Weymouth, James 4:5 says He "yearns jealously over us." I seriously doubt if, this side of heaven, we will ever know how great is the power of the force we could have utilized in this life: the power of the Holy Spirit, which we tap through prayer.

When we yield ourselves totally every moment of every day to Jesus Christ as Lord, the wonder-working power of the Holy Spirit in our lives and witness will be overwhelming. It is at this point of surrender that the secret of purity, peace, and power lies. I believe it also carries with it what George Cutting used to call Safety, Certainty, and Enjoyment. It also conveys the thought of outward achievement and inward rest.

Yes, as the Spirit of love the Holy Spirit is grieved when we sin, because He loves us.

Quenching the Spirit

To blaspheme the Spirit is a sin committed by unbelievers. Grieving and quenching the Spirit are sins committed by believers. Now we must consider what is meant by quenching the Spirit.

Paul's terse admonition is this: "Do not quench the Spirit" (1 Thess. 5:19). The word *grieve* suggests the sense of being hurt, of being made sorrowful. This has to do with the way we bruise the heart of the Spirit in our individual lives. The word *quench* means "to put out, to put a damper on." It is pertinent to the Scripture's reference to the Holy Spirit as a fire. When we quench the Spirit, we put the fire out. This does not mean we expel Him, but that we extinguish the love and power of the Spirit as He seeks to carry out His divine purpose through us. We may quench Him in a number of ways, but the figure of fire suggests two aspects by way of warning.

A fire goes out when the fuel supply is withdrawn. When we do not stir up our souls, when we do not use the means of grace, when we fail to pray, witness, or read the Word of God, the fire of the Holy Spirit is banked. These things are channels through which God gives us the fuel that keeps the fire burning. And the Holy Spirit wants us to use those gifts to maintain His burning in our lives.

The second way to put out a fire is to extinguish it, by throwing water on it or smothering it with a blanket or a shovelful of dirt. In a similar way, willful sin quenches the Spirit. When we criticize, act unkindly, belittle the work of others by careless or unappreciative words, we smother the fire and put it out. This happens many times when there is a fresh, new, or different movement of the Spirit of God—perhaps not using the old traditional methods in proclamation or service. For example, when some Christians sometimes seek to block what God may be doing in a new way.

I want to be very clear at one point: No Christian *must* sin. Yet, conversely, he has not been rendered *incapable* of sinning. I believe a Christian *can* sin, but he does not *have to*. It is possible to keep the fire burning; it is possible to avoid grieving the Spirit. God never would have told us to reject evil acts if in point of fact we could not help but do them. Thank God we need not sin, even though we can sin!

I do not know their source, but the following words about the Holy Spirit have been a help to me: "Resist not His incoming; grieve not His indwelling; quench not His outgoing. Open to Him as the Incomer; please Him as the Indweller; obey Him as the Outgoer in His testimony of the things concerning Christ, whether through yourself or others."

Have you in any sense grieved the Spirit, or quenched the Spirit in your life? These are serious matters, and they call for our careful attention. If this has been the case, realize that now is the time to confess these to God, and repent of them. And then walk each day in the fullness of the Spirit, sensitive to His leading and power in your life.

11. Gifts of the Spirit

When our children were growing up, Christmas morning would find the Christmas tree surrounded by gifts. They had been selected lovingly according to each child's enjoyment and need. Each would be opened with anticipation and excitement— accepted with expressions of love and appreciation—enjoyed and used (depending on age) all day. Alas, however, (again depending on age) by evening jealousy and squabbling had begun.

Is this not somewhat true of spiritual gifts (with the exception that spiritual gifts were given for service, not for personal enjoyment)? Still, the spiritually immature wind up eyeing with a bit of jealousy gifts which they have not received. Sometimes there is a touch of smugness and pride on the part of the receiver. But the spirit in which the gift was given cannot be judged by the attitudes of the receivers.

The New Testament lists "the gifts of the Spirit" in three passages—Romans 12:6–8; 1 Corinthians 12:8–10; and Ephesians 4:11. (There is a fourth listing in 1 Peter 4:10, 11, although it seems to duplicate material included in the previous lists.)

Gifts and the Body

The Bible teaches that every redeemed person is given at least one gift by the Holy Spirit: "Now there are varieties of gifts, . . . But to each one is given the manifestation of the Spirit for the common good" (1 Cor. 12:4, 7). God holds us responsible for the way we use our gifts.

131

The apostle Paul likens the Church to our physical bodies, where each member has a unique function yet all parts work together. Paul said, "For the body is not one member, but many. If the foot should say, 'Because I am not a hand, I am not a part of the body,' it is not for this reason any the less a part of the body. . . . But now God has placed the members, each one of them, in the body, just as He desired." Paul continued by saying that "there are many members, but one body. And the eye cannot say to the hand, 'I have no need of you'; or again the head to the feet, 'I have no need of you' " (1 Cor. 12:14–21). He added that even those members of the body that seem the most feeble or the least needed are necessary parts of the perfect body. They are all essential for the body's proper functioning.

As with the human body, so the body of Christ is a complete organism made by God. Yet each member of the body is unique. There can never be another "you" or "me." In a sense, your gift or mine is unique. God often gives similar gifts to different people, but there is a uniqueness about this that makes each of us distinct from any other person who has ever lived. And if any one of us is missing, the body is incomplete, lacking some part.

The Meaning of Charisma

The New Testament uses the Greek word *charisma* (plural, *charismata*) to speak of the various gifts God has given by the Holy Spirit to Christians. Actually, the word "charisma" has come into our English language to describe someone who has a certain indefinable quality which attracts people to his personality. We speak of certain well-known people as having charisma. A biblical illustration might be Apollos (Acts 18:24–28). This New Testament evangelist and Bible teacher seemed to have charisma, in its modern English sense. The apostle Paul lacked it. However, both men had definite spiritual gifts—*charismata*—that God had supernaturally given them. In the worldly sense charisma is an intangible influence that no one can put his finger on. But in the biblical use of the word *charisma*, it means "a gift of holy grace." Thus the word *charisma* in the Bible has a different meaning from the one the world thinks of when it says a man has "charisma."

The word *charismata* is the plural of *charisma* and, except for one passage in 1 Peter, is found only in the writings of the apostle Paul. If we define it precisely, it means "manifestations of grace," and is translated, "gifts." This word was used to denote the various spiritual gifts given to individuals for the benefit of the Church, and these gifts are the subject of this chapter. In Ephesians 4 Paul uses two other words translated "gifts," *dorea* and *doma*. They are similar to *charismata* and indeed to a fourth word for "gifts," *pneumatika*, which, precisely defined, means "things belonging to the Spirit." These various Greek terms lie behind our single English translation, "gifts," and mean about the same thing.

The Origin of Spiritual Gifts

Before dealing with the gifts of the Spirit more specifically I must emphasize one point. These gifts come to us from the Holy Spirit. He chooses who gets which gifts, and He dispenses them at His good pleasure. While we are held accountable for the use of any gifts He gives us, we have no responsibility for gifts we have not been given. Nor are we to covet what someone else has or be envious of that person. We may wish to have certain gifts and even ask for them, but if it is not the will of the Holy Spirit, we will not get what we ask for. And if we are dissatisfied because the Holy Spirit does not give us the gifts we want, we sin. In my case I believe God has given me the gift of evangelism, but I did not ask for it.

If I had the gift of evangelism and failed to use it, it would be a sin for me. If, on the other hand, someone else does not have the gift of evangelism, and yet is disgruntled because he does not have it, he also is sinning. There are many things I cannot do very well, but that is because there are some gifts I do not have, nor should I be discontented. The gifts you and I have are the ones God has seen fit to give us, and we should seek to discover and use them for His glory.

One other point should be stressed. We have talked about the fruit of the Spirit (and will have three chapters devoted to the fruit), and we have shown that every one of the fruits of the Spirit should be characteristic of every single Christian. But the gifts of the Spirit are different. Every believer should have the same fruit as every other believer, but not every believer will have the same gifts as every other believer. No, the Holy Spirit distributes the gifts in such a way that every believer has at least one gift which is uniquely his. You may have been given a certain gift by God, but it would be a mistake for you to say everyone else should have that same gift.

Spiritual Gifts and Talents

In studying the three passages where the gifts are listed, we find a total of about twenty. In addition, the Old Testament mentions a number of gifts not listed in the New Testament. Many of these seem quite similar to natural abilities or talents people may have, although others are clearly spiritual in character.

Certainly, most of us know of people who have a special gift of "music" which is not listed among these twenty. Moreover, many people wonder what the difference is between a spiritual gift and a natural talent. One may have the talent of making beautiful handicrafts; another may have a talent for music. Actually, most people have talents of one kind or another, and these too come from the Creator.

It appears that God can take a talent and transform it by the power of the Holy Spirit and use it as a spiritual gift. In fact, the difference between a spiritual gift and a natural talent is frequently a cause for speculation by many people. I am not sure we can always draw a sharp line between spiritual gifts and natural abilities—both of which, remember, come ultimately from God. Nor do I believe it is always necessary to make a sharp distinction. On most occasions, however, in the context we are discussing, the gifts I have in mind are supernatural ones the Spirit gives a person for the good of the Church.

A gift might also be called a "tool" or an instrument that is to be used, rather than a piece of jewelry for decoration, or a box of candy for personal enjoyment. We could think of the different types of tools a carpenter uses, or the different types of tools a surgeon needs. These "tools" have been given to people for use in the functioning of the Body of Christ.

There's an interesting passage in Exodus 31 about Bezalel. The Bible says, "And I have filled him with the Spirit of God in wisdom, in understanding, in knowledge, and in all kinds of craftsmanship, to make artistic designs for work in gold, in silver, and in bronze, and in the cutting of stones for settings, and in the carving of wood, that he may work in all kinds of craftsmanship" vv. 3–5). This indicates that many of the skills and talents that people have are gifts of God.

This unique ability of Bezalel, given by the Spirit, included not only manual skill but also the intellectual wisdom and understanding essential to all art. Artistic talent of every kind is a divine gift. "Every good thing bestowed and every perfect gift is from above, coming down from the Father of lights, with whom there is no variation, or shifting shadow" (James 1:17). God has given to mankind aesthetic faculties which, like all the human faculties, were corrupted by man's rebellion against God in the Garden of Eden—but they are still there!

Purpose of Gifts

Paul says that the purpose of these spiritual gifts is, "for the equipping of the saints for the work of service, to the building up of the body of Christ" (Eph. 4:12). In other words, God has given each of us a task to do, and supernatural gifts to equip us for it. If we fail to perform this task we face censure at the "judgment seat of Christ."

Scripture teaches that every believer will someday have to stand before the judgment seat of Christ to give an account of how faithfully he used his gifts, as well as his personal life before God and man. This is called the "bema" or the judgment seat of Christ: "For we must all appear before the judgment seat of Christ, that each one may be recompensed for his deeds in the body, according to what he has done, whether good or bad" (2 Cor. 5:10). This will not be a judgment for the unbelieving world. That is called the Great White Throne judgment. This will be a special judgment for Christians. Our sins have been atoned for by Christ on the cross, but after salvation every work must come into judgment. The result is reward or loss (1 Cor. 3:11–15) "but he himself [the believer] shall be saved."

In 1 Corinthians 12:7, the apostle Paul says the gifts are given "for the common good" so we are not to use them selfishly. Instead, we are to use them to help each other. As Paul says in Philippians 2:3, 4, "Do nothing from selfishness or empty conceit, but with humility of mind let each of you regard one another as more important than himself; do not merely look out for your own personal interests, but also for the interests of others."

God has also designed the gifts to help "unite" the body of Christ. Just before listing the gifts in Ephesians 4:3–7, the apostle Paul urges us to be "diligent to preserve the unity of the Spirit in the bond of peace. There is one body and one Spirit, just as also you were called in one hope of your calling; one Lord, one faith, one baptism, one God and Father of all who is over all and through all and in all. But to each one of us grace [a special gift] was given according to the measure of Christ's gift." Notice how Paul emphasizes unity by repeating the word "one."

Thus the gifts of the Spirit should never divide the body of Christ; they should unify it.

How to Recognize Your Gift

I am often asked, "How can I discover what gift I have?" And "How can I utilize my gift to the best advantage?" I would make the following suggestions:

First, realize that God has given you at least one spiritual gift, and He wants you to know what it is and to use it for His glory. Paul wrote to young Timothy and said, ". . . kindle afresh the gift of God which is in you" (2 Tim. 1:6). Just as the first step in being filled with the Spirit is understanding that God has given us the Spirit, so the first step in finding our spiritual gifts is understanding God's provision.

Second, I believe the discovery of our spiritual gifts should be a matter of careful and thoughtful prayer on our part. We should pray that God will guide us to know our spiritual gifts. Also we should be sure we are willing to make use of our spiritual gifts in a way that is honoring to God. For example, if God showed you that you had the gift of teaching others, would you be willing to put that gift to use in a Sunday school class? If we find we are reluctant to know God's gifts because we are afraid of what He might call us to do with them, this needs to be faced and confessed before God.

Along with this is a third step, which involves an intelligent understanding of what the Bible says about spiritual gifts. It is my prayer that this book will be a reliable guide, but there is no substitute for firsthand study of the Bible's teaching on the gifts of the Spirit.

A fourth step in finding out your spiritual gifts involves a knowledge of yourself and your abilities. There may be certain experiences in your personal background which would tend to lead you one way or another. We may find we like to do certain things, and we may discover we are good at them. There are few short-cuts here; we simply have to discover specific ways in which our gifts begin to emerge. Often it is good to try a variety of situations—for example, in various ministries of the church. Other people can help us. For example, we may not be aware of an ability we have to be a good listener and counselor to people. But as time goes along we find more and more people coming to us and sharing their personal problems with us; we also may find other Christians telling us they think we have certain gifts along this line.

The process of discovering our spiritual gifts may be a lengthy one, and we may even find gifts emerging as the years go by and we confront new opportunities and challenges. However, we cannot let that discourage us. God wants to use us, and we will never be used by Him in the fullest way until we know our gifts and have committed them to Him. Actually, I believe a person who is Spirit-filled—constantly submitting to the Lordship of Christ—will come to discover his gifts with some degree of ease. He wants God to guide in his life, and that is the kind of person God stands ready to bless by showing him the gifts the Holy Spirit has bestowed on him.

Humbly and gratefully accept the gift God appears to have given you, and use it as fully as possible. We should accept ourselves as we are and use the gifts we have. Our gift may call us to service in some prominent position, with its own difficulty and danger. But it may also mean we are to serve in some humble sphere. I rather like David Howard's comment: "God has not called a spiritual elite to carry out the work of the ministry, bypassing the ordinary believer in the church. Rather, '*to each* is given the manifestation of the Spirit for the common good' (1 Cor. 12:7 [RSV])."[1]

This does not do away with the office of elder or bishop, or the deacon either, for that matter. It simply means that the laity as well as elders and deacons have a role to play and obligations to discharge in the congregation.

What we have said so far lays the groundwork for discussing

each gift Paul lists. When it comes to the gifts of the Spirit mentioned by the apostle Paul, we see that he does not group gifts by category and no grouping I'm familiar with is wholly satisfactory. In the rest of this chapter we will limit ourselves to those five gifts listed in Ephesians 4:11 (apostle, prophet, evangelist, pastor, and teacher); several of these are also mentioned in 1 Corinthians 12:28. In a separate chapter we will deal with other gifts mentioned in 1 Corinthians 12 and Romans 12. A further chapter will deal with the sign gifts.

Apostle

The Greek word for this gift means "one sent with a commission." John R. W. Stott says, "The word 'apostle' is probably used in *three senses* in the New Testament. . . . [*Firstly,*] in the general sense that all of us are sent into the world by Christ and thus share in the apostolic mission of the church (Jn. 17:18; 20:21), all of us are in the broadest term 'apostles'. . . . [*Secondly,*] the word is used at least twice to describe 'apostles of the churches' (2 Cor. 8:23; Phil. 2:25), messengers sent on particular errands from one church to another. In this sense the word might be applied to missionaries and other Christians sent on special missions. . . . [*Thirdly,*] the gift of apostleship which is thus given precedence must refer, therefore, to that small and special group of men who were 'apostles of Christ', consisting of the Twelve (Lk. 6:12, 13), together with Paul (e.g. Gal. 1:1), . . . They were unique in being eyewitnesses of the historic Jesus, especially of the risen Lord. . . . In this primary sense, therefore, in which they appear in the lists, they have no successors, in the very nature of the case, although there are no doubt 'apostles' today in the secondary sense of 'missionaries'."[2] (italics mine)

Dr. Merrill C. Tenney has suggested that a present-day missionary may have this gift in its secondary meaning if he is a church planter. He would then need (1) to be sent with a message, (2) to be responsible to establish a church, and (3) to exercise authority in setting policies and enforcing them. I have a friend in the Caribbean who has spent a lifetime going from one community to another establishing churches. During his life he has established more than fifty. There are hundreds, and perhaps thousands, of men and women of God throughout the world today who are doing just that—even though the church may meet in a storefront building or a home.

Prophet

The English word *prophecy* derives from the Greek word meaning "public expounder." In apostolic times the gift of prophecy had two parts. One concerned the communication of words from God to men through the prophet. This was a supernatural gift. And in order for men to discern between false and true prophets, the Spirit gave the gift of "discerning the spirits" to other believers. The very fact that a prophet spoke by revelation virtually assured the existence of false prophets, too, as we note from both Old and New Testaments. New Testament Christians were not to despise prophesying but they were told to test all things.

According to 1 Corinthians 14:3, the second part of the prophetic office was the edification, instruction, consolation, and exhortation of the believers in local congregations. The prophet, who was usually an itinerant, took precedence over the local minister. But as time went on the gift of prophecy was exercised by local ministers who preached the Word of God for the edification of their parish members.

The gift of prophecy in the first sense, that of foretelling or predictive prophecy, no longer exists to the extent it did in first century Christianity.

I am aware of the evidence for rare instances in which Christians believe they have been given foreknowledge about future events. Hans Egede (1686–1758), the pioneer missionary to Greenland, was said to have prophesied the coming of a vessel with food at a time when starvation was close at hand. And the vessel came as he predicted. But instances of this sort are rare, not ordinary and frequent. I would not wish to rule out such occurrences as impossible to a sovereign God, though they are not binding on believers as scriptural prophecy. Also, I would think of them as distinct from what is the normal or ordinary function of the gift of prophecy today, which is the ability to understand and to engage in the exposition of the Word of God.

God no longer directly reveals "new truth"; there is now a back cover to the Bible. The canon of Scripture is closed. I understand the gift of prophecy to be used "in the extended sense of presenting God's people truths received, not by direct revelation, but from careful study of the completed and infallible Word of God."[3]

It is the work of the Holy Spirit to illumine the minds of those who are called to the prophetic office so they understand the Word of God and apply it with a depth impossible to those who do not have the gift of prophecy. It may sound like new truth freshly revealed—but to be biblical it must be based on the Word of God. There is a difference between doctrine and direction. There is nothing new in doctrine, but God does give new directions, which many times are mistaken as prophecies.

When prophecy is mentioned in connection with speaking in tongues another dimension appears. As I understand it from some of my brethren, individuals in the congregation might prophesy in tongues and then be interpreted by someone who has that latter gift. I am willing to grant that possibility, with the understanding that it does not involve *new* revelation but something the Holy Spirit would do that would be dynamically related to the written Word of God. The gift of prophecy deserves a stronger emphasis, perhaps, than that of either pastor or evangelist. Apparently, the New Testament prophets instructed, exhorted, rebuked, and warned of judgment.

I listened to a tape sometime ago that was reputed to be a new prophecy by an outstanding charismatic leader. However, upon listening to the tape I found that almost everything he said was biblically based. It was nothing new—only his emphasis was new. He gave biblical truth in a dramatic way, applying it to our own world.

In my own preaching I have done all these things. And I have encountered some evangelists whom I thought were prophets/ evangelists/teachers/pastors; they had all these gifts and the gifts overlapped. The Old Testament prophets foretold the future, especially the future as it related to judgment to fall on cities and nations, or to the coming of Messiah. The New Testament prophets had ministries more like that of the evangelists. They proclaimed the Word of God and called upon people to repent of their sins; they disturbed people in their sins. The apostle Paul devotes a large portion of 1 Corinthians 14 to the subject of prophecy. The people of Corinth were so taken with the sign gifts that Paul chose to emphasize the importance of prophecy.

One word of caution, however. The Scriptures plainly teach that we are to exercise the gift of discernment—because many false prophets will appear. As a matter of fact, both in the writings of Jesus and the apostles, there is warning after warning that false prophets would appear, especially as we approach the end of the age. Many of them will be wolves in sheep's clothing. They will often fool God's own people. Thus the Christian must have those who can distinguish between false and true prophets. Paul was concerned about the Corinthians because they seemed to have little discernment, and they welcomed anyone as a true prophet of Christ. "For if someone comes to you and preaches a Jesus other than the Jesus we preached, or if you receive a different spirit from the one you received, or a different gospel from the one you accepted, you put up with it easily enough. . . . such men are false apostles, deceitful workmen, masquerading as apostles of Christ" (2 Cor. 11:4, 13 NIV).

There is a sense in which every Christian should be discerning, ascertaining truth from falsehood. This is so because every Christian should be rooted in the Bible, and he should know what the Bible teaches. However, the Bible also indicates some Christians have the gift of discernment in special measure.

What about people who claim to foretell the future? I have often been asked this question. The requirement (or test) of the true prophet (the forthteller) in the Scriptures was that he be 100 percent accurate. Not 50 percent. Not 75 percent. Not even 99 percent. But 100 percent accurate.

Evangelist

The term "evangelist" comes from a Greek word meaning "one who announces good news."

In his excellent book, *Good News Is for Sharing,* Leighton Ford points out something that comes as a surprise to some Bible students. The word translated "evangelist" occurs only three times in the New Testament: (1) Luke called Philip an evangelist (Acts 21:8); (2) Paul said God gave evangelists to the churches (Eph. 4:11); (3) he also urged Timothy to "do the work of an

evangelist" (2 Tim. 4:5). The gift of evangelism, then, is simply a special ability in communicating the gospel.

The evangelist's message almost necessarily centers around the "content" of the gospel. The evangelist primarily is a "messenger"; he is a deliverer of "the good news." Incidentally, the evangelist in his proclamation may teach and do the work of a pastor, but his primary message centers in the death, burial, and resurrection of Christ, His coming again, and the need for all men everywhere to repent and believe.

The evangelist is the special proclaimer of the good news that God was in Christ reconciling the world to Himself. The Church through history has missed great blessings because some denominations have not as clearly recognized the gift of the evangelist as they have that of the teacher or pastor. Indeed, sometimes evangelists have been ignored or opposed by churches, as in the case of John Wesley, whose mission was rejected by his own church. Despite this, in almost every generation God has raised up evangelists, who often have had to pursue their calling outside the structured church.

Caricatures of evangelists abound because false evangelists in the Elmer Gantry image have libeled the hundreds of true ones throughout the world. But then the same can be said of some pastors, or teachers, who turn out to be false. A well-known pastor, teacher, or evangelist is often a special target of Satan. The higher the visibility, the easier the target. That's the reason those well known for their gifts need to be surrounded by prayer constantly on the part of God's people.

True evangelism speaks to the intellect and may or may not produce emotion, but its main job is to speak to the will. At times the gifts of teaching and evangelism are given to the same person. Some of the most effective evangelists I have known were essentially teachers who informed the minds of people even as they pricked their consciences by their use of the Word of God. I have known many teachers and expository preachers who claimed they were not evangelists—but indeed they did have the gift of evangelism! For example, though the late Dr. Donald Grey Barnhouse was a pastor/teacher, I have met many people who received Christ through his ministry.

Unfortunately, some evangelists spend too much time thinking and even planning about how to achieve visible results. This is an easy trap to fall into. Evangelists rightly desire to see results, but the gift itself is not a guarantee that these will be immediate.

The Reverend James R. Graham, Sr., pioneer missionary to China, proclaimed the gospel for three years without seeing results. When asked if he ever became discouraged, he replied, "No. 'The battle is the Lord's, and He will deliver it into our hands.' "

Nowhere do the Scriptures tell us to seek results, nor do the Scriptures rebuke evangelists if the results are meager. Men and women do make decisions wherever the gospel is proclaimed; whether publicly or privately, some say yes, some say no, and some procrastinate. No one ever hears the gospel proclaimed without making some kind of decision!

We should never forget that Noah was a preacher of righteousness. Yet after an evangelistic and prophetic ministry of 120 years only those in his immediate family believed and entered the ark (Heb. 11:7). On the other hand, some who obviously had the gift of evangelism have modestly subdued their gift because they are afraid of being accused of nonintellectualism, emotionalism, commercialism, or being too concerned with statistics. These are subtleties of Satan to keep the man with the gift of evangelism from being used.

For example, I remember there was a time in my own ministry when we quit keeping statistics (due to criticism). We found almost immediately that the public press exaggerated what was happening, and often used the wrong terminology. For example, we were in one city and the newspaper the next day reported, "1,000 saved at Billy Graham Crusade." Two things were wrong with that headline. First, only God knows whether they were saved or not—that is the reason we call them inquirers and not decisions. Second, it was not 1,000, but less than 500 (over half of those who came forward were trained counselors). Thus, we went back to giving accurate statistics.

Evangelism is not limited to professional evangelists, that is, those whose lives are wholly spent in this calling. The gift of evangelism is also given to many lay people. Philip is the only person in the Bible who was called an evangelist, and he was a deacon! In some sense every Christian who is not called to the vocation of evangelism is still called upon to do the *work* of an evangelist.

People often misunderstand the methods of evangelism. One

can use hundreds of different methods, but it is the message that counts. Let us take note, however, of what evangelists cannot do. They cannot bring conviction of sin, righteousness, or judgment; that is the Spirit's work. They cannot convert anyone; that is the Spirit's work. The evangelist can invite men to receive Christ, and exhort them. But the effectual work is done by the Spirit as He works on the minds, hearts, and wills of the unsaved. We are to take care of the possible and trust God for the impossible.

Yet there is more. If the evangelist is to carry on a truly effective ministry to the glory of the Lord, the message must be backed by a Spirit-filled, fruit-producing life. Jesus promised, "Follow Me, and I will make you become fishers of men" (Mark 1:17). He provides the strength, through the Spirit. I urge all Christians to do the work of an evangelist—whether they go into full-time evangelism or not! I believe they have no option. It is a command from our Lord Jesus Christ, and the general injunction of Scripture. "Go therefore and make disciples of all the nations, baptizing them in the name of the Father and the Son and the Holy Spirit, teaching them to observe all that I commanded you; and lo, I am with you always, even to the end of the age" (Matt. 28:19, 20).

Pastor

The Bible does not often use the word *pastor*. In the Old Testament it occasionally translates the Hebrew word for shepherd. The New Testament uses the word *pastor* only once with the root idea of "shepherd" (Eph. 4:11). Here it is closely linked with the Old Testament translation of the word for shepherd. It is also closely linked with the word for teacher. Forms of the underlying Greek word also appear in two other places.

Among many Christians the word *pastor* is one of the most commonly preferred designations for ordained clergy. Its use is consistent with the ministry of our Lord who applies the term "shepherd" to Himself. So those called to the pastoral ministry by the Holy Spirit are undershepherds of the sheep.

Jesus Christ is called "the good shepherd" (John 10:11), and "the great Shepherd of the sheep" (Heb. 13:20). Peter talks about the "Chief Shepherd" who will someday appear (1 Peter 5:4). If Jesus is the chief shepherd, then there must be assistant shepherds; these include ministers of the gospel and unordained saints in the congregation who have gifts of counseling, guiding, warning, and guarding the flock. A number of people have acted as spiritual shepherds in my own life although they were never formally ordained to the ministry.

Many youth counselors, Sunday school teachers, and leaders of home Bible studies and Christian nurture groups actually perform functions that are part of the pastoral gift. Three of Paul's letters, 1 and 2 Timothy and Titus, were called pastoral epistles. They tell the shepherds how to watch over the flock. In our crusades, we use a "shepherd plan": Each person who comes forward as an inquirer talks to a trained counselor (or shepherd). This person may be a layman or an ordained pastor. We ask the counselor (or shepherd) to follow up with letters, phone calls, and visits until the inquirer is either in a warm Christian atmosphere, has made other Christian contacts, or is in a nurture group or prayer group. If he is in forced solitude (in prison), the shepherd teaches him to study the Bible on his own.

I believe that thousands of Christians throughout the world who will never become pastors of churches do have the gift of a pastor that can be used to assist the clergy in their work. Those who have the gift should use it as fully as possible, remembering that failure to do so is to grieve the Holy Spirit. Many pastors of churches are overworked and could use a little help. Each of us might well ask his pastor what to do to help him.

Teacher

The Greek word in Ephesians 4:11 for the gift of teacher means "instructor." When the message of the gospel has resulted in conversions, the new Christians must then be taught. In the Great Commission (Matt. 28:18–20), the command to disciple is followed immediately by the injunction, "teaching them to observe all that I commanded you."

One of the great needs in the Church at the present hour is for more teachers of the Bible. Yet this, too, is in the sovereign hands of God. Teaching is simply a Spirit-given ability to build into the lives of Christians a knowledge of God's Word and its application to their thinking and conduct. Teaching has for its goal the conformity of Christians to the likeness of Jesus. It can and should be done both simply, compassionately, and searchingly. Many years ago I had two doctrine professors. Both had earned doctors' degrees and were scholars in their own right. Both had one thing in common. When they taught their classes, they did it with such great brokenness and compassion that often tears would come to their eyes. I have long ago forgotten a great deal of what they taught, but I still remember those "tears."

Along this line, I am told that Paul's Greek phrasing of the list of gifts in Ephesians 4 suggests such a close connection between the gift of pastor and teacher that his words could almost be translated "pastor-teacher" as if it were one gift. This reinforces the idea that the spiritual teacher must have a compassionate sensitivity to the needs of the taught.

Some of the best teachers of the Word to whom I have listened have not had much formal education. By contrast, some of the poorer teachers have had Ph.D. degrees in various biblically related disciplines, but they lacked the teaching gift with which to communicate their knowledge. It is unfortunate that some seminaries fall into the secular world's qualifications for teachers— and some of the best Bible teachers do not have earned degrees. Therefore they are not qualified to teach in a modern seminary. I believe to the extent that this is practiced it could be dangerous to the future of the Church. That does not mean God does not use our intellectual abilities when they are committed to Him, but spiritual teaching, like all spiritual gifts, is a supernatural ability the Holy Spirit gives, not a university degree. In recent years I have changed my emphasis somewhat: in my proclamation of the gospel I have emphasized the cost of discipleship and the need for learning. God has providentially brought into being thousands of Bible classes as a result of our emphasis in the preparation and follow-up of our Crusades. Likewise, God has raised up hundreds of evangelical Bible schools and seminaries throughout the world. But the Church still lacks enough teachers. Yet I believe that the Spirit has given the gift of teaching to hundreds and perhaps thousands of people who either do not know they have the gift, or are not using it!

The gift of teaching may be used in all kinds of contexts—from a theological seminary and Bible school to a Sunday school class or home Bible study. The important thing for a person who has this gift is to use it whenever and wherever God leads.

One of the first verses of Scripture that Dawson Trotman, founder of the Navigators, made me memorize was, "The things that thou hast heard of me among many witnesses, the same commit thou to faithful men, who shall be able to teach others also" (2 Tim. 2:2 KJV). This is a little like a mathematical formula for spreading the gospel and enlarging the Church. Paul taught Timothy; Timothy shared what he knew with faithful men; these faithful men would then teach others also. And so the process goes on and on. If every believer followed this pattern, the Church could reach the entire world with the gospel in one generation! Mass crusades, in which I believe and to which I have committed my life, will never finish the Great Commission; but a one-by-one ministry will.

Apostle—prophet—evangelist—pastor—teacher: five of the gifts of the Holy Spirit. But perhaps you are saying, "I'm not a pastor or an evangelist. These are someone else's gifts, not mine. What do they have to do with me?" They have much to do with you!

First, it may be God *has* given you one of these gifts. God may be calling you to be a pastor, or an evangelist, or a teacher of the Bible. Perhaps you are a young person whom God is calling to the mission field. You may be older, and God wants to use you to teach a Sunday school class or a home Bible study group.

Second, the Bible commands us to support those whom God has called as leaders in the Church. For example, you should pray regularly for your pastor, for missionaries, and for others who are involved in God's work. "Pray on my behalf" the apostle Paul said (Eph. 6:19). Let them know you are supporting their work and are interested in what God is doing through them.

Third, learn from those God has placed in positions of Christian leadership. "Remember those who led you . . . imitate their faith. . . . Obey your leaders" (Heb. 13:7, 17). Give thanks to God for the gifts He has given to these leaders "for the equipping of the saints for the work of service, to the building up of the body of Christ" (Eph. 4:12).

12. Further Gifts of the Spirit

In the last chapter we studied the gifts Paul lists in Ephesians 4. Next we will consider others that he mentions in 1 Corinthians 12 (which are somewhat duplicated in Romans 12) where we find the primary list of gifts, the ones probably best known to most of us. Because the sign gifts (such as tongues) have caused so much controversy, we will deal with them in a separate chapter.

We must note first that Paul says, "Now there are varieties of gifts, but the same Spirit" (v. 4). Whatever I say about the gifts is based on a crucial presupposition: these gifts are supernatural gifts from the Spirit. The Christian himself cannot manufacture or produce them in any way. This does not mean, of course, that we should understand the gifts apart from the written Word of God. We are to study the Word and apply it.

The Spirit grants some people special wisdom, knowledge, faith, and the like, but the granting of these special gifts does not mean other Christians are barren. Rather, such spiritual gifts are often heightened forms of a rudimentary ability God gives all Christians. The gift of wisdom illustrates this. We all have some spiritual wisdom, but a person with this *gift* has wisdom in a very special degree. On the other hand, I believe the gift of healing or miracles is one a believer has or does not have. And God gives such a gift to very few, a policy He appears to have followed throughout the history of the Church. At any rate, we must now consider the first two spiritual gifts Paul mentions in 1 Corinthians 12.

We can possess three kinds of wisdom. The first comes to us naturally. The second comes from learning, so it is something we can be taught. But the highest kind of wisdom comes directly from

God and is associated with the particular work of the Holy Spirit. Though He is the fountainhead of all truth from whatever source, yet He gives believers wisdom in a unique way—through the Scriptures. In addition, He gives a special gift or capacity for wisdom to some.

Dr. Merrill C. Tenney of Wheaton College defines this gift as "the ability to make correct decisions on the basis of one's knowledge."

This then leads us to a second gift, the gift of knowledge, which concerns acquaintance with spiritual information. Yet we all know believers with striking information about God and doctrine, but who do not know how to apply this to practical situations. I have a friend whose head is crammed full of biblical knowledge, yet the tragic mistakes he has made in judgment have almost destroyed his ministry. For this reason, the gifts of wisdom and knowledge must work together, that is, they illustrate the need for those with varying gifts to cooperate.

Jesus discusses a case where a believer may need both gifts. He says, "And when they bring you to trial and deliver you up, do not be anxious beforehand what you are to say; but say whatever is given you in that hour, for it is not you who speak, but the Holy Spirit" (Mark 13:11 RSV). Time after time Jesus' disciples had to defend themselves before mobs, governors, princes, and kings; the apostle Paul may have made his defense before Caesar himself. That knowledge which is the gift of the Spirit is based on long hours of disciplined study in which God teaches us. But the capacity to apply what we learn to actual situations goes beyond study and comes directly from the Holy Spirit. Wisdom is the gift from the Spirit which shows us how to use knowledge. Paul defended himself by using both. In doing this he illustrated Peter's advice about "always being ready to make a defense to every one who asks you to give an account for the hope that is in you, yet with gentleness and reverence" (1 Peter 3:15).

It is interesting that Peter also said we are to "grow in the grace and knowledge of our Lord and Savior Jesus Christ" (2 Peter 3:18). Through our communion with God we gain a higher knowledge and a higher wisdom than the world has. And believers given these in a peculiar degree can consider that they have the gift of knowledge or wisdom.

All of us face pressures, dilemmas, and problems for which we have no answer humanly speaking. A board of twenty-six capable men and women, both black and white, handles the personnel and financial affairs of our evangelistic association. From the very beginning of our ministry we have tried to be scrupulous in the way our business affairs are handled. Time after time in our board meetings when we reached an impasse about priorities, or when we were faced with critical financial needs, or had to face an unjust attack from some quarter, we would get on our knees to ask God for wisdom. He gave us answers immediately again and again. Every fellowship of believers needs at least one person with the gift of wisdom to aid in practical decisions. Such a person would often be the one, after we had prayed, who came up with the direction for the right decision we should make.

Faith

Faith comes from a Greek word meaning faithfulness or steadfastness: "To another faith by the same Spirit" (1 Cor. 12:9). In this passage the apostle Paul assumes the existence of saving faith. The Scripture says, "By grace you have been saved through faith" (Eph. 2:8). We are also told that "we walk by faith, not by sight" (2 Cor. 5:7). However, faith in 1 Corinthians 12 is a very special gift the Holy Spirit gives at His good pleasure.

We must distinguish between the grace of faith and the gift of faith. The grace of faith means that we can believe God will do whatever He has promised to do in His Word. All Christians have the grace of faith. Therefore, if we do not have faith in what the Bible promises, we sin. But many things come into our lives concerning which there are no specific promises from the Word. Therefore, when we pray, we add, "if it be Thy will." But sometimes the Holy Spirit gives us the gift of faith to believe for things about which the Bible is silent. If we do not have this special gift of faith, it is not sin.

We see a classic example of the gift of faith in the life of George Muller of Bristol, England, who cared for thousands of orphans over a period of many years. Muller refused to ask anyone for a single penny, but he prayed the money in. This is the gift of faith described by Jesus when He said, "If you have faith as a mustard seed, you shall say to this mountain, 'Move from here to there,' and it shall move; and nothing shall be impossible to you" (Matt. 17:20).

At times in my own ministry it has seemed to me that I was a man of little faith, and yet there have been a number of occasions when the Holy Spirit has given me the special gift of faith and forced me into seemingly impossible situations where there was no specific promise from God in the Word.

For example, in our 1957 New York Crusade, Madison Square Garden had been packed out night after night for six weeks and thousands had made their commitment to Christ. However, though we were scheduled to close at the Yankee Stadium on July 20, a burden grew in the hearts of a few of us that the Crusade should continue. Some felt that returning to the Garden after the Yankee Stadium would be anticlimactic; people would no longer be interested, especially with vacation time at hand.

I became so terribly burdened that I found it impossible to sleep at night. I knew that the ultimate decision would be up to me and my longtime colleague, Cliff Barrows, before God. Finally, one night while on my knees before God I said, "Lord, I do not know what is right, but by faith I am going to tell the committee tomorrow we shall go on." I called Cliff on the phone and he indicated God seemed to be saying the same thing to him.

Based on that decision we continued on for ten more weeks, ending with an open-air rally in Times Square where 75,000 people jammed the streets. The service was carried live on television and radio to the nation on prime evening time. Now, if that decision had not been made on the basis of the gift of faith from the Holy Spirit, hundreds of people who now know Christ might not have known Him.

I firmly believe there are times in all our lives when we make decisions on the basis of the will of God, and we are given faith by the Spirit to do what God wants us to do, regardless of the consequences.

Discernment of Spirits

The word *discernment* in 1 Corinthians 12:10 comes from a Greek word embodying several ideas: to see, consider, examine, understand, hear, judge closely. The New American Standard Bible calls the capacity for this gift, "the distinguishing of spirits."

As I stated in the last chapter, the Bible points out that

many false prophets and deceivers will emerge inside and out-side the Church through the ages. However, at the end of the age they will intensify their activities. Paul said, "Even Satan disguises himself as an angel of light. Therefore it is not sur-prising if his servants also disguise themselves as servants of righteousness" (2 Cor. 11:14, 15). I am convinced that hundreds of religious leaders throughout the world today are servants not of God, but of the Antichrist. They are wolves in sheep's cloth-ing; they are tares instead of wheat.

Spiritism, the occult, the worship of Satan, and the activities of demons have increased rapidly throughout the Western world. False teachings (Paul calls them "doctrines of demons" in 1 Timothy 4:1) have gone hand in hand with their rise.

The great question is: How can we know the false from the true? This is why believers need the gift of discernment, or at least respect for the opinions of those who have it. The apostle John said, "Beloved, do not believe every spirit, but test the spirits to see whether they are from God; because many false prophets have gone out into the world" (1 John 4:1). In other words, believers are to test the various spirits and doctrines that abound today. Most of all we are to test them against the standard of the Word of God, the Bible. However, God gives to some individuals extraordinary abilities to discern the truth. In 1 Corinthians 12:10 we read, "to another [is given] the dis-tinguishing of spirits."

A man named Joe Evans had this gift, I believe. I always called him "Uncle" Joe. He was probably the closest friend of Dr. V. Raymond Edman, the late president of Wheaton College. Many times the three of us (and sometimes members of my team) knelt down for long and glorious periods of prayer when we were faced with challenges, opportunities, or problems. At certain periods in my ministry I have been tempted to accept offers to move from evangelism to some other field. Many times, offers came through "an angel of light." I needed discernment. Since I did not always have it myself, one person to whom I went was "Uncle" Joe so I could profit from his special gift of discernment. I sought his advice and prayer. It is important to realize that a person with the gift of discernment can often tell the difference between what is of God and what is not. Such a person can often point out false teachings or false teachers

—he has an almost uncanny ability to perceive hypocrisy, shallowness, deceit, or phoniness.

Certainly, this gift enabled Peter to see through the hypocrisy of Ananias and Sapphira. He also saw through Simon of Samaria who claimed to be converted and baptized in the Spirit but who turned out to be a counterfeit (Acts 8:9ff). Paul warned that "in later times some will fall away from the faith, paying attention to deceitful spirits and doctrines of demons" (1 Tim. 4:1).

Scripture teaches us everywhere that anything religious should be evaluated very carefully; that even the churches to which we go must be examined to see if they are sound in the faith.

Helps

The gift of "helps," mentioned in 1 Corinthians 12:28, gains its name from the Greek word having the idea of supporting, or assisting.

We have an example of the use of helps when the apostles decided to appoint deacons to take over the business affairs of the church (Acts 6). Their duties consisted primarily in waiting on tables and in the distribution of funds to the poor. The use of this gift makes it possible for thousands of lay people to engage in helping to promote the kingdom of God in such ways as counseling, prayer, handling the business affairs of the church and parachurch organizations, and witnessing. But, also, "helps" embodies the idea of social service, such as assisting the oppressed who suffer from social injustice and caring for orphans and widows. It could mean preparing a meal for a sick neighbor, writing a letter of encouragement or sharing what we have with someone in need. Helps is the gift of showing mercy. It also carries with it the idea of helping in some of the ordinary activities of Christian service so that others, endowed with other gifts, can be released to utilize them more freely. "If anyone serves, he should do it with the strength God provides, so that in all things God may be praised through Jesus Christ" (1 Peter 4:11 NIV).

During my early crusades I had a compulsion to be involved in virtually all aspects of our evangelism ministry. Obviously, this meant demands so heavy upon me that I was physically exhausted most of the time. I remember how Dawson Trotman, whom I had asked to head our counseling, came to me one night. "Billy," he said, "you are wearing yourself out." He added, "Why can't we go at this as a team? Let Cliff Barrows lead the singing, you do the preaching, and trust me and those I have trained to do the counseling." I agreed to give it a try. This was one of the most momentous and profitable decisions of my life. For the first time I began to realize that God can and does use others to take charge of certain phases of the work of evangelism just as effectively as he could use me or Cliff Barrows or some of the other leaders on our team. This is an illustration of how God can use all the gifts to help one another, but that the gift of "helps" is special.

My later study of Scripture showed me that even our Lord gathered a team of people around Him and then sent them out on one occasion to minister two by two. Mark was the helper for Paul and Barnabas (Acts 12:25). Paul traveled continually with a team of workers, without whom he could never have carried on his ministry effectively. At the end of his letters Paul usually mentioned some of those faithful helpers. In Romans the list contains more than a score of names, many of them women. Writing to the Philippians, Paul mentions Epaphroditus who "ministered to my wants" (Phil. 2:25 KJV).

While I was writing this chapter, my wife Ruth and I, along with Grady and Wilma Wilson, were the guests of Mr. and Mrs. Bill Mead of Dallas, Texas. Every morning we had a Bible study. One morning Grady Wilson suggested that we break into our regular Bible study schedule and go instead to the Book of Philemon. I thought this was rather strange, but we went along with him. As we studied Philemon I prayed, "Thank you, Lord, for giving me a perfect illustration of one who had the gift of helps." The example was Onesimus, the slave. Paul wrote to his master Philemon and said, Onesimus was "useful . . . to me" (Philem. 11).

Do you have the particular gift of "helps"? You could be a businessman faithfully serving on a board of a parachurch organization or missionary society. Or you could be involved in a Bible society or be a trustee or deacon of a church. One could be a busy housewife and mother. Another could be a student.

A relative of mine named Uncle Bo used to take every Saturday afternoon to clean the little church in the heart of Charlotte where he was a member. He mowed the grass and cut the hedges. Few people ever noticed the helps he gave so cheerfully. This was about all he could do. He couldn't preach; he couldn't teach; he had a difficult time praying in public; but he had the gift of helps. And God used him.

The Gift of Governments

This gift gains its name from the Greek word carrying the idea of steering, piloting, or directing. Some versions call it the gift of administrations (1 Cor. 12:28). Certain people have been given the gift of leadership that is recognized by the Church.

The Scriptures teach that churches must have government; they require leadership, whether professional or nonprofessional. Christ spent more than half His time with just twelve men, developing them into leaders who would carry on His work after He ascended to heaven. Wherever the apostles went they appointed leaders over the churches they founded. The Scripture says that Paul and Barnabas "appointed elders for them in every church" (Acts 14:23). In 1 Timothy 3:1–7 Paul gives qualifications for "bishops" (KJV). The word for "bishop" is thought by many to be equivalent to "pastor," carrying the idea of overseer, superintendent, or governor.

While some churches and assemblies attempt to conduct the work of the Lord without an appointed leadership, I believe this is virtually impossible. Some Christian groups do not have an appointed ordained leader. Yet services are conducted decently and in order, and the other ministries of the group are carried out. There are those who exercise leadership, even if the official titles are not given to them. If we do not recognize this gift it leads to confusion, and it appears to me to be unbiblical since it hinders the work of the Holy Spirit who gives men the gift of government. The writer of the Book of Hebrews went so far as to say, "Obey your leaders, and submit to them" (Heb. 13:17). Certainly he was talking about those who had authority in the Church.

The qualifications of a leader are listed several times in the New Testament. He must not be dictatorial, egotistical, or dogmatic; he is to be anything but that. Rather he is to be humble, gracious, courteous, kind, and filled with love; yet at times he must be very firm. For this reason the gift of knowledge combined with wisdom is necessary. Further, the leadership idea outlined in the New Testament is decisively in opposition to the notion of great pomp and pageantry. Rather, it emphasizes the graces of humility and service.

The Lord Jesus Christ is the most perfect example of a governor, or a leader. "For even the Son of Man did not come to be served, but to serve, and to give His life a ransom for many" (Mark 10:45). He humbled Himself to become a servant (Phil. 2:7); He washed the disciples' feet and then said, "A servant is not greater than his master" (John 13:16 RSV). Jesus, by example, tells us that every true leader should be a helper, a servant, or even a bondslave. We are exhorted to, "through love serve one another" (Gal. 5:13). This is a command, not a suggestion, and applies with special force to leaders.

The End of the Matter

God did not ordain that the Church should drift aimlessly in the seas of uncertainty without compass, captain, or crew. By His Spirit He has provided for the operation of the Church in history through the gifts of His Spirit, and we are told to "earnestly desire the greater gifts" (1 Cor. 12:31). Whether the Holy Spirit gives us one or several, it is important for us to do two things: First we should recognize the gift or gifts God has given us. Second, we should nurture those gifts and do everything, humanly speaking, to improve them as we use them. One who has the gift of prophecy should be better able to fill this role with the passage of every year of his life. And the person with the gift of wisdom should be wiser at the end than he was at the beginning.

Some day all of us will give account of the way we have used the gifts God has given. The person to whom much has been given will find much required of him. Let's use our gifts as fully as possible and wait with expectation for our Lord's "Well done, good and faithful servant" (Matt. 25:21 RSV) at the judgment of the saints.

13. The Sign Gifts

I think a word of explanation and caution will be helpful here in connection with the so-called sign gifts listed in 1 Corinthians 12:9, 10. By "sign gifts" I mean those gifts of the Holy Spirit which are often obvious outward indications or signs of the working of God. The sign gifts include *healings, miracles,* and *tongues.* They seem to rate the most attention in the Church today, exciting the imagination and producing outward manifestations that attract multitudes.

One Christian leader said that if he heard a clergyman down the street was preaching the gospel, he would just turn on his T.V. and go back to watching his favorite program. But if he was told that someone down the street was performing miracles, he would drop everything to see what was happening. Why is this? Simply because we seem to be fascinated by the spectacular and the unusual. This kind of curiosity is not necessarily good or helpful, but it is, nevertheless, very common.

It is interesting to note that in the Bible's four discussions of the gifts of the Spirit (Rom. 12:6–8; 1 Cor. 12:8–10; Eph. 4:11; and 1 Peter 4:10, 11), these sign gifts are listed together only in the first letter to Corinth, a church that was abusing at least one of these gifts. Christians should remember that the Holy Spirit did not intend gifts to be misused so that they become divisive, or disrupt our fellowship. When this occurs the greatest of all manifestations of the Spirit, love, is diminished.

Healing

The Holy Spirit gives the gift of healing (literally, the gift of cures). Many cases of healing appear in the Old Testament, and certainly the New Testament is full of instances when Jesus and His disciples healed the sick. Throughout the history of the Christian Church countless instances of physical healing have been recorded.

The ministry of physical healings through spiritual means is sometimes associated with faith healers. Many of these claim to have the gift of healing or at least some special power. Tens of thousands of people flock to these healers. And thousands more are urged to write certain radio and television preachers who claim to have this gift of healing. Indeed, mass attention has been focused in recent years on the Christian faith and physical healing.

Yet sickness and infirmity are a part of life: no one can escape them at last. All people, including the most famous faith healers, get sick, and all eventually die. Kathryn Kuhlman, the famous faith healer, died early in 1976. For years she had suffered from a heart condition, and late in 1975 underwent open heart surgery from which she never recovered. People were healed under her ministry. She was not. Sickness brought death to her at last.

However, we must distinguish the operation of what the Bible calls the gift of healing from a second method of healing. Some place their emphasis on the faith of the one who needs healing —telling him it will happen if only he believes. By this they mean more than those who believe that forgiveness, cleansing, and acceptance with God spring from the atoning work of Jesus on the cross. They think that any Christian who becomes ill can claim healing by faith. Note that this has nothing to do with the gift of healing as such. Such teachers may believe, for example, that physical healing for disease is in the atonement of Jesus Christ. To them the death of Christ on the cross not only results in the offer of forgiveness for our sins, but also physical healing for the body. Both, they believe, come to us by faith.

This kind of healing has to do with *faith* rather than just the gift of healing itself.

In support of this position it is pointed out that the Old Testament foretold the coming of the Messiah and said of Him, "And by His scourging we are healed" (Isa. 53:5). Personally I do not believe the Scripture makes it clear to us that Christ's work on the cross included physical healing. The passage found in Isaiah 53:5 is quoted once in the New Testament in 1 Peter 2:24: "And He Himself bore our sins in His body on the cross, that we might die to sin and live to righteousness; for by His wounds you were healed." It seems clear from this that the "healing" of the Savior is primarily spiritual in nature, not physical.

Some Christians, regardless of whether they believe God heals through the spiritual gift or through the exercise of faith alone, believe it is unnecessary to consult a physician when they are ill, except possibly as a last resort. Several avenues are open to them: They can believe God for healing, in which case it does not involve the gift of healing but rather the gift of faith. Or they may go to someone whom they believe has the gift of healing. The gift of healing means that a person so gifted can do exactly what Jesus did; by that power which is his as a gift from the Holy Spirit he can make the sick well immediately and permanently: a broken arm is mended instantly, a cancer disappears, the process of pneumonia stops and the lungs become well.

Healing from illnesses must be considered from a broader perspective, I feel. James teaches that all good gifts come from above. I believe that healing can and may come from God through the gift of healing and the gift of faith, but it also comes from Him through the use of medical means. Paul told Timothy to take some medicinal wine for his stomach problems (1 Tim. 5:23). We must keep in mind that Luke was a physician and accompanied Paul on many of his trips, and probably gave him medical help.

I know the Lord has used physicians and medicine to cure illnesses I have suffered. Furthermore, we must be open to the idea that it may not be the will of God for us to be cured of all our infirmities, something true of the apostle Paul (see 2 Cor. 12:7–10). I think Christians should therefore use God-given wisdom to determine whether they should seek the use of natural means or rely solely on prayer or those with the genuine gift of healing.

If medication is not available, or if doctors have pronounced a case incurable, and God lays it on our hearts to look to Him in simple faith for the impossible, then we must follow His leading. But this leading must come from God, not the urging of fellow Christians.

However, if medication and doctors are available, to ignore them in favor of asking God to heal seems to me to border on presumption.

I had a friend who was struck with a deadly disease. The doctors knew there was no hope. He knew there was no hope. So he sent for one he knew to have the gift of healing. After prayer and spiritual counseling, the healer laid her hands on my friend. Immediately he felt what seemed to be an electric shock, and he was healed instantly. When he was checked by the doctors, all evidence of the disease had disappeared.

Overjoyed, he became totally taken up with the sign-gifts: healing, miracles, speaking in tongues and their interpretation. The person and work of Christ were all but ignored. The fruit of the Spirit was not in evidence. Three years later the disease recurred with a vengeance. This time God did not choose to heal him. He died slowly, bitterly disillusioned, as if all glory plus the Lord Himself were not awaiting him.

Prudence differs from presumption, and we ought not tempt God. If a sick Christian resorts to faith for healing, he should be certain God has given him that faith. Lacking it, he ought to seek the help of physicians. And in my judgment it is normal for a Christian to use the medical help God provides. Medicine and physicians (such as Luke) are of God, too.

Sometime ago I conversed with a psychiatrist of impeccable qualifications. In the conversation he underscored a well-known fact: People suffer from both organic and functional diseases. Under the latter category the medical books list many diseases which have no organic basis but are psychosomatic. Yet they do produce outward physical ailments which cannot be cured by ordinary medical treatment; they can be cured, however, when the mind is treated. When the mind is made well, the physical manifestations stemming from this functional situation disappear. The Romans had a famous saying: *mens sana in corpore sano,* a sound mind in a sound body. A diseased mind can produce disease in the body. A healthy mind will keep the body from functional diseases that derive from disease of the mind.

Having said all this, I do know that God heals under certain circumstances in accordance with His will. My own sister-in-law is an outstanding example. She was dying of tuberculosis. The X-rays showed the seriousness of her condition, but she asked her surgeon father for permission to discontinue medical treatment because she believed God was going to heal her. It was granted, and some godly men and women anointed her with oil and prayed the prayer of faith. Then a new series of X-rays was taken, and to the astonishment of the physicians at the sanatorium she no longer showed any signs of active tuberculosis. Immediately she began to gain weight, and thirty-five years later she is an active Bible teacher, a healthy person. Obviously, she was healed. But note that the healing came, not through someone who had the gift of healing, but through faith.

It is interesting to note that Jesus did not always heal people the same way. On some occasions He simply spoke the word and the healing took place. At other times He used what might be considered *means*. Jesus took the hand of Simon Peter's mother-in-law, and she was healed instantly (Matt. 8:15). When Jesus raised Lazarus from the dead, He cried out with a loud voice, "Lazarus, come out" (John 11:43 RSV). But Jesus healed the man born blind in quite a different way: He mixed clay and spittle, spread it on the eyes of the blind man, and commanded him to wash it off in the pool of Siloam (John 9:1ff). In the case of the centurion's servant, the sick man was not even near Jesus when he was healed (Matt. 8:5ff). And the woman with the issue of blood was healed simply by touching the garment of the Lord (Matt. 9:18ff).

The laying on of hands or the anointing with oil has both spiritual and psychological significance. The sick and those who anoint them must not suppose that the healing is due to the laying on of hands, the anointing with oil, their own personal faith, or even their prayers. The healing is from God and is of God. "The *Lord* will raise him up" (James 5:15, italics mine).

But God does not always choose to heal us. As I have said, I can find no evidence in Scripture that it is the will of God to heal all people of all illnesses. If the Holy Spirit gives a sick person or someone who is praying for a sick person the gift of faith that the person will be healed, then we can be sure the person will be healed. But God does not always give the gift of faith. This means that sick people and their loved ones should certainly pray for the one who is ill, but in the absence of the gift of faith they must pray, "If it be Thy will." I believe that true faith involves a complete surrender of our life to the will of God, whatever it is, even when God does not choose to heal us. This means we are willing to be healed, or willing to remain afflicted, or willing to die—willing for whatever God wants!

We have the classic example of Job who was afflicted with boils from head to foot. Satan was responsible for this, but it is interesting to note that Satan had to get God's permission before he could even touch Job's possessions, much less Job.

Yet the Book of Job is the result of the situation. What would believers have done down through the centuries without this tremendous account?

Then there is the example of Amy Carmichael of India who spent over fifty years ministering to children. The last twenty years of her life were spent in bed in almost constant pain due to an injury from a severe accident. Yet it was during these years that she did all her writing—poems, devotional books, and accounts of the ministry of the Dohnavur Fellowship. These books continue to minister to thousands throughout the world though she has long since gone to be with the Lord. Had she not been confined to her bed, she would never have had the time to write.

I have attended a number of healing meetings. Some sickened me because of the emotional hysteria present. I have also attended healing meetings where the services were conducted decently and in order. At those, I have witnessed the quiet moving of the Spirit of God in a way that could offend no one. In meetings like that the Spirit used God's servants with special gifts to do His will.

Every sickness, every infirmity, and every wrong thing in our lives can be traced back to original sin. But this does not mean that those of us who experience these difficulties do so because we have been guilty of overt transgressions. Certainly in some cases we do suffer from illnesses that are the direct or indirect result of some evil we have committed. But not always.

One day Jesus encountered a man who was blind from birth. And it was His disciples, not the Pharisees or the Sadduccees who asked this question, "Who sinned, this man or his parents, that he should be born blind?" (John 9:2). Even Jesus' disciples could not conceive of blindness that was not a direct result of sin. Jesus told them, "It was neither that this man sinned, nor his parents; but it was in order that the works of God might be displayed in him" (v. 3).

When we see someone with an infirmity or illness, we should be careful not to assume he is suffering because of his sin. Many illnesses are not the result of the person's sin. Accidents or inherited defects can cause sickness. Neither the sin of a retarded baby or its parents caused its misfortune, though all illness arises from original sin. God never meant for us to get sick and die, but man's rebellion against God in the Garden of Eden changed all that. We must remember, too, that the devil spitefully tries to use every sickness to hinder our fellowship with God, to cause us to have a neurotic sense of guilt, or even to charge God with injustice, lack of love for us, or harshness.

At the same time we have the promise of God that some day all the effects of sin on this creation will be destroyed, including sickness. "And He shall wipe away every tear from their eyes; and there shall no longer be any death; there shall no longer be any mourning, or crying, or pain; the first things have passed away" (Rev. 21:4).

Many Christians do suffer physical, mental, and even spiritual illnesses from time to time. Chronic physical impediments, minds disposed to periods of depression, or weak spirits subject to doubt all cause acute suffering. God's help is available for those impediments, and His sympathy and understanding abound. We can expect the Holy Spirit to be present and to work in our lives. "The Spirit also helpeth our infirmities" (Rom. 8:26 KJV), and through Hebrews 4:16 God promises us help: "Let us therefore draw near with confidence to the throne of grace, that we may receive mercy and may find grace to help in time of need."

In circumstances like these the Holy Spirit takes over. He is called "the divine Paraclete." The Greek word *parakletos* occurs five times in the New Testament. Four times it is translated "helper" (John 14:16, 26; 15:26; 16:7) and once "advocate" (1 John 2:1). It means "one who walks by our side as our counselor, helper, defender, and guide."

The Holy Spirit *does* help us in the midst of our sicknesses, infirmities, and weaknesses. Sometimes these very sicknesses indicate that we are Spirit-filled. Three times the apostle Paul asked God to remove the "thorn" that gave him great difficulty, but God answered, "No." He also said, "My grace is sufficient for you, for power is perfected in weakness" (2 Cor. 12:9). Paul responded quickly, "Most gladly, therefore, I will rather boast about my weaknesses, that the power of Christ may dwell in me" (2 Cor. 12:9). He went even further: "I am well content with weaknesses, with insults, with distresses, with persecutions, with difficulties, for Christ's sake; for when I am weak, then I am strong" (2 Cor. 12:10). Paul, even while being filled with the Holy Spirit, bore a sickness in his body that God allowed him to suffer for His glory.

So if God allows a sickness and refuses healing, we should accept it with gratitude. And we should ask Him to teach us all He wants us to learn through the experience, including how to glorify Him in it.

Paul's experience teaches us a lesson concerning healing in relation to the atonement of our Lord. Matthew says that "He took our infirmities and bore our diseases" (Matt. 8:17 RSV). This is absolutely true. By His death on Calvary we are assured that we shall be delivered from every infirmity and every disease. But God permits some of us to be afflicted with infirmities and diseases now. So we know that deliverance from them was never meant for all God's people, and for all diseases at all times, including today.

There are a growing number of churches that hold occasional healing services. When I inquired about these healing services, it was explained that few of the healings had to do with physical illness—rather they deal with relationships, memories, attitudes, guilt feelings. As a result, marriages have been healed; parents reconciled with children; employers with employees.

To summarize, there is no doubt in my mind that there is a gift of healing—that people are healed in answer to the prayer of faith—and that there are other healings, such as healings of relationships. There is also need for a word of caution. There are many frauds and charlatans in the fields of medicine and faith healing. Again, one must have spiritual discernment.

Miracles

The gift of performing miracles takes its key term, "miracles," from a Greek word meaning "powers" (2 Cor. 12:12). A miracle is an event beyond the power of any known physical law to produce; it is a spiritual occurrence produced by the power of God, a marvel, a wonder. In most versions of the Old Testament the word "miracle" is usually translated "a wonder" or "a mighty work." Versions of the New Testament usually refer to miracles as "signs" (John 2:11) or "signs and wonders" (John 4:48; Acts 5:12; 15:12).

Clearly, the wonders performed by Jesus Christ and the apostles authenticated their claim of authority and gave certitude to their message. And we must remember that people did ask Jesus and the apostles this question, "How do we know that you are what you say you are, and that your words are true?" That was not an improper question. And at strategic moments God again and again manifested Himself to men by miracles so they had outward, confirming evidence that the words they heard from God's servants were true.

One notable case that illustrates this principle has to do with Elijah on Mount Carmel. He was engaged in a terrible battle in which the people of Israel had to decide between God and Baal. Elijah challenged the priests of Baal to set up an altar and lay an animal sacrifice on it. He told the people of Israel they should look for a confirming sign to convince them whether the true God was Baal or the Lord. The priests of Baal cried out in desperation to their god, but nothing happened. Then Elijah poured barrels of water over the animal sacrifice on his altar, and God sent fire from heaven that consumed the sacrifice in spite of the water. This was a miracle!

Paul argues that men could know he was an apostle when he said, "The signs of a true apostle were performed among you with all perseverance, by signs and wonders and miracles" (2 Cor. 12:12). The Holy Spirit gave the gift of performing miracles to the early apostles as an evidence that they were Christ's messengers for a special task: that of ushering in a new era in mankind's history.

However, it has always interested me that many of the great men of both the Old and New Testaments performed no miracles. John the Baptist illustrates this: "And many came to Him; and they were saying, 'While John performed no sign, yet everything John said about this man was true.' And many believed in Him there" (John 10:41, 42). So though John performed no miracles, he exalted the Lord Jesus Christ, whom many then received. Remember that Jesus said of John, "Truly, I say to you, among those born of women there has not arisen anyone greater than John the Baptist" (Matt. 11:11).

Why do we not see the spectacular miracles today that we read about in the Bible? Are few such miracles occurring because our faith is small—or could it be that God does not will the spectacular right now? Could it be that signs and wonders were gifts particularly appropriate to the special circumstances of the early Church? I think so. And today when the gospel is proclaimed on the frontiers of the Christian faith that approximate the first century situation, miracles still sometimes accompany the advance of the gospel. As indicated by both the prophets Hosea and Joel, as we approach the end of the age we may expect miracles to increase.

Yet Jesus, referring to His miracles, told the disciples they would perform "greater works than these" (John 14:12). What could be greater than the works He did: healing the sick, restoring sight to the blind, raising the dead, casting out demons? It has been said, "Jesus did not come to preach the gospel but in order that there might be a gospel to preach."

Because of His death and resurrection we now have a gospel that can provide forgiveness of sins and the transformation of lives. A transformed life is the greatest of all miracles. Every time a person is "born again" by repentance of sin and faith in Jesus Christ, the miracle of regeneration is performed.

This is not to reject the further truth that in some places in the world the Holy Spirit has sovereignly appointed certain people to be workers of miracles. I have just stated that as we approach the end of the age I believe we will see a dramatic recurrence of signs and wonders which will demonstrate the power of God to a skeptical world. Just as the powers of Satan are being unleashed with greater intensity, so I believe God will allow signs and wonders to be performed.

Tongues

A leading minister in the Church of Scotland lay in the Intensive Care Unit of a Glasgow infirmary. He knew that his life hung in the balance—at any minute he might be seeing his Lord face to face. And so, he began talking to Him. As he did, he found himself praying in a language he had never heard before. After confiding this to a friend, he never mentioned it again. He recovered to serve His Lord for several more years.

A frantic young wife and mother, for whom everything had gone wrong one day, sat up in her bed that night literally "fussing at God."

"Have you ever heard of praying in tongues?" she paused to ask my wife when she was recounting the incident. Ruth nodded. "Well, I never had. I'd never heard of it. I'd never asked for it. I didn't even know what was happening. And suddenly it was as if I were orbiting the earth in a spaceship and as I passed over each continent I thought of the Christians there, mentioning the missionaries I knew by name. In this way I circled the entire globe. Then I glanced at the clock, thinking I had been praying at least thirty minutes. To my amazement it was dawn. And I was refreshed. The burden was lifted. The frustration, the anger, the complaining—it was all gone. And I felt as if I'd had a good night's sleep."

A Sunday school class was studying the person and work of the Holy Spirit in a neighborhood where speaking in tongues had become a divisive issue among believers. After one particularly exciting meeting the college Sunday school teacher was asked to speak on the Holy Spirit. One by one the students shared their experience with this phenomenon. The teacher, recalling the class some months later, mentioned three people who stood out in his memory. One, whose testimony had the ring of truth to it, for a few months after his experience became totally preoccupied with tongues, speaking of little else, and doing his best to see that other believers had the same experience. Eventually, however, he leveled off, realizing that the Holy

Spirit has been given to enable us to glorify the Lord Jesus in differing ways. Today he is a uniquely gifted minister of the gospel.

A second class member, who also claimed to speak in tongues, was expelled from his college a few weeks later for open, repeated, and unrepentant immorality.

A third who stands out in the teacher's memory was a recently converted street-fighter from one of our large cities. After the class, he had taken the teacher to one side and confided that he had been in the same meeting where he had recognized the language spoken. When the teacher asked him what language it was, he replied, "The language I used to hear when I assisted my grandmother who was a spirit medium." The teacher told me he thought these cases illustrated three sources for what are called tongues: (1) the Holy Spirit; (2) psychological influence; (3) satanic influence.

While I do not pose as an expert on the subject of tongues, my opinions have come from my study of the Bible and from my experience and conversations with many people. Of one thing I'm certain: neither the Holy Spirit nor any of His gifts were given to divide believers. This does not mean that we ought not have our own opinions about what the Bible teaches on tongues. Or that we should not have local congregations in which prominence is given to tongues as well as those in which tongues are not prominent. But I am certain about one thing: when the gift of tongues is abused and becomes divisive, then something has gone wrong. Sin has come into the body of Christ.

Historical Background

For almost a century speaking in tongues has been given an important role among many Christians and certain churches. For them tongues-speaking is related to the life of the Christian subsequent to conversion.

It is true, however, that thousands of so-called "charismatic" believers have never spoken in tongues. Yet they are accepted as true believers in the Lord Jesus. Thus, among many churches which consider themselves charismatic, speaking in tongues is not regarded as an essential sign of having been born again. They agree that regenerated believers have been baptized into the body of Christ by the Spirit, of which water baptism is an outward sign. At the time of regeneration the Spirit took up His abode in their hearts. But for them the baptism in the Spirit is something that occurs after regeneration.

More recently the neo-Pentecostal or charismatic movement has come into being. Many of these people hold their memberships in mainline denominations and some of them are Roman Catholics. They agree with Pentecostal churches in their emphasis on healing and often accept speaking in tongues as a sign of baptism with the Holy Spirit, an experience occurring subsequent to regeneration. But the old-time Pentecostal churches are bothered because they do not always see a change in life style among the neo-Pentecostals, something they cherish as being intrinsic to the Spirit-anointed life.

No one can escape the fact that the neo-Pentecostal emphasis has brought Protestants and Roman Catholics closer together in some parts of the world, not on the basis of having worked out their theological disagreements on matters like justification by faith, the sacrifice of the Mass, or the infallibility of the Pope, but on the basis of speaking in tongues and baptism with the Holy Spirit. However, I have met many Roman Catholics, like Protestants, who call themselves charismatic but have never spoken in tongues. For them it has been a new discovery of a personal relationship with Christ.

The Biblical Data on Tongues

Speaking in tongues (or "glossolalia," a term formed from the equivalent Greek words) is mentioned in *only two* New Testament books: The Acts of the Apostles and Paul's First Letter to the Corinthians (though it is mentioned in Mark 16:17, which most scholars believe is not in the original manuscripts). The word seems to be used in two different ways. One way is found in connection with the events at Pentecost, when the promised coming of the Holy Spirit occurred. A careful study of that passage in Acts 2 indicates that the "tongues" were known languages which were understood by foreign visitors in Jerusalem. Thus the little band of Christians was given a supernatural ability to speak in other languages.

What happened at Pentecost? The second chapter of Acts

tells us that four things took place which signaled the advent of the new age. First, a sound from heaven like that of a violent wind filled the house. Second, something that looked like tongues of fire sat on each one of the people in the upper room. Third, all of them were filled with the Holy Spirit. Fourth, all of them spoke in tongues as the Spirit gave them the ability to do so. These tongues were languages known to the people from all over the Roman Empire who had come to Jerusalem for Pentecost. Some believe that the miracle took place in the ears of the hearers. Others believe that the apostles were given a supernatural gift of speaking in a foreign language that they did not know. Whatever position we take, a "miracle" took place!

The same basic word for "filled" appears in Acts 4:8 where Peter, "filled with the Holy Spirit" (speaking in tongues is not mentioned), preached his short sermon to the high priest and the rulers of the Jews. The same root word is used in connection with John the Baptist in Luke 1:15 where the Scripture says that "he will be filled with the Holy Spirit, while yet in his mother's womb." However, we have no record that John ever spoke in tongues. In Paul's conversion experience we are told that Ananias came to him "that you may regain your sight, and be filled with the Holy Spirit" (Acts 9:17). His sight then returned, he was baptized, and "immediately he began to proclaim Jesus in the synagogues, saying, 'He is the Son of God' " (Acts 9:20). Again, speaking in tongues is not mentioned.

Acts 19 recounts the story of Paul at Ephesus. He found some believers there who had heard nothing about the Spirit's coming. We are then told that "when Paul had laid his hands upon them, the Holy Spirit came on them, and they began speaking with tongues and prophesying" (Acts 19:6). Here the Scripture does not say they were filled with the Spirit. At any rate they spoke with tongues and prophesied, though there were no tongues of fire nor rushing mighty wind as at Pentecost. Moreover, the account in Acts 19 does not say whether the tongues spoken were languages the people there understood nor does it say interpreters were present. At least we can assume they spoke in tongues used somewhere in the world.

When I go to a foreign country, I speak in English. This is an unknown tongue to the majority of my listeners. For example, in northeast India I spoke to many thousands at each meeting;

seventeen separate interpreters were used to translate my message into seventeen different dialects so that the people could understand my "unknown tongue." In my judgment this is analogous to what happened at Pentecost, except there it was a divine miracle. Either a given speaker spoke in a language certain listeners knew, or the Holy Spirit interpreted what was being said to each listener in his own language, the miracle then being in his capacity to understand.

"Unknown" Tongues in 1 Corinthians

In 1 Corinthians speaking in tongues appears to be something quite different from the occurrences in the Acts of the Apostles, although the same Greek word is used in Acts and 1 Corinthians to speak of "tongues."

At Pentecost the disciples spoke in tongues known to the people visiting Jerusalem. The Spirit-empowered speakers did not know these languages, but their listeners did. However, in 1 Corinthians the listeners did not hear a language they knew, so interpreters were required. The question is whether or not the tongues in 1 Corinthians were known languages. Some Bible students suggest they were, while others say they were simply some form of ecstatic utterance unrelated to any known human language. Personally, I lean toward the latter position. Actually, however, it probably makes little difference in our understanding of the passage, although some point out that if the Corinthian gift of tongues was a known language, then it is unrelated to much of what is labeled as "tongues" today. The fact that "interpretation" is seen as a spiritual gift makes me believe that the gift of tongues mentioned in 1 Corinthians was not a known language which might be understood by someone who naturally spoke that language.

First Corinthians 13 has its own puzzle. Paul mentions tongues of men and of angels. Now it should be apparent that angelic tongues are not known to any of us, yet the implication is there that some might speak in such tongues. However, in Corinthians Paul speaks of tongues as a gift that comes from the Holy Spirit, so He might give someone the ability to speak an angelic tongue. Of course, Paul makes it quite plain that not everyone is given this particular gift. It is for these reasons that

I have difficulty linking the filling of the Holy Spirit to a second baptism and to a necessary accompanying sign, speaking in tongues. I cannot see solid Scriptural proof for the position that tongues as a sign is given to all who are baptized with the Spirit while tongues as a gift is given only to some.

Furthermore, I sometimes think the modern usage of the term "charismatic" may be incorrect. In 1 Corinthians, the Greek word for gifts God gives believers is *charismata*. No one can get such a gift by himself. According to Paul, the gifts, as we shall see in a moment, come from the sovereign operation of the Spirit of God "distributing to each one individually just as He wills" (1 Cor. 12:11). Paul says, "For by one Spirit we [for that is what the Greek says] were all baptized into one body" (1 Cor. 12:13). But in addition to this the Spirit distributes gifts to the various members of the body. Thus, every believer gets some gift. And *every* believer is therefore a charismatic!

Moreover, Paul does not indicate that any one gift belongs to every believer. He says only that each receives "some" gift. He does tell the Corinthians to "covet" (which Cruden's Concordance defines as "to earnestly desire") the best gifts, however. And in 1 Corinthians 13 he insists that any gift unaccompanied by love is worthless.

Observations on the Gift of Tongues

Concerning the gift of tongues as mentioned in 1 Corinthians 12:30 and the lengthy discourse on the subject in 1 Corinthians 14, the following points must be noted:

First, there is a definite gift of tongues apparently different from the one expressed at Pentecost because no interpretation was required there. And other signs accompanied it: the tongues as of fire and the violent rushing wind. These are nowhere mentioned in connection with the gifts of the Spirit in 1 Corinthians.

Although there is honest disagreement among Christians about the validity of tongues today, I personally cannot find any biblical justification for saying the gift of tongues was meant exclusively for New Testament times. At the same time, it easily becomes a misunderstood and even divisive issue; the fact that Paul found it necessary to deal with it at such length in 1 Corinthians 12–14 is testimony to this. (While stressing it was the least of the gifts, Paul also devoted the most space to discussing it of any of the gifts.) Therefore, when it does occur today it must be surrounded very carefully with the biblical safeguards Paul sets forth.

Also, while the gift of tongues may occur today as a valid spiritual gift, this does not mean every manifestation of tongues is according to the will of God and should be approved uncritically by us.

Second, it should be stressed, as is clearly indicated in 1 Corinthians 12–14, that tongues is a gift of the Holy Spirit, not a fruit of the Spirit. As we shall see, the fruit of the Spirit outlined in Galatians 5:22, 23 should mark every Christian who is walking in the Spirit. On the other hand, gifts are distributed among believers by the sovereign will of God. Therefore, it is a gift that some may have but not others. I simply cannot find any biblical reason for saying that tongues is a gift God desires to give to all believers. Some may be given the gift, while many others will not be given it. It would be wrong for someone who has not been given the gift of tongues to feel he is somehow a "second-rate" Christian, or earnestly covet this gift if God has not seen fit to give it to him. It would be equally wrong for someone who has this gift to try to compel others to have it, or to teach that everyone must experience it.

Third, the gift of tongues mentioned in 1 Corinthians 12–14 is clearly one of the less important gifts of the Spirit—in fact, it appears to be the least important. The reason for this is that it often does not give any spiritual benefit to other believers. The other gifts clearly are exercised to build up and strengthen the body of Christ, however. While tongues may do this in a public worship service (if there is an interpreter present), the other gifts are more directly involved in the mutual strengthening of believers.

This is why the gift of tongues should not be thought of as the high point of Christian maturity. In fact, millions of spiritually mature Christians have never spoken in tongues, and many who have spoken in tongues are not spiritually mature.

Fourth, the gift of tongues is not necessarily a sign of the baptism of the believer by the Holy Spirit into the body of Christ. That is especially true in 1 Corinthians, because these people had already been incorporated once-for-all into the body of Christ. Nowhere in the Bible do I find it said that the gift of tongues is a necessary evidence of being baptized with the Holy Spirit into Christ's body, the Church. Even in Acts where speaking in tongues is mentioned there is no indication it was necessary evidence that one had been baptized with the Holy Spirit.

In like manner the gift of tongues is not necessarily to be equated with being filled with the Spirit. We may be Spirit-filled and never speak in tongues. The filling of the Spirit may result in many different experiences in our lives, of which tongues on occasion may be only one evidence. Some of the most Spirit-filled Christians I have ever known had never experienced the gift of tongues, but they were no less filled with the Spirit.

Fifth, both the Bible and experience warn us that the gift of tongues may easily be abused and in fact may be dangerous. For example, the gift of tongues has often led to spiritual pride. Perhaps someone experiences the gift of tongues and immediately believes he is better or more spiritual than other believers who have not been given this gift. Such an attitude is directly contrary to the proper attitude of a Spirit-filled believer.

Other dangers should be mentioned. For example (as has been indicated), tongues may easily lead to divisiveness. Often this happens because of pride or because a person with the gift of tongues tries to force it on others. On the other hand, it is possible for some people to be proud because they don't speak in tongues, and that is equally wrong!

One of the greatest dangers in this matter of tongues is imbalance. That is, sometimes a person who has experienced this gift will become almost completely absorbed or preoccupied with tongues. The other gifts of the Spirit are forgotten (except, perhaps, the other sign gifts which are also spectacular or impressive), and there is often little interest in holy living and the fruit of the Spirit. Some who insist on making it their central focus to call others to seek this gift, fail to show any interest in evangelism, an emphasis the Spirit wants to give. I am thinking, for instance, of a small group of tongues-speaking people who rarely win other souls to Christ. They wait until someone else does the soul-winning, and then approach the new convert in an effort to persuade him that he must speak in tongues to grow in the Lord.

Still another danger is that some would see an experience of speaking in tongues as a short-cut to spiritual power and maturity. A member of my staff was in seminary with a young man who was going to various meetings constantly hoping to get the gift of tongues. When asked why he wanted this gift, he said it was because he felt a deep lack of power and fellowship with God, and he thought this would give him both spiritual power and a sense of God's presence. When asked if he prayed with any frequency, or read his Bible regularly, or spent much time in fellowship with other believers, he admitted he did not do any of these. God had given him the means of spiritual growth—prayer, the Bible, fellowship—but he was unwilling to be disciplined enough to make use of them. For him, tongues would be a short-cut to spiritual maturity. It was probably no accident that he dropped out of seminary shortly after this and gave up his plans to become a minister.

One final danger might be mentioned, and that is the possibility that the gift may sometimes be counterfeited. This may be due to deliberate deception, or possibly because the "gift" sometimes has its sources not in God but in our psychological make-up. It also may be the result of demonic activity.

Perhaps it should be noted that the ancient Greek oracle of Delphi spoke what might be called "tongues," as did the priests and priestesses at the great temple above Corinth. Dr. Akbar Abdul-Haqq tells me it is not an uncommon phenomenon in India among non-Christian religions today.

Also, there are certain well-substantiated instances of demon-possessed people given the ability to speak in certain known languages with which they were totally unfamiliar when in their right minds. The Bible records how Pharaoh's magicians were able to duplicate God's miracles up to a certain point.

No wonder John says, "Do not believe every spirit, but test the spirits to see whether they are from God" (1 John 4:1). We have already gone into this in the discussion of the gift of discernment in chapter 12.

Even Christians have counterfeited this gift. One girl who attended a charismatic meeting wanted desperately to receive the gift of tongues as had so many of her friends. So, having been raised in another country, she prayed in that native language, pretending it was the operation of a spiritual gift. The others thought she had received the gift of tongues. As a result, in this little circle where speaking in tongues was so important, she was finally accepted!

No experience—no matter how much it may mean to us, or how impressive it may seem to be—must take the place of God's Word in our lives. Our experiences must always be judged in light of the Bible; we must not judge the Bible by our experiences. God the Holy Spirit has given us the Bible, and no gift which is truly from the Holy Spirit will contradict the Bible.

Sixth, what about the private, devotional use of tongues as a means of praising God and experiencing His fellowship? A number of friends have told me that after they had prayed for a long period of time, they suddenly found themselves speaking in an unknown language. For the most part they have kept it private and have not said everyone else must have the same experience. They have not said that all Christians must speak in tongues as a sign of spiritual maturity. Everyone knew that Corrie ten Boom had spoken in tongues, but she never talked about it and never discussed it. She often rebuked those who did talk about it excessively.

Actually, the Bible has little to say about this. The private use of tongues is implied by Paul when he remarks that "I speak in tongues more than you all; however, in the church I desire to speak five words with my mind, that I may instruct others also, rather than ten thousand words in a tongue" (1 Cor. 14:18, 19). Some have suggested that Paul's command to "pray at all times in the Spirit" (Eph. 6:18) involves praying in tongues, but the emphasis on specific prayer requests (in which the mind is clearly at work concentrating on the subjects of the prayer) in this passage would indicate this is not what is implied by Paul.

In conclusion, I must say I cannot help but be impressed by the wide differences of opinion about tongues on the part of the people who would call themselves charismatic. Many feel it is utterly wrong to say that tongues are essential to being baptized or filled with the Holy Spirit. A large group of evangelicals do not even regard tongues as a relevant gift of the Spirit today, just as the office of the apostolate is no longer a relevant gift.

I know of one Bible conference ministry which has been greatly used of God, but it would not knowingly invite to its platform anyone, however gifted and acceptable he might be in evangelical circles, who professed to speak in tongues. Others may disagree with this policy, but the leaders of this ministry are sincere in their convictions and should be respected for their views.

On the other hand, many evangelicals who do not themselves profess to speak in tongues now adopt an entirely neutral stance. They have seen the charismatic movement penetrate deeply into all the denominations with great blessing and renewal. So they are prepared to recognize that all the supernatural gifts of 1 Corinthians 12 are relevant today and therefore to be accepted as gifts of the Spirit.

In fairness to some of my charismatic friends I must add that even though I disagree with them on the issue of the "baptism with the Spirit" as accompanied by the sign of tongues, yet I do know and teach the need for believers to be filled with the Spirit. Setting aside the issue of tongues as the necessary sign, we may be talking about a phase of the same experience. In my judgment the Bible says that any believer can enjoy the filling of the Holy Spirit and know His power even though he or she has not had any sign such as speaking in tongues. On the occasion of a particular infilling, tongues may be a sign God gives some, but I do not find that it is a sign for all. I do think it is important, though, for each of us to hold our opinion without rancor and without breaking our bonds of fellowship in Jesus Christ. We worship the same Lord, and for this we are grateful.

In 1 Corinthians 14 Paul certainly says that prophesying is greater than speaking in tongues. At the same time he says, "Do not forbid to speak in tongues" (1 Cor. 14:39). Paul apparently spoke in many different tongues, but he did not emphasize this unduly. We must be careful not to put the Holy Spirit into a position where He must work our way. The Holy Spirit is sovereign; He gives His gifts as He wills! Peter Wagner says: "It must be remembered that the body of Christ is universal, with many local manifestations. Spiritual gifts are given to the body universal, and therefore certain ones may or may not be found in any particular local part of the body. This explains why, for example, a local church or even an entire denomination may not have been given the gift of tongues, while other parts of the body might have it."[1]

To summarize. *First,* there is a real, as contrasted with a counterfeit, gift of tongues. Many of those who have been given this gift have been transformed spiritually—some temporarily and some permanently!

Second, God uses tongues at certain times, in certain places, especially on the frontiers of the Christian mission, to further the kingdom of God and to edify believers.

Third, many are convinced that we may be living in what Scripture calls "the latter days." Both Joel and Hosea prophesy that in those days great manifestations of the Spirit and many of the sign gifts will reappear. We may be living in such a period of history. Certainly we cannot blind ourselves to the fact that many of the sign gifts which vindicate the authenticity of the gospel are reappearing at this hour.

Many years ago in a class discussion at the Florida Bible Institute a teacher said something on the subject of tongues that has stayed with me. He advised his students to "seek not; forbid not."

Indeed, tongues *is* a gift of the Spirit. Today there are Presbyterians, Baptists, Anglicans, Lutherans, and Methodists, as well as Pentecostals, who speak or have spoken in tongues—or who have not, and do not expect to.

But if tongues is the gift of the Holy Spirit, it cannot be divisive in itself. When those who speak in tongues misuse it so that it becomes divisive, it indicates a lack of love. And those who forbid it do the Church a disservice because they appear to contradict the teaching of the apostle Paul. Those believers who do speak in tongues and those who do not should love each other and work for the greater glory of God in the evangelization of the world, remembering one thing: those who do speak in tongues and those who do not *will* live with each other in the New Jerusalem.

Is this a gift God has seen fit to give you? Don't let it be a source of pride or preoccupation. Become grounded in the whole Word of God. And above all, learn what it means to love others, including believers who may not agree with your emphasis.

Is this a gift you do not have? Don't let it preoccupy you either, and don't let it be a source of division between you and other believers if at all possible. There may be other believers who have a different emphasis from you, but they are still your brothers and sisters in Christ.

Above all, we are called to "walk by the Spirit, and you will not carry out the desire of the flesh" (Gal. 5:16).

The sign gifts—healings, miracles, and tongues—probably attracted as much attention in the first century as they do today. They also sometimes caused confusion and abuses just as they do today. Nevertheless, God the Holy Spirit gave them to some within the Church, to be used for His glory. They must never be exploited for selfish reasons, nor must they ever become sources of either division or pride. We are not to become preoccupied or obsessed with them, and most of all whenever gifts of this nature are given, they must be used strictly in accordance with the principles God has set forth in the Bible. This should also contribute to the unity of the Spirit. And if God chooses to give these gifts to some today, we should always pray that they will be used "for the common good" (1 Cor. 12:7) and the furtherance of the kingdom of God.

14. The Fruit of the Spirit

A handful of men had been waiting at a dock on the Thames since five o'clock that bitter cold winter morning. Along with scores of others, they had been selected to unload a docked freighter. This was done by balancing a wheelbarrow on planks that stretched from the dock to a barge and from the barge to the freighter. Among the working men, unknown to them, was a clergyman. Deeply concerned for the men of that area, he had decided that the only way he could communicate with them was to live and work among them. Dressed like them, he denied himself even a cup of hot tea before leaving his room, and went without an overcoat. He knew the men who would be standing in line for jobs along the docks that day would not have had the comfort of a cup of tea, and would, for the most part, be inadequately clothed.

In the days before he landed a job, he learned what it was to be treated as a stranger. He learned what it was to stand all day in the cold and the fog, only to be told there were no jobs available. These men would have to go back to inadequate lodgings and face hungry families without so much as a piece of bread for them.

But this day he had been fortunate and was hired. On his twelfth trip, as he was crossing the plank with his loaded wheelbarrow, it began to jiggle so that he lost his footing and fell into the Thames, amid roars of laughter on all sides.

Fighting to control his temper, he managed finally to struggle to his feet, grinning as he did so. One of the workmen (the cul-

180

prit who had jiggled the plank) had shouted, "Man overboard," and stood there laughing. As he watched the unrecognized clergyman struggling good-naturedly in the mud, some better impulse seemed to move him to drop some empty boxes into the slush and jump down to help the man out. His would-be rescuer's first remark justified the clergyman's attitude which the Holy Spirit had prompted.

"You took that all right," his former tormenter said as he helped the clergyman to clamber onto the boxes. He did not have the accent of a cockney, for he was not the usual docker.

"You haven't been long at this game," the clergyman remarked.

"Neither have you," replied his tormenter-turned-rescuer. The clergyman agreed, then invited the man to accompany him to his rooming house.

As they talked, the clergyman learned to his amazement that the man had once been a highly successful physician, but due to heavy drink he had lost a thriving practice and his lovely wife and family. The outcome of the story was that the clergyman was able to lead this man to Christ and eventually see him reunited with his family.

Perhaps this is what the fruit of the Spirit is all about. If life were always kind to us, if people were always pleasant and courteous, if we never had headaches, never knew what it was to be tired or under terrific pressure, the fruit of the Spirit might go unnoticed.

But life is not always like that. It is in the midst of difficulties and hardships that we especially need the fruit of the Spirit, and it is in such times that God may especially work through us to touch other people for Christ. As we bear the fruit of the Spirit in our lives, others will see in us "the family likeness of his Son" (Rom. 8:29, Phillips) and be attracted to the Savior.

It is no accident that the Scriptures call the Third Person of the Trinity the *Holy* Spirit. One of the main functions of the Holy Spirit is to impart the holiness of God to us. He does this as He develops within us a Christlike character—a character marked by the fruit of the Spirit. God's purpose is that we would "become mature, attaining the full measure of perfection found in Christ" (Eph. 4:13, NIV).

Fruit: God's Expectation

God the Holy Spirit uses the word *fruit* frequently in Scripture to denote what He expects of His people in the way of character. We have noted in the chapters on the gifts of the Holy Spirit that believers are given various gifts. I may have a gift someone else does not have, while another person may have been given gifts I do not have. However, when we come to the Bible's teaching on the fruit of the Spirit, we find there is a basic difference between the *gifts* of the Spirit and the *fruit* of the Spirit.

Unlike the gifts of the Spirit, *the fruit of the Spirit is not divided among believers.* Instead, *all* Christians should be marked by *all* the fruit of the Spirit. The fruit of the Spirit is God's expectation in our lives. This is clearly seen in many passages of Scripture. In Matthew 13 Jesus told the familiar parable of the seed and the sower. He likens the work of anyone who declares the Word of God—a pastor, teacher, evangelist or any other Christian—to a man sowing seed. Some seed falls by the wayside and is eaten by the birds; some falls on rocky ground and withers in the sun; still other seed begins to grow but is choked by thorns. The fourth group of seeds falls into good soil, takes root, and brings forth fruit abundantly. So you and I are to bear fruit, as the Word of God begins to work in our lives in the power of the Spirit.

It is interesting that the Bible talks of the *fruit* of the Spirit rather than *fruits*. A tree may bear many apples, but all come from the same tree. In the same way, the Holy Spirit is the source of all fruit in our lives.

Put in simplest terms, the Bible tells us we need the Spirit to bring fruit into our lives because we cannot produce godliness apart from the Spirit. In our own selves we are filled with all kinds of self-centered and self-seeking desires which are opposed to God's will for our lives. In other words, two things need to happen in our lives. *First,* the sin in our lives needs to be thrust out. *Second,* the Holy Spirit needs to come in and fill our lives, producing the fruit of the Spirit. *"Put to death,* therefore, whatever belongs to your earthly nature: . . . as God's chosen people, holy and dearly loved, *clothe yourselves* with compassion, kindness, humility, gentleness and patience" (Col. 3:5, 12 NIV, italics mine).

Let me use an illustration. Many people have a fence around their home with a gate for entering and leaving. Remember, a gate can be used for two purposes: it can be opened to let people in, or it can be shut to keep people out.

Spiritually our lives are like this gate. Inside our lives are all sorts of things that are wrong and unpleasing to God. We need to let these things out, and allow the Holy Spirit to come in and control the very center of our lives. But we do not have the power even to open the gate. Only the Holy Spirit can do that, and when He does—as we yield to Him and look to Him for His fullness— He not only comes in but He helps us thrust out the evil things in our lives. He controls the gate, and as He purges the heart of its wickedness He can bring in new attitudes, new motivations, new devotion and love. He also strengthens the door with bars that keep out evil. So the works of the flesh depart and the fruit of the Spirit comes in. The Scripture says that the Holy Spirit wants us to have fruit—and then more fruit, and even much fruit.

In his book, *The Fruit of the Spirit,* Manford George Gutzke compares the fruit of the Spirit to light: "All the colors of the rainbow are in every beam of sunlight. They all are there at any one time. They may not always come into vision, but they are all present. It is not necessary to think of them as being so many separate colors. Just as these colors of the rainbow are present in light, so these traits of personal conduct are in the working of the Holy Spirit."[1]

How the Fruit Grows

How does the Holy Spirit work in our lives to produce the fruit of the Spirit? There are two passages of Scripture especially helpful in answering this question.

The first passage is Psalm 1, which compares the godly man to a tree planted by a river: "But his delight is in the law of the Lord, and in His law he meditates day and night. And he will be like a tree firmly planted by streams of water, which yields its fruit in its season, and its leaf does not wither; and in whatever he does, he prospers" (Ps. 1:2,3). Here the bearing of spiritual fruit is clearly related to the place the Word of God has in our lives. (Notice, it does not just say read, but meditate.) As we read and meditate on the Bible, the Holy Spirit—who, we remember, inspired the Bible—convicts us of sin which needs to be purged and directs us to God's standard for our lives. Apart from the Word of God there will be no lasting spiritual growth or fruit-bearing in our lives.

The second passage is found in John 15, where Jesus compares our relationship to Him to the branches of a vine. "Abide in Me, and I in you. As the branch cannot bear fruit of itself, unless it abides in the vine, so neither can you, unless you abide in Me. I am the vine, you are the branches; he who abides in Me, and I in him, he bears much fruit; for apart from Me you can do nothing" (John 15:4,5).

There are many wonderful truths in this passage, but there are several points we should especially notice. First, this is a command to every believer: "Abide in Me." By that is meant we are to have the closest, most intimate relationship with Christ, with nothing coming between us. This is one reason why the disciplines of prayer, Bible study, and fellowship with other believers are so important.

Also, this tells us that we can *only* bear spiritual fruit if we abide in Christ: "Apart from me you can do nothing." It may be possible for us to make use of the *gifts* of the Spirit even when we are out of fellowship with the Lord. But we cannot display the *fruit* of the Spirit all the time when our fellowship with Christ has been interrupted by sin. We can see, then, how crucial it is to be filled with the Spirit, and we are being filled as we abide in Christ, the vine. The secret of abiding is obedience. As we, through obedient living, abide in Christ, the life of Christ (like the life-giving sap in a vine) flows into us, producing fruit to the glory of the Father and the nourishment and blessing of others.

I believe there is something about this relationship which we cannot fully understand. If we were to ask a branch on a grapevine, "How do you grow such luscious fruit?" the branch would probably reply, "I don't know. I don't grow any of it; I just bear it. Cut me off from this vine and I will wither away and become useless." Without the vine the branch can do nothing. So it is with our lives. As long as I strain and work to produce the fruit of the Spirit from within myself, I will end up fruitless and frustrated. But as I abide in Christ—as I maintain a close, obedient, dependent relationship with Him—God the Holy Spirit works in my life, creating in me the fruit of the Spirit. That does not mean we instantly become mature, bearing all the fruit of the Spirit fully and immediately. The fruit on a fruit tree takes time to mature, and pruning may be necessary before fruit is produced in quantity. So it may be with us.

My wife and I enjoy the beautiful trees surrounding our house in North Carolina. In the autumn most leaves drop off and are blown away, but thousands of the old dead leaves cling to the branches even in March and April. However, when the sap in the trees begins to flow, the new leaves form—and life and power pulsate and surge through every living branch. Then all of the old dry leaves fall off, unnoticed. What an analogy for the Christian! "Old things have passed away; behold, new things have come" (2 Cor. 5:17).

Furthermore, each summer we cut down some of the trees that obstruct the view or keep out the sunlight. And some have been badly damaged during the winter storms. Similarly, we have trees in our lives to which the axe must be laid—trees which either lie rotting on the ground or produce only ugly sights. Jesus said, "Every plant which My heavenly Father did not plant shall be rooted up" (Matt. 15:13). We have a few fruit trees on our property. We take special care of those with the best fruit—pruning, feeding, and spraying at proper times. A good tree brings forth good fruit and should be kept. But whether a tree is worth keeping or cutting down depends on the distinction Jesus made. He said, "You will know them by their fruits" (Matt. 7:20 RSV).

Then there are a few grapevines. Some years we pick only a small crop of substandard grapes for personal use. But we do not cut the vines down. Rather, we prune them carefully. Then the next year the vines bring forth more and better fruit. Similarly, as the pruning process goes on in our lives under the guidance of the Holy Spirit, the vines, speaking spiritually, are useful for the production of more spiritual fruit.

Remember, the picture in John 15 is of the Lord Jesus as the vine, we as the branches, and God as the husbandman, or gardener.

Verse three says, "You are already clean because of the word which I have spoken to you," or as J. B. Phillips translates it, "Now, you have already been pruned by my words." There is no better way for the child of God to be pruned than through studying and applying the Bible to his own heart and situation. Somehow God can correct us, tell us where we have fallen short and gone astray, without once discouraging us.

In the Acts of the Apostles we read of Apollos whose earnestness, love, and great gift of oratory appealed to the hearts of Priscilla and Aquila. However, he was immature and unprepared to lead others into the deeper Christian life. He had progressed barely beyond the baptism of John. But this godly couple, instead of laughing at his ignorance or decrying his lack of understanding of true biblical orthodoxy, took him into their home and in love expounded the way of the Lord more perfectly to him (Acts 18:26). Then he began to use his great gifts for the glory of God and the winning of souls. He left an indelible impression on the early Church and helped promote the kingdom of God in the first century.

Are you abiding in Christ? This is the primary condition God sets down for us before we can really bear the fruit of the Spirit. Is there any unconfessed sin in your life which is keeping you from a close walk with Christ? Is there any lack of discipline? Is there any broken relationship with another person which needs healing? Whatever the cause may be, bring it to Christ in confession and repentance. And then learn what it means each day to "Abide in Me."

15. The Fruit of the Spirit: Love, Joy, Peace

Of all the passages in the Bible which sketch the character of Christ and the fruit which the Spirit brings to our lives, none is more compact and challenging than Galatians 5:22, 23. "But the fruit of the Spirit is love, joy, peace, patience, kindness, goodness, faithfulness, gentleness, self-control." In the next three chapters we will examine in detail the meaning of each of these. For purposes of study, we can divide these nine words into three "clusters" of fruit. Love, joy, and peace make up the first cluster. They especially speak of our Godward relationship. The second "cluster"—patience, kindness, and goodness—especially are seen in our manward relationship, i.e. our relationship with other people. The third "cluster" of faithfulness, gentleness, and self-control are especially seen in our inward relationship—the attitudes and actions of the inner self.

At the same time, of course, these three "clusters" are all related to each other, and *all* should characterize our lives. And all *will* characterize our lives when we abide in Christ and allow the Holy Spirit to do His work in us.

The Fruit of the Spirit: Love

There should be no more distinctive mark of the Christian than love. "By this all men will know that you are My disciples, if you have love for one another" (John 13:35). "We know that we have passed out of death into life, because we love the brethren" (1 John 3:14). "Owe nothing to anyone except to love one another; for he who loves his neighbor has fulfilled the law" (Rom. 13:8).

No matter how else we may bear our testimony for the Lord Jesus Christ, the absence of love nullifies it all. Love is greater than anything we can say, or anything we can possess, or anything we can give. "If I speak with the tongues of men and of angels, but do not have love, I have become a noisy gong or a clanging cymbal. And if I have the gift of prophecy, and know all mysteries and all knowledge; and if I have all faith, so as to remove mountains, but do not have love, I am nothing. And if I give all my possessions to feed the poor, and if I deliver my body to be burned, but do not have love, it profits me nothing" (1 Cor. 13:1–3).

The greatest chapter on love in the Bible is 1 Corinthians 13. Its description of love should be written in letters of gold on every Christian heart. If any chapter of the Bible should be memorized besides John 3, it is 1 Corinthians 13. When we reflect on the meaning of love, we see that it is to the heart what the summer is to the farmer's year. It brings to harvest all the loveliest flowers of the soul. Indeed, it is the loveliest flower in the garden of God's grace. If love does not characterize our lives, they are empty. Peter said, "Above all, keep fervent in your love for one another, because love covers a multitude of sins" (1 Peter 4:8).

In his little book, *The Four Loves,* C. S. Lewis discusses the different Greek words translated "love" in English. When Scripture describes God's love for us and the love God wants us to have, it often uses the Greek word *agape* (pronounced ah-*gah*-pay). *Agape* love is found everywhere in the New Testament. When Jesus said, "Love your enemies," Matthew in his Gospel used the word *agape*. When Jesus said we were to love one another, John used the word *agape*. When Jesus said, "Thou shalt love thy neighbor," Mark used the word *agape*. When the Scripture says, "God is love," it uses the word *agape*. The New Bible Dictionary defines *agape* love in Greek as "that highest and noblest form of love which sees something infinitely precious in its object."[1]

God's greatest demonstration of *agape* love was at the cross where He sent His Son Jesus Christ to die for our sins. Since we are to love as God does, believers should have *agape* love. But we do not have it naturally, nor can we develop it, for the works of the flesh cannot produce it; it must be supernaturally given to us by the Holy Spirit. He does this as we yield ourselves to the will of God.

We should be clear about one thing concerning *agape* love. All too often today love is seen only as an emotion or feeling. Certainly there is emotion involved in love, whether it is love for others or love for God. But love is more than an emotion. Love is not a feeling—love is doing. True love is love which *acts*. That is the way God loves us: "For God so loved the world, that He *gave* His only begotten Son" (John 3:16, italics mine). "Little children, let us not love with word or with tongue, but in deed and truth" (1 John 3:18).

Love is, therefore, an act of the will—and that is why our wills must first be yielded to Christ before we will begin to bear the fruit of love. Bishop Stephen Neill has defined love as "a steady direction of the will toward another's lasting good."[2] He points out that much human love is really selfish in nature, while *agape* love involves self-giving. As Neill says:

"The first love [human love] says, 'I wish to make my own something that another has, and which it is in his power to give me.'

"The second love [God's love] says, 'I wish to give to this other, because I love him.'

"The first love wishes to make itself richer by receiving a gift which some other can give.

"The second love wishes to make another richer by giving all that it has.

"The first love is a matter of feeling and desire. This love comes and goes as it will; we cannot call it into being by any effort of our own.

"The second love is much more a matter of the will, since to give or not to give is largely within our power."[3]

We are to love as the Good Samaritan loved (Luke 10: 25–38), which is nothing less than love finding its best demonstration in action. This is a love which reaches out to all—wives, husbands, children, neighbors, and even people we have never met on the other side of the world. It will include those who are easy to love, because they are like us, and those who are hard to love because they are so different. It will even extend to people who have harmed us or brought sorrow to us.

A young wife and mother whose husband had become unfaithful and left her to live with another woman was bitter and full of resentment. However, as she began to think about the love of Christ for us she found a new love growing in her for others—including the woman who had taken her husband. At Christmas time she sent the other woman one red rose with a note: "Because of Christ's love for me and through me, I can love you!" This is *agape* love, the fruit of the Spirit.

The command to love is not an option; we are to love whether we feel like it or not. Indeed, we may say that love for others is the first sign that we have been born again and that the Holy Spirit is at work in our lives.

Certainly above all, love should be the outstanding mark among believers in every local congregation. Dr. Sherwood Wirt has written: "I have learned there is no point in talking about strong churches and weak churches, big churches and little churches, warm churches and cold churches. Such categories are unrealistic and beside the point. There is only a loving church or an unloving church."[4]

It can be so easy at times to say we love people, and be completely honest and sincere in our expression. But so often we don't see the lonely person in the crowd, or the sick or destitute man or woman whose only hope of escape may be the love we can give through Christ. The love God would have us show reaches down to each person.

A friend of ours is a well-known singing star. I have noticed that when he enters a room full of people he does not look around to find the people he knows. He looks for the little guy, unknown, uneasy, out of place, and he walks right over, hand out, his rugged face alight with a kindly smile as he introduces himself, "Hello, I'm . . . ."

As a young boy growing up in Boston a dear friend of mine of many years, Allan Emery, had an experience which made a deep impression upon him. His father received a call saying a well-known Christian had been found at a certain place drunk on the sidewalk. Immediately his father sent his chauffered limousine to pick the man up, while his mother prepared the best guest room. My friend watched wide-eyed, as the beautiful coverlets were turned down on the exquisite old four-poster bed, revealing the monogrammed sheets.

"But, mother," he protested, "he's drunk. He might even get sick."

"I know," his mother replied kindly, "but this man has slipped and fallen. When he comes to, he will be so ashamed. He will need all the loving encouragement we can give him."

It was a lesson the son never forgot.

Jesus looked at the multitudes of people and was moved with compassion for each of them. He loved as no human is able to love. His love engulfed the whole world, the whole human race, from time's beginning to end. His love knew no bounds, no limit, and no one was excluded. From the lowliest beggar to the greatest monarch, from the deepest sinner to the purest saint—His love embraced them *all*. Nothing but the Spirit of God working in our lives can produce such fruit, and it will be evident in our public as well as private lives.

The Fruit of the Spirit: Joy

Returning from his young son's grave in China, my father-in-law wrote to his mother in Virginia, "There are tears in our eyes, but joy in our hearts." The joy which the Spirit brings to our lives lifts us above circumstances. Joy can be ours, even in the midst of the most trying situations.

The Greek word for joy is used repeatedly in the New Testament to denote joy from a spiritual source such as "the joy of the Holy Spirit" (1 Thess. 1:6). The Old Testament likewise uses phrases like "the joy of the Lord" (Neh. 8:10) to point to God as the source.

Just before Calvary our Lord met with His disciples in the Upper Room. He told them He had spoken as He did "that My joy may be in you, and that your joy may be made full" (John 15:11). Bishop Stephen Neill has remarked: "It was because they were a joyful people that the early Christians were able to conquer the world."[5]

Today's world is joyless, full of shadows, disillusionment, and fear. Freedom is rapidly disappearing from the face of the earth. Along with the loss of freedom, a great many of the superficial joys and pleasures of life are also disappearing, but this need not alarm us. The Scriptures teach that our spiritual joy is not dependent on circumstances. The world's system fails to tap the *source* of joy. God, by His Spirit, directs His joy to our bleak, problem-riddled lives, making it possible for us to be filled with joy regardless of our circumstances.

America's Declaration of Independence speaks of "the pursuit of happiness," but nowhere in the Bible are we told to pursue this. Happiness is elusive, and we don't find it by seeking it. It comes when outward conditions are favorable, but joy goes much deeper. Joy is also different from pleasures. Pleasures are momentary, but joy is deep and abiding despite the worst circumstances of life.

Not only are we given the source of joy which is the person of Christ, but we are assured that it is constantly available to the Christian, no matter what the circumstances.

I once visited Dohnavur in South India where Amy Carmichael had lived for fifty years, caring for hundreds of girls originally dedicated to temple service. As I said earlier, she was bedridden for the last twenty years of her life, during which time she wrote many books that have blessed millions. Joy filled her sick room so that everyone who visited her came away praising God. In her book *Gold by Moonlight* she said, "Where the things of God are concerned, acceptance always means the happy choice of mind and heart of that which He appoints, because (for the present) it is His good and acceptable and perfect will."[6]

Even after her death, when I visited the room where she had served the Lord for twenty years, writing from her bed, I was asked by her former nurse to lead in prayer. I began, but was so overwhelmed by a sense of God's presence I broke down (a thing I seldom ever do). So I indicated to my companion that he should continue. The same thing happened to him. As I left that room, I sensed the joy of the Lord in my own heart. Many times I have visited sick people to encourage them. Some suffered from terminal illnesses. Strangely enough, I have come away blessed in my own soul by their contagious joy.

Deep joy crowned the apostle Paul's final testimony as he wrote his last letter to young Timothy from death row. Despite the suffering he had endured, the horror of prison, and the frequent threat of death, the joy of the Lord filled his heart.

Charles Allen puts it this way, "Just as all the water in the world cannot quench the fire of the Holy Spirit, neither can all the troubles and tragedies of the world overwhelm the joy which the Spirit brings into the human heart."[7]

It has been said that "Joy is the flag that flies above the palace when the King is in residence."

The Fruit of the Spirit: Peace

Peace carries with it the idea of unity, completeness, rest, ease, and security. In the Old Testament the word was *shalom.* Many times when I meet Jewish friends I greet them with *"Shalom."* And often, when I greet my Arab friends I use a similar term that they use for peace, *salam.*

Recently as I watched the televised report of passengers disembarking from a hijacked plane, I saw terror, horror, and fear on their faces. But one woman had a little child in her arms, calmly sleeping through it all. Peace in the midst of turmoil.

Isaiah said, "Thou wilt keep him in perfect peace, whose mind is stayed on thee: because he trusteth in thee" (Isa. 26:3 KJV). This is the picture of any Christian who stands alone on the battlefield, by faith garrisoned round about with God's holy weapons, and in command of the situation. Such a man is not troubled about the future, for he knows who holds the key to the future. He does not tremble on the rock, for he knows who made the rock. He does not doubt, for he knows the One who erases all doubt.

When you and I yield to worry, we deny our Guide the right to lead us in confidence and peace. Only the Holy Spirit can give us peace in the midst of the storms of restlessness and despair. We should not grieve our Guide by indulging in worry or paying undue attention to self.

There are different kinds of peace, such as the peace of a graveyard, or that of tranquilizers. But for the Christian, peace is not simply the absence of conflict, or any other artificial state the world has to offer. Rather it is the deep, abiding peace only Jesus Christ brings to the heart. He describes it in John 14:27: "Peace I leave with you; My peace I give to you; not as the world gives, do I give to you." This is the peace that can come only from the Holy Spirit.

The peace *of* God that can reign in our hearts is always preceded by peace *with* God, which must be the starting point. When this is so, the peace of God can follow. From this standpoint, Christ's work of salvation has two stages: First He was able to end the war between sinful man and the righteous God. God indeed was angry with man because of his sin. But Jesus by His blood made peace. The war ended; peace came. God was satisfied. The debt was cancelled, and the books were balanced. With his accounts settled, man was set free, if willing to repent and turn in faith to Christ for salvation. God is now able to look on him with favor.

But Jesus Christ not only freed us from bondage and war. He also made possible a further stage—we can have the peace *of* God in our hearts here and now. For us, peace with God is not simply an armistice; it is a war ended forever; and now the redeemed hearts of former enemies of the cross are garrisoned with a peace that transcends all human knowledge and outsoars any wings of flight we can possibly imagine.

Concerning the peace of God, Spurgeon said: "I looked at Christ, and the dove of peace flew into my heart; I looked at the dove of peace, and it flew away." So we should not look at the fruit itself, but at the source of all peace, because Christ through the Holy Spirit wisely cultivates our lives to allow us to bring forth peace. The greatest psychiatric therapy in the world is appropriating what Jesus promised, "I will give you rest"—or peace (Matt. 11:28). King David became living proof of the spiritual therapy for the soul which the Holy Spirit dispenses when he said, "He maketh me to lie down" (Ps. 23:2 KJV). This is peaceful resting. But David continues, "He restoreth my soul." This is peaceful renewing. Though men continue to seek peace, they will not find it until they come to the simple realization that "Christ is peace."

A woman full of despair and frustration wrote me that her case was hopeless because God could not possibly forget all her gross sins. In reply I said that although she felt forsaken by God and others, He had not forsaken her, but had allowed distress and despair to flood her heart so she might realize her need for God's forgiveness and peace. She wrote later that she jumped up and down with delight when she realized she could have God's peace. Jesus said that not our peace but His peace makes the difference: "My peace I give to you; not as the world gives" (John 14:27).

In Romans Paul gives us these wonderful words, "May the God of hope fill you with all joy and peace in believing, so that by the power of the Holy Spirit you may abound in hope" (15:13 RSV). How can joy and peace be any better described? Indeed the fruit of the Spirit is peace—do you have it in your heart?

16. The Fruit of the Spirit: Patience, Kindness, Goodness

The first cluster of the fruit of the Spirit has a primary Godward relationship with outward results others can see. Thus, we speak of the love of God, the joy of the Lord, and the peace of God. The second cluster—patience, kindness, and goodness—has to do with the kind of Christians we are in our outward relationships. If we are short-tempered, unkind, and rude, we lack the second cluster of the fruit of the Spirit. But when the Spirit controls us, He works to transform us so that the buds of patience, kindness, and goodness begin to blossom and then to be fruitful.

The Fruit of the Spirit: Patience

The English word *patience* (or *long-suffering* in the King James Version) comes from a Greek word that speaks of a person's steadfastness under provocation. Inherent in the word is the thought of patiently enduring ill-treatment without anger or thought of retaliation or revenge. Thus, this part of the fruit of the Spirit is seen in our relationship to our neighbors. It is patience personified—love's patience. If we are irritable, vengeful, resentful, and malicious to our neighbors, we are short-suffering, not long-suffering. And when that condition exists, the Holy Spirit is not in control.

Patience is the transcendent radiance of a loving and tender heart which, in its dealings with those around it, looks kindly and graciously upon them. Patience graciously, compassionately and with understanding judges the faults of others without unjust criticism. Patience also includes perseverance—the ability to bear up under weariness, strain, and persecution when doing the work of the Lord.

Patience is part of true Christlikeness, something we so often admire in others without demanding it of ourselves. Paul teaches us that we can be "strengthened with all might, according to his glorious power, unto all patience and longsuffering with joyfulness" (Col. 1:11 KJV). Patience in our lives springs from God's power based upon our willingness to learn it. Whenever we are selfish, or when anger or ill will begins to build, or when impatience or frustration overtakes us, we must recognize that we are the source of our problems, not God. We must refuse, renounce, and repudiate the situation immediately. It comes from the old sinful nature.

Patience and Testing

Patience is closely related to testings or trials in the Bible, and that is only logical. We may be patient in ordinary life, but how do we react when trials come? It is then that we especially need the fruit of the Spirit—patience. This is one reason why the Bible tells us that trials can be good for us, because they allow us to be strengthened, and especially they allow patience to be developed by the Spirit. "Consider it all joy, my brethren, when you encounter various trials, knowing that the testing of your faith produces endurance" (James 1:2, 3).

If this is true, we should welcome trials and testings when they come, because they force us to draw more and more upon the source of all strength, producing more of the patience which is the fruit of the Spirit. It is the regular exercise of patience and longsuffering in the small day-to-day frustrations and irritations which prepares us to endure when the great battles come.

Inner erosion of the heart leaves us vulnerable to the cunning, and often disguised, attacks of Satan. But the heart that has learned to call *instantly* in prayer on the Holy Spirit at the first sign of temptation has no reason to fear any such erosion. In a short time prayer will become so automatic and spontaneous that we will have uttered the prayer almost before we are aware of the need. The Bible says we are to be "patient in tribulation; continuing instant in prayer" (Rom. 12:12 KJV). For me, the best time to pray is the *very moment* a tense situation or an unspiritual attitude overtakes me. God the Holy Spirit is always there, ready to help me gain victory in the spiritual battles I face—big or small. However, in order for prayer to become an involuntary, or subconscious reaction to my problem, I must voluntarily and consciously practice it day after day until it becomes an integral part of my being.

A dear friend and trusted counselor once told me that sometimes the greatest test comes to us when we ask God the question, "Why?"

As Charles Hembree has pointed out, "In the full face of affliction it is hard to see any sense to things that befall us and we want to question the fairness of a faithful God. However, these moments can be the most meaningful of our lives."[1]

One of God's great servants, Paul Little, was killed in an automobile accident in 1975. I immediately asked God, "Why?" Paul was one of God's outstanding young strategists and Bible teachers. He was a theological professor, a leader of Inter-Varsity Christian Fellowship, and a former member of our team. I am sure his wife, Marie, must have asked in the agony of her heart, "Why?" And yet, a few months later when she came to our team retreat, she manifested a marvelous spirit as she shared her victory with the wives of our team members. Instead of our comforting her, she was comforting us.

We may suffer affliction or discipline, yet the Psalmist said, "Weeping may last for the night, but a shout of joy comes in the morning" (Ps. 30:5). No Spirit-filled Christian will fail to evince long-suffering and patience if he has faithfully endured "the fellowship of His sufferings" (Phil. 3:10).

In order for the fruit to appear in our lives God allows us to face chastening, discipline, affliction, and persecution. Had Joseph not been sold into slavery by his brothers who hated him, and been wrongly accused by Potiphar who put him in prison, he would not have developed the fruit of patience and long-suffering that was to become the hallmark of his life. Even after he had told Pharaoh's cupbearer he would be restored to the king's court and asked him to tell Pharaoh of his unjust imprisonment, he had to wait two more years for release from prison.

As we wait upon the Lord, God may sometimes seem slow in coming to help us, but He never comes too late. Paul wrote, "For momentary, light affliction is producing for us an eternal weight of glory far beyond all comparison" (2 Cor. 4:17). Jesus told His disciples, "By your perseverance you will win your souls" (Luke 21:19). It is this long-suffering and patience that the Holy Spirit uses to bless others.

We must guard against one thing, however, when we speak about long-suffering. Sometimes we use it as an excuse for failing to take specific action when it is called for. Sometimes we enjoy a kind of neurotic self-flagellation because we don't want to face the truth, and we mistakenly call it long-suffering. But Jesus vigorously "drove out all who sold and bought in the temple, and he overturned the tables of the money-changers and the seats of those who sold pigeons" (Matt. 21:12 RSV). Moreover He furiously castigated the scribes and the Pharisees (Matt. 21:13ff). It is the Spirit-filled Christian who knows when to have "righteous indignation" and when to be patient, and who knows when long-suffering becomes an excuse for inaction or a crutch to hide a defect of character.

The Fruit of the Spirit: Kindness

Kindness, or *gentleness,* is the *second segment* of the fruit that grows outward. This term comes from a Greek word referring to the kindness that pervades and penetrates the whole nature. Gentleness washes away all that is harsh and austere. Indeed, gentleness is love enduring.

Jesus was a gentle person. When He came into the world, there were few institutions of mercy. There were few hospitals or mental institutions, few places of refuge for the poor, few homes for orphans, few havens for the forsaken. In comparison to today, it was a cruel world. Christ changed that. Wherever true Christianity has gone His followers have performed acts of gentleness and kindness.

The word gentleness occurs only a few times in our English Bible. It is spoken of in connection with the three persons of the Trinity. In Psalm 18:35, it is the gentleness of God; in 2 Corinthians 10:1, the gentleness of Christ; and in Galatians 5:23, the gentleness of the Holy Spirit.

Charles Allen points out: "In one's disdain of sin, one can be harsh and unkind toward a sinner. . . . Some people seem to have such a passion for righteousness that they have no room left for compassion for those who have failed."[2]

How easy it is to be impatient or harsh toward those who may have failed in life! When the hippie movement began in America, many people reacted to it with a critical and unloving attitude toward the hippies themselves. The Bible teaches us otherwise. Jesus would have responded to them with loving "kindness" or "gentleness." The only people with whom He dealt harshly were the hypocritical religious leaders, but to everyone else He manifested a wonderful gentleness. Many sinners on the verge of repentance have been disillusioned by a pharisaical and coldly rigid Christianity that hangs on to a legalistic religious code minus the quality of compassion. But Jesus dealt tenderly, gently, and kindly with everyone. Even small children sensed His gentleness and approached Him eagerly and without fear.

Paul told his young friend Timothy, "The servant of the Lord must not strive; but be gentle unto all men" (2 Tim. 2:24 KJV). James said, "The wisdom that is from above is first pure, then peaceable, gentle, and easy to be entreated" (James 3:17 KJV).

Some claim that gentleness is a sign of weakness, but they are wrong! Abraham Lincoln was well-known for his gentleness and humility, but it can never be said that he was weak. On the contrary, it was the combination of his great strength of character and his gentle and compassionate spirit that made him the great person he was.

In *Fruits of the Spirit,* Hembree says, "In our age of guided missiles and misguided men there is desperate need for us to learn how to share gentleness. It seems strange that in an age when we can reach the moon, bounce signals off far planets, and receive pictures from whirling satellites we have great difficulty communicating tenderness to those about us."[3]

The logical place to turn for guidance and instruction in such things of the Spirit is the minister in the pulpit, and the compelling need of this generation is to be exposed to great preaching. But however eloquent, however well prepared, and however gifted any preacher may be, if his ministry lacks tenderness and gentleness, he will be unable to lead many people to Jesus Christ. The gentle heart is the broken heart—the heart that weeps over the sins of the bad as well as the sacrifices of the good.

The Fruit of the Spirit: Goodness

The *third element* in this trio is *goodness*. This is derived from a Greek word referring to that quality found in the person who is ruled by and aims at what is good, that which represents the highest moral and ethical values. Paul writes, "For the fruit of the light consists in all goodness and righteousness and truth" (Eph. 5:9). He also says, "To this end also we pray for you always that our God may count you worthy of your calling, and fulfill every desire for goodness and the work of faith with power; in order that the name of our Lord Jesus may be glorified in you" (2 Thess. 1:11, 12). Again Paul says in commending the church in Rome, "And concerning you, my brethren, I myself also am convinced that you yourselves are full of goodness, filled with all knowledge, and able also to admonish one another" (Rom. 15:14).

As I said in an earlier chapter, on the grounds that surround our home we have a number of fresh water springs. One spring sends forth a never ending supply of pure water, and from it we get the water for our house. The comment of the man who tested it was, "It's the purest water I've ever found." A good heart, like a good spring, perpetually pours out goodness.

The word "good" in the language of Scripture literally means "to be like God," because He alone is the One who is perfectly good. It is one thing, however, to have high ethical standards but quite another for the Holy Spirit to produce the goodness that has its depths in the Godhead. The meaning here is more than just "doing good." Goodness goes far deeper. Goodness is love in action. It carries with it not only the idea of righteousness imputed, but righteousness demonstrated in everyday living by the Holy Spirit. It is doing good out of a good heart, to please God, without expecting medals and rewards. Christ wants this kind of goodness to be the way of life for every Christian. Man can find no substitute for goodness, and no spiritual touch-up artist can imitate it.

Thoreau wrote, "If a man does not keep pace with his companions, perhaps it is because he hears a different drummer. Let him step to the music which he hears, however measured or far away."[4] As Christians we have no alternative but to march to the drumbeat of the Holy Spirit, following the measured steps of goodness, which pleases God.

We can do good deeds, and by practicing principles of goodness can witness to those around us that we have something "different" in our lives—perhaps something they themselves would like to possess. We may even be able to show others how to practice the principles of goodness in their own lives. But the Bible says, "Your goodness is as a morning cloud, and as the early dew it goeth away" (Hosea 6:4 KJV). True goodness is a "fruit of the Spirit," and our efforts to achieve it in our own strength alone can never succeed.

We should be careful that any goodness the world may see in us is the genuine fruit of the Spirit and not a counterfeit substitute, lest we unwittingly lead someone astray.

We must be constantly aware that Satan can take any human effort and twist it to serve his own purposes, but he cannot touch the spirit that is covered by the blood of Christ and rooted deep in the Holy Spirit. Only the Spirit can produce the goodness that can stand up under any test.

Goodness is never alone so far as the outward facets of the fruit of the Spirit are concerned, but it is always accompanied by patience and kindness. These three go together and all were beautifully manifested in the life of the One who is the perfect prototype of what you and I ought to be. By the power of the Holy Spirit these traits of character become part of our lives that we might remind others of Him.

17. The Fruit of the Spirit: Faithfulness, Gentleness, Self-Control

Authentic Christian living has its own order of priority in our lives: God first, others second, self third. It is proper, therefore, when speaking about the third cluster of the fruit of the Spirit to focus our attention upon the *inward man.* The Spirit works *in* us that He might work through us. "Being" is far more important than "doing." But when we are what we should be inside, we will bring forth fruit, more fruit, and much fruit. This is the ultimate purpose the apostle Paul had in mind when he wrote, "It is God who is at work in you, both to will and to work for His good pleasure" (Phil. 2:13). He also says, "He who began a good work in you will perfect it until the day of Christ Jesus" (Phil. 1:6).

The third cluster of the spiritual fruit has to do with the inward man. It includes faithfulness, gentleness, and self-control.

The Fruit of the Spirit: Faithfulness

The reference to faithfulness (or "faith" in the KJV) is not to faith exercised by the Christian, but rather to *faithfulness* or *fidelity,* produced by the Holy Spirit in a yielded Christian life.

The same word occurs in Titus 2:10 where it is translated "fidelity" in the King James Version. This trait of character is highly commended in Scripture. Fidelity in little things is one of the surest tests of character, as our Lord indicated in the parable of the talents: "You were faithful with a few things, I will put you in charge of many things" (Matt. 25:21). Morality is not so much a matter of magnitude, but of quality. Right is right, and wrong is wrong, in small things as well as in big things.

Peter contrasts those who walk faithfully with God over against those who become entangled again with the pollution of the world. He writes, "For it had been better for them not to have known the way of righteousness, than, after they have known it, to turn from the holy commandment delivered unto them. But it is happened unto them according to the true proverb, The dog is turned to his own vomit again; and the sow that was washed to her wallowing in the mire" (2 Peter 2:21, 22 KJV).

The Third Epistle of John contains only fourteen verses. Diotrephes and Demetrius are the two main characters. The faithful follower was Demetrius who is described as receiving a "good testimony from everyone, and from the truth itself" (v. 12). He is commended because in word and in truth, in practice and in precept, he followed the Lord faithfully.

A familiar expression in industry is "turn around time," the time that elapses between the receipt of an order and the day it is delivered. Many Christians will some day regret the self-imposed time lag that came between the point when God first showed them His plan for them, and the point when they took action. The ancient Israelites could have completed their journey from Egypt to Canaan in a few months. Instead, the journey took forty years and a whole generation died because of their unfaithfulness.

Lack of faithfulness is actually a sign of spiritual immaturity. One sign of emotional immaturity is the refusal to accept responsibility. A young person may want all the privileges of adulthood, but refuse to accept the responsibilities. The same thing is true spiritually. God has given us certain responsibilities as mature Christians. When we are disobedient and refuse to accept these responsibilities, we are unfaithful. On the other hand, when we are faithful, it means we have accepted the responsibilities God has given us. This is a sign of spiritual maturity, and it is one of the important fruits the Spirit brings to our lives.

Surely most of us grow at a slower rate than we should because we refuse to allow the Holy Spirit to control all areas of our lives. Rather, our faithful obedience to allow God the Holy Spirit to remove any vile habit or developing infection should be immediate. We can become impatient when we discover it takes so long to become like Him, but we should be patient and faithful, for becoming like Him is worth waiting for. However, even if we could become totally mature Christians I am not sure that we would be conscious of it. Who of us can claim total perfection in this life? But we know that when we stand with Him in eternity, we will be glorified with Him. And the Holy Spirit will begin to perform the deeper work of God's plan in our lives any time we are willing to faithfully say "yes" to His will!

The Scriptures are replete with stories of men like Abraham (Heb. 11:8–10), who were faithful in their walk before God. The entire eleventh chapter of Hebrews should be studied as it recounts the men and women whom God calls faithful.

It is dangerous to tempt God, as did "unfaithful" men in the day of Amos. To them God declared, "Behold, days are coming . . . when I will send a famine on the land, not a famine for bread, or a thirst for water, but rather for hearing the words of the Lord" (Amos 8:11).

Rather we should heed the advice of James: "Blessed is a man who perseveres under trial; for once he has been approved, he will receive the crown of life, which the Lord has promised to those who love him" (1:12). James later says, "One who looks intently at the perfect law, the law of liberty, and abides by it, not having become a forgetful hearer but an effectual doer, this man shall be blessed in what he does" (1:25).

Over and over we are admonished to be *faithful*. As we saw earlier we read in the Bible about a number of judgments at the end of this age. One of these is called the judgment seat of Christ. Someday all Christians will stand before Jesus Christ to give an account of the works we have done since our conversion. We will be judged, not on the basis of how successful we were in the eyes of the world, but on how faithful we were in the place God put us. The apostle Paul indicates this in 1 Corinthians 3:9–16: faithfulness will be the basis on which God renders judgment.

Sometimes the greatest test of our faithfulness is how much time we spend reading the Scriptures, praying, and living in accord with the principles of righteousness when we have been blessed with prosperity. A devout Christian surprised me recently by saying, "It's hard to be a faithful Christian in modern-day America." It is so easy to forget and to forsake our God in the midst of prosperity and especially when materialism is rampant. This is the reason Jesus told us that it is hard for rich men to enter the kingdom of God. Rich men can be saved—but the Bible talks about "the deceitfulness of riches" (Matt. 13:22). The burdens and cares of this world often interfere with our faithful walk before the Lord. In the midst of material prosperity we should beware lest we fall into the same pitfall as the Laodiceans, who incurred God's wrath and displeasure because they felt they had need of nothing since they were materially rich (Rev. 3:17). "But those who want to get rich fall into temptation and a snare and many foolish and harmful desires which plunge men into ruin and destruction. For the love of money is a root of all sorts of evil, and some by longing for it have wandered away from the faith, and pierced themselves with many a pang" (1 Tim. 6:9, 10).

If we could carve an epitaph on the tombstone of the apostle Paul, it might read: "Faithful unto death." As he awaited execution Paul could say without hesitation, "I have fought a good fight, I have finished my course, I have kept the faith: Henceforth there is laid up for me a crown of righteousness, which the Lord, the righteous judge, shall give me at that day" (2 Tim. 4:7, 8 KJV). Whatever the failures of Paul and however short he fell of perfection, he knew that he had been faithful to the Lord to the end.

This wonderful segment of the cluster of the fruit of the Spirit—faithfulness—constitutes faithfulness to our testimony, faithfulness to our commitments and calling, and faithfulness to the commands of Christ. And the ultimate reward for faithfulness is given in Revelation 2:10: "Be faithful until death, and I will give you the crown of life."

The Fruit of the Spirit: Gentleness

The word gentleness here (or in the KJV, meekness) comes from a Greek word meaning "mild; mildness in dealing with others." Jesus said, "Blessed are the gentle, for they shall inherit the earth" (Matt. 5:5). Nowhere in Scripture does this word carry with it the idea of being spiritless and timid. In biblical times gentleness or meekness meant far more than it does in modern day English. It carried the idea of being tamed, like a wild horse that has been brought under control. Until tamed by the Holy Spirit Peter was a rough and ready character. Then all of his energy was used for the glory of God. Moses was called the meekest of men, but prior to God's special call to him he was an unbroken, high-spirited man who needed forty years in the desert before he was fully brought under God's control. A river under control can be used to generate power. A fire under control can heat a home. Meekness is power, strength, spirit, and wildness under control.

In another sense, gentleness can be likened to modesty in that it is the opposite of a flamboyant and self-indulgent spirit. Rather, it displays a sensitive regard for others and is careful never to be unfeeling for the rights of others.

Gentleness enjoys a quiet strength that confounds those who think of it as weakness. This is seen in the response of Jesus following his arrest—throughout His trial, torture, and crucifixion he endured the emotional and physical pain inflicted mercilessly by his captors and taunting spectators. "He was oppressed and He was afflicted, yet He did not open His mouth; Like a lamb that is led to slaughter, and like a sheep that is silent before its shearers, so He did not open His mouth" (Isa. 53:7). Meekness is referred to as love under discipline. Charles Allen states, "God never expects us to be less than we really are. . . . Self-belittlement is an insult to the God who made us. Meekness comes another way. . . . Pride comes from looking only at ourselves, meekness comes through looking at God."[1]

All Christian growth, including meekness, takes place in the heavy atmosphere of hostility. This kind of spiritual poise and inward quiet strength as a growing work of the Holy Spirit does not come on a playground, but on a spiritual battleground.

In still another definition of meekness, David Hubbard says that meekness is making ourselves consistently available to those who count on us; we are at peace with our power, so we do not use it arrogantly or hurtfully. When speaking of meekness, DeWitt Talmadge said, "As the heavens prophetically are taken by violence, so the earth is taken by meekness, and God as proprietor wants no tenants more or grants larger leases than to the meek of heart and spirit."

In his appraisal of Andrew Murray, the great Keswick speaker, Dr. V. R. Edman states in his book, *They Found the Secret,* "Such indeed is the abiding life that draws its sustenance and strength from the Vine. By the refreshing and reviving flow of the Holy Spirit through that life there is prayer that prevails, preaching that is powerful, love that is contagious, joy that overflows, and peace that passes understanding. It is the adoration that is stillness to know God for one's self. It is the obedience that does the Saviour's bidding in the light of the Word. It is the fruitfulness that arises spontaneously from abiding in the Vine."[2]

Another illustration that has helped me to understand gentleness is the iceberg. I have seen some of them from shipboard when crossing the Atlantic. However high an iceberg may be above the water line, the greater part of it is submerged. Icebergs are particularly formidable and destructive when they drift along the sea lanes.

But the greatest threat to icebergs comes from something beneficent, the sun. The sun's rays bring warmth to life, and death to icebergs. As gentleness is a powerful force, so the sun proves to be more powerful than the mightiest iceberg. God's gentleness, or meekness, in us permits the rays of the sun of God's Holy Spirit to work on our icebound hearts, transforming them into instruments for good and for God. Spiritually, the gentle, Spirit-filled Christian is a prism through whom the rays of the sun's spectrum are gathered to minister to the icebergs of our carnality.

How do you and I apply gentleness to ourselves? Jesus set before us His own example by calling upon us to be "gentle and humble in heart" (Matt. 11:29).

First, we do not rise up defensively when our feelings are ruffled, as did Peter when he slashed the ear of the soldier at the arrest of Jesus in the garden, only earning His Lord's rebuke (Matt. 26:51, 52).

Second, we do not crave to have the preeminence, as Diotrephes did (3 John 9). Rather, we desire that in all things Jesus Christ might have the preeminence (Col. 1:18).

Third, we do not seek to be recognized and highly regarded, or to be considered the voice of authority, as Jannes and Jambres did (2 Tim. 3:8). These magicians of Egypt rejected the Lord's authority through Moses, and opposed him just before the Exodus. "Do not think of yourself more highly than you ought, but rather think of yourself with sober judgment, . . . Be devoted to one another in brotherly love. Honor one another above yourselves" (Rom. 12:3, 10 NIV).

The enthronement of Jesus Christ in our lives makes it possible for meekness to become one of our virtues. Gentleness may be the most tangible sign of greatness displayed in us. You and I may never be respected as voices of authority; we may never gain the plaudits of the world; we may never rule or swing the baton of power. But one day the meek will inherit the earth (Matt. 5:5), for no one can take away our rightful share of God's divine and delightful bequest to us.

The Fruit of the Spirit: Self-control

Self-control (temperance in the KJV) is the third fruit in this cluster. It comes from a Greek word meaning strong, having mastery, able to control one's thoughts and actions.

John Wesley's mother once wrote him while he was a student at Oxford that "anything which increases the authority of the body over the mind is an evil thing." This definition has helped me understand "self-control."

Intemperance has brought about the fall of kings and tycoons. History illustrates this. Someone has said: "There are men who can command armies, but cannot command themselves. There are men who by their burning words can sway vast multitudes who cannot keep silence under provocation or wrong. The highest mark of nobility is self-control. It is more kingly than regal crown and purple robe."

Elsewhere it has been said:
> "Not in the clamor of the crowded street,
> Not in the shouts and plaudits of the throng,
> But in ourselves, are triumph and defeat."[3]

Past history and current public examples illustrate how the excesses of uncontrolled appetite and fleshly indulgence wreak damage in our hearts.

The sin of intemperance, lack of self-control, springs from two causes: first, physical appetite; second, mental habit.

When we think of temperance we usually think of alcohol. This is not unexpected because of the great efforts of temperance leaders who for years sought to eradicate this poison that affects so many people in the world. But somehow we silently countenance gluttony, which the Bible condemns as clearly as drunkenness. We also tend to overlook unkindness, gossip, pride, and jealousy. It is possible to be intemperate in all these areas, too. The Scripture says, "Those who live according to their sinful nature have their minds set on what that nature desires; but those who live in accordance with the Spirit have their minds set on what the Spirit desires" (Rom. 8:5 NIV). Temperance, self-control, as a fruit of the Spirit is the normal Christian life taking its exercise.

Temperance in our use of food is moderation. Temperance with respect to alcohol is soberness. Temperance in sexual matters is abstinence for those who are not married. Even for those of us who are married there may be times for temperance, when we abstain by mutual consent from legitimate sexual activity so we can give ourselves more fully to the study of God's Word, prayer, and good works (see 1 Cor. 7:5).

Temperance in regard to temper is self-control. Recently I was with a man who parked in a prohibited zone at the airport. An attendant kindly asked him if he would move the car as he was in a no-parking zone. Angrily he replied, "If you don't have police credentials, shut your mouth." This Christian was so nervous and tense from shouldering so many responsibilities that he had almost totally lost control of his temper. He was intemperate. It was just as much a sin as if he had become drunk.

Temperance in matters of dress is appropriate modesty. Temperance in defeat is hopefulness. Temperance in relation to sinful pleasure is nothing short of complete abstinence.

Solomon wrote, "He who is slow to anger is better than the mighty, and he who rules his spirit, than he who captures a city" (Prov. 16:32). The Living Bible paraphrases the latter part of that verse to read, "It is better to have self-control than to control an army." The writer of Proverbs said, "A man without self-control is as defenseless as a city with broken-down walls" (25:28 LB).

Paul taught the importance of self-control. Any athlete who would win a race must train himself to become the complete master of his body, he told his readers. He emphasized that the goal was not merely a corruptible, but an incorruptible crown: "Everyone who competes in the games exercises self-control in all things. They then do it to receive a perishable wreath, but we an imperishable. . . . but I buffet my body and make it my slave, lest possibly, after I have preached to others, I myself should be disqualified" (1 Cor. 9:25, 27).

In Peter's list of Christian virtues, he says, "Add . . . to knowledge temperance; and to temperance patience" (2 Peter 1:5, 6 KJV). All these go together. And it is quite clear that when we allow our passions to rule us, the outcome at last is far more undesirable than can be imagined during the moment of pleasurable fulfillment.

Who is to say where temperance stops and intemperance begins? Some Christians have an elastic conscience when it comes to their own foibles—and an ironbound conscience when it comes to the foibles of others. Maybe that's why it is so easy for some Christians to condemn a person who takes an occasional sip of wine but never rebuke themselves for the sin of habitual overeating. Compulsive overeating is one of the most widely accepted and practiced sins of modern Western Christians. It is easy to condemn an adulterer, but how can the one who condemns do so when he is guilty of some other form of intemperance? Should each of us not have clean hands and a pure heart in all of life? Is one form of slavery more wrong in principle than another? Are we not just as tightly bound if the chains are made of ropes as of steel?

The appetite that controls one person may differ from the appetite that controls another. But if one person submits to a craving for possessions, is he so different from others who crave sex, gambling, gold, food, alcohol, or drugs?

The need for temperance in *every* aspect of life has never been greater than it is today. At a time when violence, selfishness, apathy, and undisciplined living threaten to destroy this planet, it is imperative that Christians set an example. The world needs this example—something steadfast it can hold on to, an anchor in a raging sea.

For centuries Christians have proclaimed Christ as the anchor. If we who have the Holy Spirit living and working within us falter and fail, what hope is there for the rest of the world?

Space for Fruit-growing

We have now considered these nine wonderful facets that comprise the fruit of the Spirit: love, joy, peace, patience, kindness, goodness, faithfulness, gentleness, and self-control. It is my prayer that they will characterize your life and mine.

The Holy Spirit is already in every Christian heart, and He intends to produce the fruit of the Spirit in us. However, there must be a displacement. A boat does not sink when it is in the water, but it does sink when the water comes into the boat. We do not fail to enjoy the fruit of the Spirit because we live in a sea of corruption; we fail to do so because the sea of corruption is in us.

The internal combustion engine's worst enemy is the deadly carbon that builds up in the cylinder chamber. It reduces the power and causes the motor to lose efficiency. Oil will improve the engine's performance, but it will not remove the carbon so that the motor can run more efficiently. Mechanical surgery must be performed to remove the carbon so that the oil can do its best work and the motor perform as it was designed to do. Similarly, we must eliminate the works of the flesh from our inner lives so that deadly carbon and grit do not impair the effectiveness of our spiritual performance. One oil company advertised, "More power for smoother performance." Spiritually this is possible only as we yield our lives to the control of the Holy Spirit. We must let the searchlight of God's Word scan us to detect the abiding sins and fruitless qualities which impair our personal growth and fruitfulness.

The story is told of a man who glanced at the obituary column in his local newspaper. To his surprise he saw his own name, indicating that he had just died. At first he laughed about it. But soon the telephone began to ring. Stunned friends and acquaintances called to inquire and to offer their sympathy. Finally, in irritation, he called the newspaper editor and angrily reported that even though he had been reported dead in the obituary column he was very much alive. The editor was apologetic and embarrassed. Then in a flash of inspiration he said, "Do not worry, sir, I will make it all right, for tomorrow I will put your name in the births column."

This may sound like merely a humorous incident, but it is actually a spiritual parable. Not until we have allowed our old selves to be crucified with Christ can our new selves emerge to display the marvelous fruit characteristic of the life of Jesus Christ.

And only the Holy Spirit can make possible the out-living of the in-living Christ. The kind of persons God wants us to be can never be produced through human effort. But when the Holy Spirit fills us, He brings forth His fruit in people who manifest a growing likeness to Christ, the prototype of what we will someday be.

18. The Need of the Hour

The 1850s in America brought a marked decline in religion in the United States. The discovery of gold in California, as well as a number of other developments, had turned people's minds and hearts away from religion and toward material things. The political turmoil over slavery and the threatened disintegration of the nation also preoccupied public attention. A severe financial panic in the late 1850s led to even greater concern about material things.

In September of 1857 a quiet businessman named Jeremiah Lanphier decided to invite other businessmen to join him in a noonday prayer meeting once a week, seeking for the renewing work of the Holy Spirit. He distributed hundreds of handbills advertising the meeting, but the first day only half a dozen showed up, meeting in the rear of a church on Fulton Street. Two weeks later there were forty, and within six months some ten thousand were gathered daily for prayer in New York City alone. Awakening swept the country, and within two years an estimated one million people had professed faith in Christ.

The effects of the awakening were profound, both in individual lives and in society. Tragically, the awakening was too late to avoid the Civil War which threatened the very life of the nation. But untold good came from the awakening, including many movements for evangelism and social betterment.

The Need for Spiritual Revival

The world today is again in desperate need of a spiritual awakening. It is the only hope for the survival of the human race.

In the midst of the vast problems which face our world Christians are strangely silent and powerless, almost overwhelmed by the tides of secularism. And yet Christians are called to be "the salt of the earth" (Matt. 5:13), keeping a decaying world from further corruption. Christians are to be "the light of the world" (Matt. 5:14), illuminating the darkness caused by sin and giving guidance to a world that has lost its way. We are called to be "children of God above reproach in the midst of a crooked and perverse generation, among whom you appear as lights in the world" (Phil. 2:15).

Why are we not "salt" and "light" as we should be? Why are we not doing much more to bring the kingdom of God to the hearts and lives of humanity?

There certainly are many instances of Christians who have been touched by God, and are in turn touching the lives of others for Christ. But for every instance of that, there are many more Christians who are living defeated, joyless lives. These people have no sense of victory over sin or effectiveness in witnessing. They have little impact on those around them for the sake of the Gospel.

If, then, the greatest need of our world is to feel the effects of a spiritual awakening, the greatest need within the Christian Church throughout the world today is to experience the touch of the Holy Spirit, bringing true "revival" and "renewal" to the lives of countless Christians.

Many centuries ago God gave Ezekiel, the prophet, a remarkable vision in which he saw national Israel scattered among the nations. Israel's bones were described as many and dry. All hope for the future seemed to be gone. According to the word of the prophet, Israel might as well be buried as far as the secular world was concerned. However, Ezekiel was staggered when God asked this question: "Can these bones live?" (Ezek. 37:3). To this the prophet replied, "Thou knowest." Then the man of God was commanded to speak the word of God and the bones stood up, a great host of men who were clothed with flesh. But they still seemed strangely impotent. They lacked spirit or breath. Then the Spirit of God gave them breath and they became a mighty army.

Again we face a dark time in the history of God's people. In spite of some encouraging signs, the forces of evil seem to be gathering for a colossal assault on the work of God in the world. Satan has unleashed his power in a way perhaps unparalleled in the history of the Christian Church. If ever there was a time we needed renewal, it is now. Only God can thwart the plans of Satan and his legions, because only God is all-powerful. Only His Holy Spirit can bring true spiritual awakening which will stem the tide of evil and reverse the trend. In the darkest hour God can still revive His people, and by the Holy Spirit breathe new vigor and power into the body of Christ.

Our world needs to be touched by Christians who are Spirit-filled, Spirit-led, and Spirit-empowered. Are you that kind of Christian? Or is there in your own life the need for a new touch of the Spirit? Do you stand in need of genuine spiritual renewal within your own life? If so, know that God the Holy Spirit wants to bring that renewal to you right now.

The Time Is Now

The time for spiritual revival is *now*. We must not delay. Dr. Samuel Johnson wore a watch on which was engraved the words from John 9:4, "The Night Cometh." We Christians ought to carry written in our hearts the solemn truth of how short is our opportunity to witness for Christ and live for Him. We do not know—any of us—how much time we have left on this earth. Death may cut our lives short. Christ could come again at any moment.

I once read about a sundial on which was inscribed the cryptic message, "It is later than you think." Travelers would often pause to meditate on the meaning of that phrase. We Christians have a sundial—the Word of God. From Genesis to Revelation it bears its warning, "It is later than you think." Writing to the Christians of his day Paul said, "It is already the hour for you to awaken from sleep; for now salvation is nearer to us than when we believed. The night is almost gone, and the day is at hand. Let us therefore lay aside the deeds of darkness and put on the armor of light" (Rom. 13:11, 12).

Billy Bray, a godly clergyman of another generation, sat by the bedside of a dying Christian who had been very shy about his testimony for Christ during his life. The dying man said, "If I had the power I'd shout glory to God." Billy Bray answered, "It's a pity you didn't shout glory when you had the power." I wonder how many of us will look back over a lifetime of wasted opportunities and ineffective witness and weep because we did not allow God to use us as He wanted. "Night is coming, when no man can work" (John 9:4).

If ever we are to study the Scriptures, if ever we are to spend time in prayer, if ever we are to win souls for Christ, if ever we are to invest our finances for His kingdom—it must be *now*. "Since all these things are to be destroyed in this way, what sort of people ought you to be in holy conduct and godliness, looking for and hastening the coming of the day of God, on account of which the heavens will be destroyed by burning, and the elements will melt with intense heat! But according to His promise we are looking for new heavens and a new earth, in which righteousness dwells. Therefore, beloved, since you look for these things, be diligent to be found by Him in peace, spotless and blameless" (2 Peter 3:11–14).

The Effects of an Awakening

What would happen if revival were to break into our lives and our churches today? I believe there are at least *eight characteristics* of such an outpouring of the Holy Spirit.

1. There will be a new vision of the majesty of God. We must understand that the Lord is not only tender and merciful and full of compassion, but He is also the God of justice, holiness, and wrath. Many Christians have a caricature of God. They do not see God in all of His wholeness. We glibly quote John 3:16, but we forget to quote the following verse, "he who does not believe has been judged already" (v. 18). Compassion is not complete in itself, but must be accompanied by inflexible justice and wrath against sin and a desire for holiness. What stirs God most is not physical suffering but sin. All too often we are more afraid of physical pain than of moral wrong. The cross is the standing evidence of the fact that holiness is a principle for which God would die. God cannot clear the guilty until atonement is made. Mercy is what we need and that is what we receive at the foot of the cross.

2. There will be a new vision of the sinfulness of sin. Isaiah saw the Lord upon a throne high and lifted up, His train filling the temple, and he saw the seraphim bowing in reverence as they cried, "Holy, Holy, Holy, is the Lord of hosts, the whole earth is full of His glory" (Isa. 6:3). Then it was that Isaiah realized his own unworthiness and his utter dependence upon God. When Simon Peter, on the Sea of Galilee, realized that it was the very Lord with him in the boat, he said, "Depart from me, for I am a

sinful man, O Lord!" (Luke 5:8). The consciousness that Jesus
was God Himself brought to Peter's mind his own human sinfulness. In the presence of God, Job said, "I abhor myself" (Job
42:6 ASV).

When a man is tempted, James tells us, his own passions carry
him away and serve as a bait (James 1:14, 15). And whatever
his lust may be it conceives and becomes the parent of sin, and
sin when fully matured gives birth to death. We need to see sin
as it really is. The greatest vision of sin that a person can ever receive is to look at the cross. If Jesus Christ had to die for sin, then
sin indeed must be dark and terrible in the sight of God.

3. *There will be an emphasis on the necessity of repentance,
faith, and the new birth.* Jesus came preaching repentance and
saying that unless a man is born from above he cannot see the
kingdom of God. He said that sinners love darkness and will not
come to the light for fear their deeds will be exposed and condemned. Those whose hearts have been changed are new crea-
tures. They come to the light out of love for truth and for God.
If anyone is in Christ Jesus, he is a new creature, for the old
things have passed away and everything has become new.

4. *There will be the joy of salvation.* The prayer expressed in
the Psalm was for a requickening "That Thy people may rejoice
in Thee" (Ps. 85:6). David's desire was for a restoration of the
joy of salvation. The express purpose of Jesus for the disciples
was "that your joy may be made full" (John 15:11). When
Philip went down to Samaria and led a great spiritual awakening,
Scripture says, "There was much rejoicing in that city" (Acts
8:8). Jesus also tells us that there is joy in heaven, joy in the
presence of the angels of God over one sinner who repents (Luke
15:7). So a true revitalization of the Church would bring about
the salvation of tens of thousands of sinners, and this in turn
would bring joy in heaven as well as joy here on earth.

If there were no heaven and no hell I would still want to be a
Christian because of what it does for our homes and our own
families in this life.

5. *There will be a new realization of our responsibility for
world evangelization.* John the Baptist pointed his hearers to "the
Lamb of God" and his two disciples followed Jesus from then on
(John 1:36, 37). Andrew first found his own brother Peter and
told him that they had found the Christ. When Philip had begun

to follow Christ he went after Nathanael (John 1:40–45). The apostles were to be witnesses anywhere and everywhere, even unto the uttermost part of the earth (Acts 1:8). And when persecution scattered the church which was at Jerusalem, they went everywhere preaching Christ and the glorious gospel (Acts 8:4). One of the first and best evidences of being a true believer is the concern which we feel for others.

6. *There will be a deep social concern.* In Matthew 22:37–39, Jesus said, "You shall love the Lord your God with all your heart, and with all your soul, and with all your mind. . . . You shall love your neighbor as yourself." Our faith is not only vertical, it is horizontal. We will become interested in the hurts of those around us and those far away. But I would have to say that to a world which really wants to be saved from the consequences of its own sin and folly a revived Christianity can have only one message, "Repent." Too many people today want a brotherly world in which they can remain unbrotherly; a decent world in which they can live indecently. Too many individuals want economic security without spiritual security. But the revitalization that we long for must be biblical. If it is Christian, it will be Bible-centered. If this is true, then its leaders must have the courage of Amos to condemn those who "buy the helpless for money and the needy for a pair of sandals" (Amos 8:6).

We must lift high the moral, ethical, and social teachings of Jesus, agreeing that He offers the only standard for personal and national character. The Sermon on the Mount is for today and every day. We cannot build a new civilization on the chaotic foundation of hatred and bitterness.

7. *There will be increased evidence of both the gifts and the fruit of the Spirit.* Renewal is brought by the Holy Spirit, and when He comes in all His power upon the Church there will be clear evidences of the gifts and the fruit of the Spirit. Believers will learn what it means to minister to one another and build each other up through the gifts the Holy Spirit has given. They will be given a new measure of love for each other and for a lost and dying world. No longer will the world say that the Church is powerless and silent. No longer will our lives seem ordinary and indistinguishable from the rest of the world. Our lives will be marked by the gifts only the Holy Spirit can give. Our lives will be marked by the fruit only He can bring.

8. *There will be renewed dependence upon the Holy Spirit.* There are already evidences that this is taking place in many parts of the world. No spiritual revitalization can come without Him. The Holy Spirit is the one who reproves, convicts, strives, instructs, invites, quickens, regenerates, renews, strengthens, and uses. He must not be grieved, resisted, tempted, quenched, insulted, or blasphemed. He gives liberty to the Christian, direction to the worker, discernment to the teacher, power to the Word, and fruit to faithful service. He reveals the things of Christ. He teaches us how to use the sword of the Spirit which is the Word of God. He guides us into all truth. He directs in the way of godliness. He teaches us how to answer the enemies of our Lord. He gives access to the Father. He helps us in our prayer life.

There are things which money cannot buy; which no music can bring; which no social position can claim; which no personal influence can assure; and which no eloquence can command. No clergyman however brilliant, no evangelist no matter how eloquent or compelling, can bring about the revival we need. Only the Holy Spirit can do this. Zechariah said, "Not by might nor by power, but by My Spirit, says the Lord of hosts" (Zech. 4:6).

Steps to Awakening

If spiritual revival is the great need for many Christians today, how does it come? What are the steps to revival in our own lives and the lives of others? I believe there are three steps which the Bible sets forth.

The first step is admitting our spiritual poverty. All too often we are like the Laodicean Christians who were blinded to their own spiritual needs, "You say, 'I am rich, and have become wealthy, and have need of nothing,' and you do not know that you are wretched and miserable and poor and blind and naked" (Rev. 3:17).

Is there sin in our lives which is blocking the work of the Holy Spirit in and through us? We must not be too quick to answer "no." We must examine ourselves in the light of God's Word, and pray that the Holy Spirit will reveal to us every sin which hinders us. It may be something we are doing that is wrong—a habit, a relationship, an evil motive or thought. It may be something we are neglecting—a responsibility we are shirking or an act of love we have failed to perform. Whatever it is, it must be faced honestly and humbly before God.

The second step in spiritual renewal is confession and repentance. We can know we have sinned, and still do nothing about it. But we need to bring our sin to God in confession and repentance, not only acknowledging our sins before Him but actually turning from sin and seeking to be obedient to Him. One of the great promises of the Bible is 1 John 1:9, "If we confess our sins, He is faithful and righteous to forgive us our sins and to cleanse us from all unrighteousness." The prophet Isaiah said, "Seek the Lord while He may be found; call upon Him while He is near. Let the wicked forsake his way, and the unrighteous man his thoughts; and let him return to the Lord" (Isa. 55:6, 7).

It is no accident that some of the great awakenings in history have begun in prayer. A prayer meeting under a haystack in a rainstorm in 1806 led to the first large-scale American missionary efforts. In 1830 some 30,000 people were converted in Rochester, New York, under the ministry of Charles Finney; later Finney said the reason was the faithful praying of one man who never attended the meetings but gave himself to prayer. In 1872 the American evangelist Dwight L. Moody began a campaign in London, England, which was used of God to touch countless lives. Later Moody discovered that a humble bedridden girl had been praying. The list could go on and on.

Are you praying for revival, both in your own life and in the lives of others? Are you confessing sin to Him and seeking His blessing on your life?

The third step is a renewed commitment on our part to seek and do the will of God. We can be convicted of sin—we can pray and confess our sin—we can repent—but the real test is our willingness to obey. It is no accident that true revival is always accompanied by a new hunger for righteousness. A life touched by the Holy Spirit will tolerate sin no longer.

What is it that is hindering spiritual revival in your life today? Ultimately, of course, it is sin. Sometimes it hurts deeply to face the truth about our own lack of spiritual zeal and dedication. But God wants to touch us and make us useful servants for Himself. "Let us also lay aside every encumbrance, and the sin which so easily entangles us, and let us run with endurance the race that is set before us, fixing our eyes on Jesus, the author and perfecter of faith" (Heb. 12:1, 2). James A. Stewart has observed, "A church that needs to be revived is a church that is living below the norm of the New Testament pattern. . . . It is a tragic fact that the vast majority of Christians today are living a sub-normal Christian life. . . . the Church will never become normal until she sees revival."[1]

Are you living a "subnormal" Christian life—a life that is ineffective, lukewarm, and lacking in love for Christ and for others? Let God the Holy Spirit bring you in humility to God, confessing sin and seeking His face. Let Him touch you as you yield yourself to Him. The greatest need in the world today is for fully committed Christians.

Over 100 years ago, two young men were talking in Ireland. One said, "The world has yet to see what God will do with a man fully consecrated to Him." The other man meditated on that thought for weeks. It so gripped him that one day he exclaimed, "By the Holy Spirit in me I'll be that man." Historians now say that he touched two continents for Christ. His name was Dwight L. Moody.

This can happen again, as we open our lives to the recreating power of the Holy Spirit. No person can seek sincerely the cleansing and blessing of the Holy Spirit, and remain the same afterward. No nation can experience the touch of awakening in its midst, and remain the same afterward.

As we have seen in this book, Pentecost was the day of power of the Holy Spirit. It was the day the Christian Church was born. We do not expect that Pentecost will be repeated any more than that Jesus will die on the cross again. But we do expect pentecostal blessings when the conditions for God's moving are met, and especially as we approach "the latter days." We as Christians are to prepare the way. We are to be ready for the Spirit to fill and use us.

Notes

Chapter 1

1. Matthew Henry, *Commentary on the Whole Bible,* Vol. 1 (Old Tappan, N. J.: Fleming H. Revell Co.), p. 2.

Chapter 2

1. W. A. Criswell, *The Holy Spirit in Today's World* (Grand Rapids: Zondervan Publishing House, 1966), p. 87.
2. J. D. Douglas, ed., *Let the Earth Hear His Voice* (Minneapolis: World Wide Pub., 1975), p. 277.
3. John R. W. Stott, *Your Mind Matters* (Downers Grove, IL: Inter-Varsity Press, 1973), pp. 5, 7.
4. Ibid, p. 10.

Chapter 3

1. Al Bryant, *1,000 New Illustrations* (Grand Rapids: Zondervan Publishing House, 1960), p. 30.
2. B. H. Carroll, *Inspiration of the Bible* (New York, Chicago, London, Edinburgh: Fleming H. Revell Co., 1930), p. 54ff.
3. John R. W. Stott, *The Authority of the Bible* (Downers Grove, IL: Inter-Varsity Press, 1974), pp. 30, 40.
4. John Calvin (Trans. Ford Lewis Battles) ed. John McNeill, *Institutes of the Christian Religion* (Philadelphia: Westminster Press, 1960) Book One, Chapter 7, Sections 4 & 5, pp. 79, 80.

5. J. D. Douglas, ed., *Let the Earth Hear His Voice* (Minneapolis: World Wide Pub., 1975), p. 259.
6. Henry H. Halley, *Halley's Bible Handbook* (Grand Rapids: Zondervan Publishing House, 1962), p. 5.
7. J. B. Phillips, *Letters to Young Churches* (New York: The Macmillan Company, 1955), p. xii.

Chapter 4

1. *The Open Bible* (Nashville: Thomas Nelson, 1975), p. 988.
2. J. Gresham Machen, *The Christian Faith in the Modern World* (Grand Rapids: Wm. B. Eerdmans Co., 1947), p. 63.

Chapter 5

1. John R. W. Stott, *Baptism and Fullness* (London: Inter-Varsity Press, 1975), p. 28f.
2. David Howard, *By the Power of the Holy Spirit* (Downers Grove, IL: Inter-Varsity Press, 1973), p. 34f.
3. Ibid.

Chapter 6

1. A. T. Robertson, *Word Pictures in the New Testament*, Vol. 1 (Nashville: Broadman Press, 1930), p. 239.
2. Matthew Henry, *Commentary on the Whole Bible*, Vol. 6 (Old Tappan, N.J.: Fleming H. Revell Co.), p. 688f.
3. Ibid.
4. C. S. Lewis, *Letters to Malcolm: Chiefly on Prayer* (London and Glasgow: Collins Fontana Books, 1966), p. 22f.
5. John Wesley, *A Compend of Wesley's Theology*, eds. Burtner and Chiles (Nashville: Abingdon Press, 1954), p. 95.

Chapter 7

1. Horatius Bonar, *God's Way of Holiness* (Chicago: Moody Press, 1970), p. 93.
2. C. I. Scofield, ed., *The New Scofield Reference Bible* (New York, Oxford University Press, 1967), p. 1276.
3. Ibid, p. 1219.
4. Bonar, *God's Way of Holiness*, p. 91.

Chapter 8

1. *Keswick Week* (London: Marshall Brothers, 1907), p. 105.

Chapter 9

1. William Barclay, *The Daily Study Bible: The Letter to the Romans* (Philadelphia: Westminster Press, 1957), p. 90.
2. John R. W. Stott, *Men Made New* (London: Inter-Varsity Fellowship, 1966), pp. 49–51.
3. James H. McConkey, *The Threefold Secret of the Holy Spirit* (Chicago: Moody Press, 1897), p. 65.
4. John MacNeil, *The Spirit-filled Life* (Chicago: Moody Press, n.d.), pp. 58–59.

Chapter 10

1. "Oh For a Closer Walk," in *Christian Praise* (London: Tyndale Press, 1963), p. 337.

Chapter 11

1. David Howard, *By the Power of the Holy Spirit* (Downers Grove, IL: Inter-Varsity Press, 1973), p. 101.
2. John R. W. Stott, *Baptism and Fullness,* p. 99ff.
3. Merrill C. Tenney, ed. *The Zondervan Pictorial Encyclopedia of the Bible,* Vol. 4 (Grand Rapids: Zondervan Publishing House, 1977), p. 903.

Chapter 13

1. Peter Wagner, *Frontiers in Missionary Strategy* (Chicago: Moody Press, 1971), p. 71.

Chapter 14

1. Manford George Gutzke, *The Fruit of the Spirit* (Atlanta: The Bible For You, n.d.), pp. 10, 11.

Chapter 15

1. J. D. Douglas, ed., *The New Bible Dictionary* (London: The Inter-Varsity Fellowship, 1965), p. 753.
2. Stephen Neill, *The Christian Character* (New York: Association Press, 1955), p. 22.
3. Ibid., p. 21.
4. Sherwood Wirt, *Afterglow* (Grand Rapids: Zondervan Publishing House, 1975), p. 82.
5. Neill, *The Christian Character,* p. 29.
6. Amy Carmichael, *Gold by Moonlight* (Fort Washington, PA: Christian Literature Crusade, n.d.), p. 31.
7. Charles Allen, *The Miracle of the Holy Spirit* (Old Tappan, N.J.: Fleming H. Revell Co., 1974), p. 56.

Chapter 16

1. Charles Hembree, *Fruits of the Spirit* (Grand Rapids: Baker Book House, 1969), pp. 57, 58.
2. Charles Allen, *The Miracle of the Holy Spirit* (Old Tappan, N.J.: Fleming H. Revell Co., 1974), p. 60.
3. Hembree, *Fruits of the Spirit*, p. 74.
4. Henry David Thoreau, *Walden* (Boston: Houghton, Mifflin & Co., 1906), p. 358ff.

Chapter 17

1. Charles Allen, *The Miracle of the Holy Spirit* (Old Tappan, N.J.: Fleming H. Revell Co., 1974), p. 63.
2. V. Raymond Edman, *They Found the Secret* (Grand Rapids: Zondervan Publishing House, 1960), p. 98.
3. Henry Wadsworth Longfellow, *The Poets,* quoted from Bartlett's *Familiar Quotations* (Boston: Little, Brown, and Co., 1968), p. 624b.

Study Guide

How to Use This Book

The questions and exercises in this study guide are designed for individual study which will in turn lead to group interaction. Thus, they may be used either as a guide for individual meditation or group discussion. During your first group meeting we suggest that you set aside a few minutes at the outset in which individual group members introduce themselves and share a little about their personal pilgrimage of faith.

If possible, it is a good idea to rotate leadership responsibility among the group members. However, if one individual is particularly gifted as a discussion leader, elect or appoint that person to guide the discussions each week. Remember, the leader's responsibility is simply to guide the discussion and stimulate interaction. He or she should never dominate the proceedings. Rather, the leader should encourage all members of the group to participate, expressing their individual views. He or she should seek to keep the discussion on track, but encourage lively discussion.

If one of the purposes of your group meeting is to create a caring community, it is a good idea to set aside some time for sharing individual concerns and prayer for one another. This can take the form of both silent and spoken petitions and praise.

Introduction: Man's Cry—God's Gift

1. Dr. Graham quotes a friend who said, "I need Jesus Christ for my eternal life, and the Holy Spirit for my internal life." Discuss the implication of this.
2. Who promised the Holy Spirit would come?
3. At what point did the Holy Spirit come?
4. The Bible uses two words related to the Holy Spirit, "ask" and "receive." What is the difference in the relationship these two words imply?

1. Who Is the Holy Spirit?

1. What are some of the "personal" characteristics of the Holy Spirit (pp. 17–18)?

2. What are some of the characteristics of the Holy Spirit that speak of His divinity (p. 19)?
3. Read Dr. McKenna's story on pages 20–21. What are some of the explanations you have heard as to the nature of the Trinity?
4. Discuss the implications of the formula, "one times one times one equals one." Does this help you understand the Trinity?

2. When the Holy Spirit Has Come

1. When did the Holy Spirit begin His work?
2. According to Psalm 104:30, the Holy Spirit not only had a part in creation, He is also a sustainer. What are the implications of this truth?
3. Three words in the Old Testament are used to describe the work of the Holy Spirit—He *came* upon men (2 Chron. 24:20); He *rested* on men (Num. 11:25); He *filled* men (Exod. 31:3). What differences do these words imply?
4. Around whom did the Holy Spirit center His work in the Gospels?
5. What is the Holy Spirit's present work in the world? The Church?
6. What does the Holy Spirit do for the individual believer?

3. The Holy Spirit and the Bible

1. What was the Holy Spirit's place in the writing of Scripture (2 Peter 1:21)?
2. What do we mean when we say the Bible is "inspired"?
3. What portion of Scripture is profitable for application (2 Tim. 3:16)? Discuss.
4. What do we mean when we say the Bible is "authoritative"?
5. How long will the Bible be authoritative (Isa. 40:8; John 10:35)?
6. How complete is God's Word (Rev. 22:18, 19)?
7. What effect does the Bible have on believers (read Heb. 4:12; John 15:3; Ps. 119:9, 11)?

4. The Holy Spirit and Salvation

1. What part does the Holy Spirit play in a person's salvation (John 3:6, 8)?
2. Define "sin" in your own words.
3. Discuss the role of the Holy Spirit as described by Jesus in John 16:8–11.
4. Who does the work of regeneration in the life of the believer?
5. What are some of the flawed ways in which people try to regenerate themselves?
6. What are the four steps to being born again? Analyze Nicodemus's experience.

5. Baptism with the Spirit

1. Discuss Dr. Graham's statement, "I have become convinced that there is only one baptism with the Holy Spirit in the life of every believer, and that takes place at . . . conversion" (p. 62).
2. Discuss the difference between a concept of once-and-for-all "filling" by the Spirit and the idea of "re-filling." How does this differ from the baptism of the Spirit?
3. Discuss Dr. Graham's further point: "Baptism with the Spirit is connected with our *standing* before God, not our current subjective *state;* with our *position* and not our *experience*" (p. 63).
4. Read Acts 8:17, 9:17, 19:1–7 and discuss these events in the light of the chapter's subject.
5. How do modern believers share in the Pentecost event?
6. Read Ephesians 4:4–5. Here Paul seems to be saying that there is only one baptism, implying that once we are baptized into the body of Christ, the process need not be repeated, only appropriated. The writer of Hebrews goes further to add that teachings about the baptism and repentance are elementary and are meant to be the foundation for going on to maturity. Read Hebrews 6:1–3 and make a list of these elementary teachings.

6. The Seal, the Pledge, and the Witness of the Spirit

1. What two spiritual facets does Dr. Graham isolate in his discussion of the sealing of the Holy Spirit (p. 75)?
2. What do you see in the seal of the Holy Spirit in terms of your own salvation experience?
3. Read 2 Corinthians 1:21, 22 and discuss the "pledge" of the Holy Spirit. Compare this to 2 Corinthians 5:5 and Ephesians 1:14.
4. What are the three aspects of "the witness of the Holy Spirit" that Dr. Graham points out on pages 78–79?

7. The Christian's Inner Struggle

1. Think about the two sides of your inner nature. Which seems to dominate? Why?
2. Read Dr. Graham's paraphrase on page 84. Can you identify with his experience?
3. Describe the three aspects or levels of "sanctification" as outlined on page 86. Tie this to "walking in the Spirit."
4. Discuss St. Augustine's statement: "Love God and live as you please."

5. Read Galatians 5:19–21 and Romans 1:17–22. What does the apostle Paul mean by the term, "the flesh"? Discuss the specific sins or "works of the flesh" listed in these passages. What is the secret of overcoming these problems?

8. The Fullness of the Spirit

1. What does the Bible mean when it speaks of the fullness of the Holy Spirit?
2. What is the difference between the way a bucket is filled and the filling of a natural spring or river?
3. Discuss Dr. Graham's comment on page 100, "It is not how much of the Spirit *we* have, but how much the Spirit has of *us.*"
4. What is the purpose of the "filling of the Spirit"?
5. How can we glorify God?

9. How to be Filled with the Holy Spirit

1. What is the difference between fact and feeling in terms of the Holy Spirit's presence?
2. What is it that blocks the Holy Spirit's presence in our lives?
3. What is the first step in being filled with the Holy Spirit?
4. What is the second step?
5. What is the third step?

10. Sins against the Holy Spirit

1. In what three ways do people sin against the Holy Spirit?
2. Which of the three is unforgivable?
3. Does Dr. Graham define the "unpardonable sin"? If so, what does he say it is—and is not?
4. How do we Christians "grieve" the Holy Spirit?
5. What does it mean to "quench" the Spirit?
6. Dr. Graham says it is possible for a Christian *to* sin—but he does not *have* to. Do you agree?

11. Gifts of the Spirit

1. Make a list of the gifts listed in the following passages:

Rom. 12:6–8	1 Cor. 12:8–10	Eph. 4:11

2. What is the biblical meaning of the word "charisma" as described on pages 132–133?
3. What is the difference between "gifts" and "fruit"?
4. What is the difference between "gifts" and "talents"?
5. What is the purpose of "gifts"?
6. What are the four steps in recognizing one's gift?
7. Discuss the gifts listed in the graph in question 1.

12. Further Gifts of the Spirit

1. Define the gift of wisdom and give an example from your own experience (a person or an event?). What biblical character do you think of when the word "wisdom" is mentioned?
2. What three kinds of wisdom are there?
3. How does the gift of knowledge differ from wisdom?
4. What is the difference between the "grace of faith" and the "gift of faith"?
5. Define the gift of spiritual "discernment." Examples from life? From the Bible?
6. Describe the gift of "helps" and give examples.
7. What is another name for the gift of "governments"?

13. The Sign Gifts

1. What are the three categories of "sign gifts"?
2. On page 159 Dr. Graham questions whether the "healing" mentioned in Isaiah 53:5 and 1 Peter 2:24 is physical—or primarily "spiritual." Discuss.
3. Discuss the gift of healing as it seems to be practiced today.
4. Has anyone in your family (or acquaintance) been healed?
5. Is there a difference in degree between the healing of "memories" (mental) and the healing of "bodies" (physical)?
6. Why do we not see the spectacular miracles today that we read about in the Bible?
7. What six points concerning "tongues" does Dr. Graham make on pages 172–176?

14. The Fruit of the Spirit

1. What is one of the main functions of the Holy Spirit (p. 181)?
2. How does the "fruit of the Spirit" differ from the "gifts"?
3. What is the secret of fruit-bearing?
4. Read John 15:4–5. Discuss the implications of "abiding in Christ."

15. The Fruit of the Spirit: Love, Joy, Peace

1. Discuss the "cluster" concept described on page 187.
2. Why do you think the Godward concepts come first?
3. Why do you suppose Paul lists "love" as the first fruit of the Spirit?
4. Read and meditate on Romans 15:13.
5. How does "joy" differ from happiness?

16. The Fruit of the Spirit: Patience, Kindness, Goodness

1. How does patience relate to love?
2. When does patience most come into play (p. 196)?
3. Dr. Graham says kindness is "love enduring." Discuss.
4. Why is "the gentle heart . . . the broken heart"?
5. On page 200 Dr. Graham says, "Goodness is love in action." Discuss.
6. "Good" means to be "like God." Discuss.

17. The Fruit of the Spirit: Faithfulness, Gentleness, Self-control

1. This "cluster" of fruit has to do with man's inward nature. Is there a reason this comes last of the three clusters?
2. What is the relationship of "faithfulness" to love?
3. How does "gentleness" differ from "kindness" in the second cluster?
4. Meekness or "gentleness" is "love under discipline." Discuss.
5. How do "gentle" people operate in the world (p. 207)?
6. How does self-control or temperance relate to love?
7. On page 211 Dr. Graham remarks, "Only the Holy Spirit can make possible the out-living of the in-living Christ." Discuss.

18. The Need of the Hour

1. Why are we Christians not "salt" and "light" as we should be?
2. Do you agree with Dr. Graham that most Christians lead joyless and defeated lives? If so, why is this true, do you think?
3. Who brings about revival?
4. What are the eight characteristics of a revived people (pp. 215–218)? How do these things happen?
5. What are Dr. Graham's three steps to spiritual awakening? Discuss each.